STRATEGIC
HUMAN RESOURCES
PLANNING

STRATEGIC HUMAN RESOURCES PLANNING

GEORGE E. BILES
COLLEGE OF BUSINESS ADMINISTRATION
THE AMERICAN UNIVERSITY

AND

STEVAN R. HOLMBERG
COLLEGE OF BUSINESS ADMINISTRATION
THE AMERICAN UNIVERSITY

THOMAS HORTON AND DAUGHTERS
22 Appleton Place, Glen Ridge, New Jersey 07028

ISBN 0-913878-20-0

TABLE OF CONTENTS

PREFACE

Effective human resource management and planning are increasingly being recognized as two of the most important influences on the success of the individual business firm or organization as well as the economy as a whole. Consequently, the purpose of this readings book is to synthesize systematically and present the relevant human resource management and planning literature. This book is designed to (1) facilitate awareness, knowledge, understanding, and skills concerning the relationship of human resource strategic planning to a particular organization; and (2) assist in more fully incorporating human resource planning into the overall strategic management planning of an organization.

A number of developments have increased the sensitivies of managers to the growing importance of human resource strategic planning. Legislation enacted over the past ten to fifteen years has had a major impact on all facets of human resource management and planning (for example, OSHA; the myriad of antidescrimination laws; ERISA; and amended minimum wages). The relatively rapid inflation of the 1970s has substantially increased direct costs for human resources incurred by all organizations. Indirect human resource costs have also increased dramatically due to the rises in health care costs, required social security contributions, benefit costs, unemployment insurance costs, and other such factors. The rapid rise in human resource direct and indirect costs has placed greater emphasis on human resource productivity as a means of mitigating upward pressures on prices. Finally, the past two decades have seen significant shifts in society's values, which are reflected in employee and employer perspectives towards each other and their work. The value changes are evidenced by the increase in the number of working women, the growing popularity of flexitime and part-time employment, and trends in participative management. All of these trends further add to the need for more formal human resource strategic planning if the challenges facing individual organizations and the country as a whole are to be met.

The past ten years has seen a rapid growth in the body of literature appearing in both academic and professional journals dealing with human resource strategic planning. Indeed, in 1978 the Human Resource Planning Society was created, which publishes the *Human Resource Planning* journal. For the most part, the literature has dealt with specific topics or elements within human resource strategic planning. Now there is a need to bring together this fragmented research into one comprehensive and systematically structured source.

The readings articles in this book are organized into three major parts. Collectively, these articles represent the full range and the best of current and classical research in human resource strategic planning: conceptual articles; articles dealing with specific tools or techniques; and articles which report on current practices of organizations.

Part I begins by tracing the evolving management concept of human resource strategic planning. The concepts and use of corporate/total-organization strategic planning are developed along with an overview of the human resource strategic planning subcomponent.

Part II develops the specific subelements of human resource strategic planning by providing for each subelement the requisite concepts, tools, and practical examples of their application.

Part III focuses on the future of human resource strategic planning from the perspective of both individual organizations and the economy as a whole.

An organization's success or failure will increasingly depend on its ability to manage and plan strategically its human resources. Organizations as well as individual managers will have to devote greater amounts of time and effort to managing their human resources. In seeking to provide a comprehensive and systematic approach to human resource strategic planning, this book is designed for:

- Professional managers at both top and middle management levels in business and nonprofit organizations
- Corporate personnel and industrial relations specialists
- Public and nonprofit sector human resource policy makers and personnel specialists
- Personnel management and industrial relations graduate courses, as a supplement to another textbook
- Human resource planning courses at the undergraduate and graduate levels, as the primary book
- Management and executive development programs

We express our appreciation to Dean Herbert E. Striner, College of Business Administration, The American University, for research support which assisted in the development of this book.

PART I

THE ORGANIZATION AND STRATEGIC HUMAN RESOURCE MANAGEMENT PLANNING

A two- to three-decade evolution in management thought has produced an increasing recognition that a business or nonprofit organization's success or failure depends in large part on its ability to manage and plan its human resources. The readings in Part I of this book are designed, first, to identify some of the underlying developments in the evolution of human resource strategic planning thought and practice. Second, the readings develop fundamental concepts of corporate-wide strategic planning and relate them to the human resource planning sub-component. Third, the readings examine various human resource strategic planning conceptual models and review their current use in individual organizations. In summary, Part I provides the overall perspective and framework necessary to the discussion of the specific human resource strategic planning components and methodologies.

The past two decades have seen a substantial shift from the view of the personnel function as routine record keeping to one in which personnel occupies a more significant position within corporate management, with responsibilities for human resource management and planning. The many causes for the role change and rising importance of the chief personnel executive have also resulted in a redefinition of how employees are regarded by both personnel managers and top management. Human resources are increasingly recognized as being equally as important as other organizational resources. Just as with other resources (capital, land, facilities, etc.), the organization has a substantial investment in its human resources. For maximum return on this human resource investment it must receive the same prudent professional management as other resource components.

The results of individual firm total productivity, when aggregated, yield the overall productivity results for the total economy. In turn, the results of aggregate output per hour of all persons (productivity) combined with hourly compensation labor cost charges yield unit labor costs. These per unit labor cost changes surface as pressures on prices, as firms seek to maintain desired profit levels. While the relatively rapid nation wide inflation trends of the 1970's have had many diverse causes, the productivity and unit labor cost trends during this time have certainly posed very significant considerations. Thus, while this readings book focuses on, and is dedicated to improving, human resource management and planning at the individual organizational level, it bears a direct relationship to the national economy.

The emerging concept of human resource strategic management and planning provides an essential component of a new management philosophy and approach. However, while necessary, it is not by itself sufficient to cause fundamental changes in management behavior. This management concept must be placed within the larger framework of a strategic corporate/total-organization management planning model which facilitates a more formal, systematic, and comprehensive consideration of human resource planning.

CORPORATE/TOTAL-ORGANIZATION STATEGIC PLANNING CONCEPTUAL MODEL

The formal strategic planning conceptual model (see Figure 1) developed in this section provides a step-by-step planning framework or process for private, nonprofit, and public sector organizations. First, the model identifies the important variables which must be considered in any truly comprehensive planning approach. Second, the model suggests the most appropriate sequence for the organization's strategic planning. Substantial problems often arise in actual planning in real organizations because major categories of planning variables (1) are not considered, (2) are considered out of sequence, or (3) include insufficient analysis of one variable which is used as the basis for analyzing the next variables in the sequence. Third, the planning model also provides for three major planning support components, which are necessary to the successful performance of the primary planning components.

Next, the overall model will be examined in greater detail.

Primary Planning Subcomponents

External Environmental Analysis. The overall strategic planning model begins with a comprehensive identification and analysis of all relevant external environmental factors. Without the formal, comprehensive monitoring, identification, assessment of potential impacts, identification of opportunities and threats, and systematic analysis, the proper external environmental variables may not even be identified, much less analyzed, thereby increasing the likelihood of major errors and potential risks for the organization.

The outputs of the external environmental planning subcomponent would be the organization's planning assumptions and target customer/constituency need definition. The planning assumptions are the written assumptions concerning specific external environmental variables which serve as the basis for all subsequent planning subcomponents. The target customer/constituency need definition specifies which of the organization's segments (customer/constituency needs) would appear to have a high potential.

Customer/Constituency Need Analysis. For more closely defining broad target customer/constituency needs, the second major subcomponent of the overall planning model employs a detailed customer/

Figure 1. Strategic Planning Total Conceptual Model

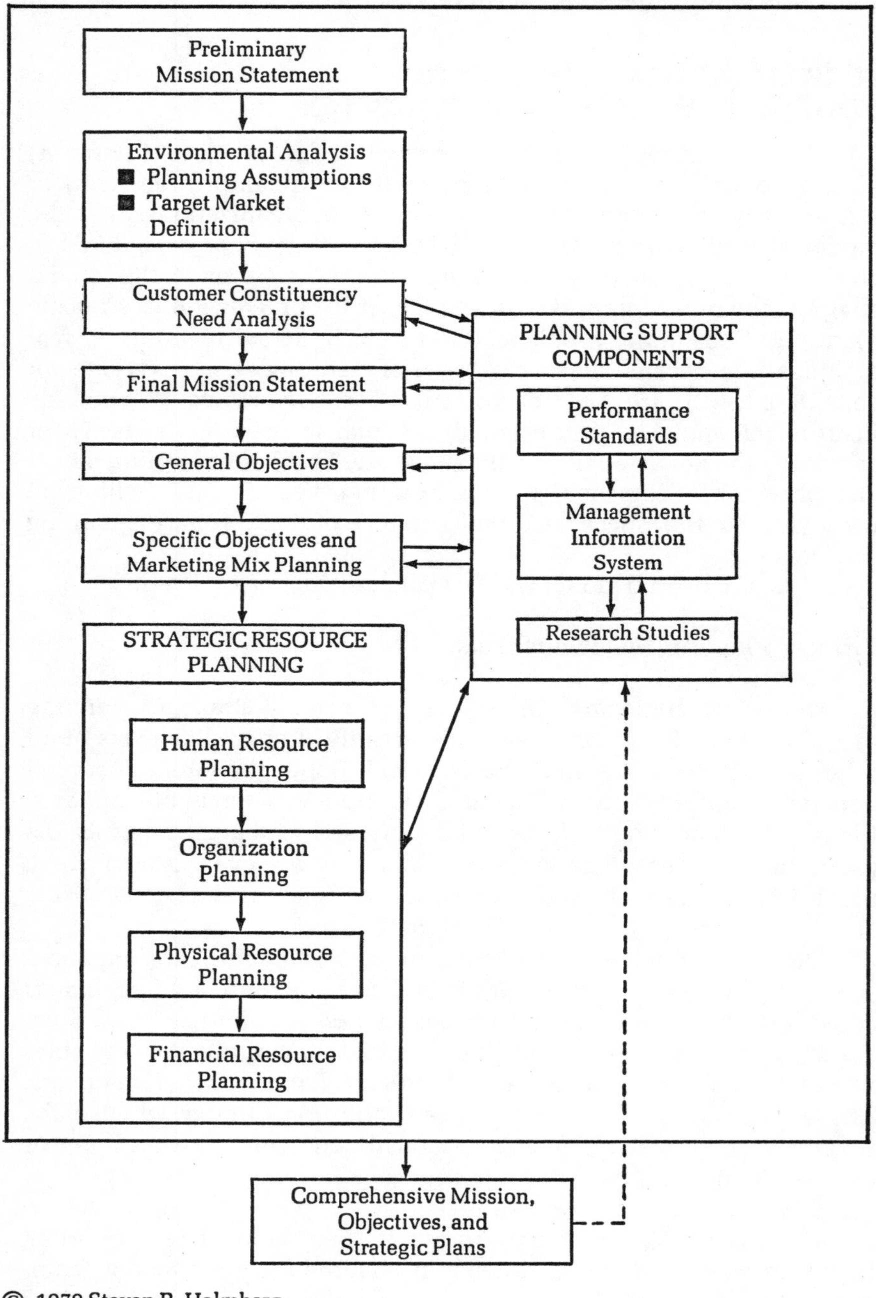

```
┌─────────────────────────────────────────────────────────────────┐
│  ┌───────────────────────┐                                       │
│  │ Preliminary           │                                       │
│  │ Mission Statement     │                                       │
│  └───────────┬───────────┘                                       │
│  ┌───────────▼───────────┐                                       │
│  │ Environmental Analysis│                                       │
│  │ ■ Planning Assumptions│                                       │
│  │ ■ Target Market       │                                       │
│  │   Definition          │                                       │
│  └───────────┬───────────┘                                       │
│  ┌───────────▼───────────┐   ┌─────────────────────────────┐     │
│  │ Customer Constituency │──►│  PLANNING SUPPORT           │     │
│  │ Need Analysis         │◄──│  COMPONENTS                 │     │
│  └───────────┬───────────┘   │  ┌───────────────────────┐  │     │
│  ┌───────────▼───────────┐   │  │ Performance           │  │     │
│  │ Final Mission Statement│◄─ │  │ Standards             │  │     │
│  └───────────┬───────────┘   │  └───────────┬───────────┘  │     │
│  ┌───────────▼───────────┐   │  ┌───────────▼───────────┐  │     │
│  │ General Objectives    │◄─►│  │ Management            │  │     │
│  └───────────┬───────────┘   │  │ Information           │  │     │
│  ┌───────────▼───────────┐   │  │ System                │  │     │
│  │ Specific Objectives and│◄─►│  └───────────┬───────────┘  │     │
│  │ Marketing Mix Planning │   │  ┌───────────▼───────────┐  │     │
│  └───────────┬───────────┘   │  │ Research Studies      │  │     │
│  ┌───────────▼───────────┐   │  └───────────────────────┘  │     │
│  │ STRATEGIC RESOURCE    │   └─────────────────────────────┘     │
│  │ PLANNING              │                                       │
│  │  ┌───────────────────┐│                                       │
│  │  │ Human Resource    ││                                       │
│  │  │ Planning          ││                                       │
│  │  └─────────┬─────────┘│                                       │
│  │  ┌─────────▼─────────┐│                                       │
│  │  │ Organization      ││                                       │
│  │  │ Planning          ││                                       │
│  │  └─────────┬─────────┘│                                       │
│  │  ┌─────────▼─────────┐│                                       │
│  │  │ Physical Resource ││                                       │
│  │  │ Planning          ││                                       │
│  │  └─────────┬─────────┘│                                       │
│  │  ┌─────────▼─────────┐│                                       │
│  │  │ Financial Resource││                                       │
│  │  │ Planning          ││                                       │
│  │  └───────────────────┘│                                       │
│  └───────────────────────┘                                       │
└─────────────────────────────────────────────────────────────────┘
              ┌───────────────────────┐
              │ Comprehensive Mission,│
              │ Objectives, and       │
              │ Strategic Plans       │
              └───────────────────────┘
```

© 1979 Stevan R. Holmberg.

constituency need analysis. The factual identification of the need structure of the organization's current and potential customers or constituencies is an essential element if planning is to be successful. Often, managers simply assume that they "know" what the customer or constituency wants. This subjective "knowledge" is typically based solely on intuitive feel and experience without any systematic research efforts to actually determine and document customer/constituency need structures.

If sufficient information on current and potential customers is currently not available, steps must be taken at this early stage in the planning process to develop a formal process for filling this information gap.

Mission and Objectives. The customer/constituency need analysis planning subcomponent in conjunction with the external environmental analysis forms the basis for determining the organization's mission statement. In specifying the reasons for the organization's existence, the mission statement establishes the scope for the organization's activities in terms of a selection of target customer/constituency segments. The mission statement also provides the overall direction for the organization and the framework for subunit cohesion of general objectives and strategies.

Product, Service, or Program Mix. Once the organization's mission and general objectives are established, the next step in the formal planning process is the analysis and ultimate determination of the most appropriate output, service, or program mix and their associated specific objectives. Selecting the most appropriate output, service, or program mix involves a thorough analysis of the tradeoffs in choosing one output over another. Once the decision has been made, then the organization is committed to a particular course of action.

Resource Planning. An integral part of product or program planning is planning for resources, since products or programs (and, therefore, objectives) can be achieved only through the effective application of resources. Detailed planning must be done for human, organizational, physical, and financial resources. Human resource planning involves selecting the proper mix of full and part-time employees, consultants, and others required by a particular organizational output. Organizational planning consists of structuring resources so that outputs, services, or programs can be effectively implemented. Physical resource planning develops the physical facilities needed for those outputs. Financial planning involves estimating both cost and revenue flows over time.

Planning Support Subcomponents

The primary steps in the formal strategic planning model, as illustrated in Figure 1, have three support elements that assist the planning process: (1) a management information system that provides timely and relevant information on the organization's ongoing activities; (2) a set of desired performance standards that use the factual information system and other considerations in conducting an ongoing evaluation of the organization's objectives and outputs; and (3) research studies oriented towards providing technical and nontechnical information that will be useful in all facets of strategic planning.

The final step of this strategic planning process is the organization's strategic plan document. The major segments of this document correspond to the major planning components. Central to all of the underlying analysis and the resulting strategic plans represented in a strategic planning document is the human resource strategic planning subcomponent, which will be examined in detail in the next section.

Figure 2. Human Resource Strategic Planning

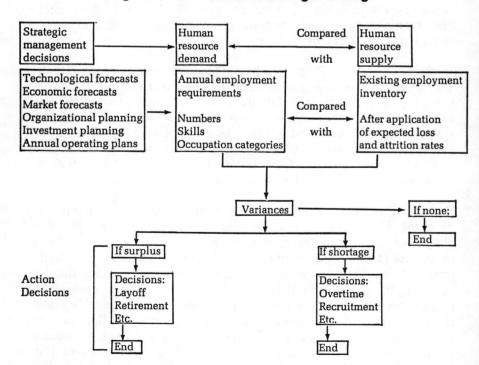

Source: William F. Glueck, *Personnel: A Diagnostic Approach*, Revised Edition, (Dallas: Business Publications, Inc., 1978), p. 89.

HUMAN RESOURCE STRATEGIC PLANNING

Human resource strategic planning, as illustrated in Figure 1, takes place within the overall corporate/total-organization strategic planning model. Consequently, strategic management decisions concerning the organization's mission, objectives, and output strongly condition and frame the human resource planning decisions, as illustrated in Figure 2. These strategic management decisions provide the basis for analyzing human resource demand versus its supply. In general terms, human resource demand is translated into annual employment requirements while human resource supply is developed as the existing personnel skills inventory. To the extent that there are variances between the human resource requirements and supply, strategies must be developed to close these gaps.

The interaction between the major questions which frame strategic management decisions and those which relate to human resource planning are illustrated in Figure 3. The issues raised by these questions will be interrelated and addressed in the readings articles which appear in this part as well as the more specifically focused articles which appear in Part II.

Figure 3. The Interaction Between Strategic Management Decisions and Employment Planning

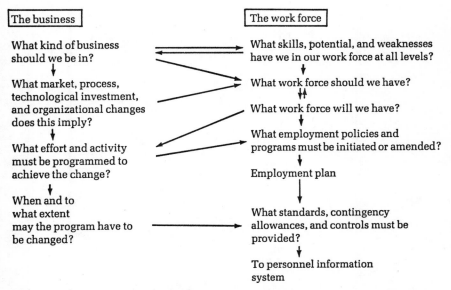

Source: B. L. Donald, "Manpower and a Planned Future," in *Planning for Human Resources,* ed. Charles Margerison and David Ashton (London: Longmans, Green & Co., 1974).

CHAPTER 1
INTRODUCTION TO HUMAN RESOURCE PLANNING: A NATIONAL AND INDIVIDUAL ORGANIZATIONAL PERSPECTIVE

Towards Human Resources Management
Arthur J. Daltas and Howard M. Schwartz

Over the last decade there has been a gradual increase in management awareness of, and sensitivity to, what has historically been called "the personnel function." Today, management literature refers to it as "human resources management."

A Complex Function for a Complex Environment

While the title change for some firms reflects a tendency to use the current management buzzword, for many firms a very real change in attitude has taken place regarding personnel activities. The shift that has occurred has taken the personnel manager from being an administrator of company regulations and policies regarding employees to one of being a manager (and planner) of the human resources "assets" of the firms. This shift has been brought about by several factors: spiralling wage and benefit costs, increasingly complex governmental regulations, rapid change in technological, competitive and economic environments, the explosion of technical and managerial knowledge and the increasing need, in many businesses, to find better ways to manage rapidly changing tasks involving the coordination of many diverse specialists.

Any firm faces a wide range of choices in structuring its approach to human resources management. In our experience, human resources objectives are best established after a careful review of the way in which

Arthur J. Daltas and Howard M. Schwartz are vice-presidents at the Cambridge Center for Organization Development, Inc., Cambridge, Massachusetts.

human resources problems are likely to constrain business results. Once such an assessment is undertaken, top management can further consider ways in which its approach to human resources management might provide a competitive edge. Finally, the values, aspirations, and leadership styles of top management can be analyzed to insure that human resources objectives aim at developing an organizational environment consistent with both top management's own philosophy and its view of the company's future growth and development.

For example, the rapidly changing business, social, and political environment will continue to demand that the business strategy of any large company emphasize both the revitalization of some of its traditionally strong areas and the creation of new sources of profits from entirely new entities and methods of operation. Some of these changes which will drastically affect the human resources of a company are:

A. Internally
   1. New departments
   2. New business
   3. Expansion of some existing functions
   4. Contraction of other functions
   5. Increased turnover and transfers of personnel
   6. Increased decentralization and divisional automony
B. Externally
   1. Employees changing employers more frequently
   2. Changes in the skills mix of the work force
   3. More stringent employment and safety laws
   4. Higher expectations of workers at all levels
   5. Increased union emphasis on job security and extended benefits

These factors in turn will cause constant changes in the corporation's need to focus on such human resources concerns as the numbers of people affected, types of skills needed, working relationships between people and departments, forms of compensation and rewards, appropriate organizational structures, and methods of motivation and control. To deal effectively with these concerns, organizations will have to use new and better means for dealing with people. To some extent, current capabilities will have to be expanded and accented while new capabilities will have to be developed. Some of these changes will include:

1. Realizing that the function plays a strategic role, not a status quo role, by linking its skills and activities with the business plans of the organization.

2. Providing information about the human assets of the firm in the right quantity and format for action-taking purposes of line management and staff specialists.

3. Automating the retrieval and analysis of personnel information centrally and locally as part of human resources management and control systems.

4. Developing performance measures for the human resource management activities carried out by both the department and line management.

5. Creating new incentives for the proper use of human resources; a continuing search for talent internally and externally and the replacement of less talented people.

6. Using individual performance appraisal methods to improve and maintain performance, not simply to record it, especially by relating it to rewards and job training and by divorcing it from promotion decisions.

7. Treating evaluations of potential in individuals as indicators for developmental training and promotion decisions.

8. Offering meaningful career planning and counseling at all levels.

9. Evaluating the structural relevance of the whole organization and its components as their roles change so that the structures fit the work, not just a chart.

10. Increasing the ability to create and staff non-traditional organizations (e.g., matrix structures).

11. Being more sophisticated in the design and programming of compensation and benefit packages.

12. Providing training which is based on corporate priorities and specific weaknesses and which is designed to have lasting, tangible effects in the context of current and future business plans.

13. Researching and testing innovative personnel programs and methodologies.

14. Increasing communication with the personnel functions of other corporations and community agencies for more effective intake and out-placement of people to mutually even out excesses and deficiencies.

15. Helping managers and employees to put their energy on tasks, not conflicts, through the effective use of mutual goal-setting, interpersonal communication, group problem solving, and conflict resolution.

16. Removing the blockages that prevent the successes of special programs within, for example, the EEO and OSHA areas, especially because these blockages are often indicative of more general organizational problems.

Problems of Implementation

A traditional personnel function is generally concerned with keeping records on, and administering to the needs of, the current work force, and to its perception of the future needs of that work force. Essentially it is an accounting function and, even though it deals in such things as employment forecasts, its insights and abilities to deal with the future are quite limited. Furthermore, traditional personnel organizations tend to view the management of the corporation's human resources as the sum of many isolated activities. As a result, many line managers have come to view the personnel organization as contributing a necessary and useful housekeeping function but having relatively little impact on the major strategic issues which affect the firm's survival and growth. Few personnel executives have learned to view their function as a set of interlocking pieces, a system which is constantly solving problems for the corporation and the people in it. Rather than viewing their organizaton as involved in a dynamic process which is constantly readjusting as needs change, many personnel managers unwittingly become custodians of status quo procedures which are not responsive to today's challenges.

The problems of making meaningful change in the direction of a human resources management approach are significant. Clarity of vision and committed top executive leadership are essential for insuring that people are as much a part of strategic planning as capital. While the problems encountered in establishing such a capability will differ considerably in each organization, our experience suggests that the following considerations have an important bearing on the success and speed with which effective human resources management can be implemented:

1. *Top management commitment is key.* Top management must understand that effective human resources management is a significant element in the firm's overall corporate strategy. This commitment should be evidenced by the Human Resources executive being positioned among the most senior executives in the company. He should be expected to play a major role in top executive debates regarding business plans and corporate strategy.

2. *Credibility and cooperation must be won.* Even with top management backing, the Human Resources VP must still gain credibility for himself and his organization by becoming relevant to the realization of corporate and division operating objectives. This is complicated by the need for many line executives to change their own behavior before results can be demonstrated. For example, before Human Resources can deliver meaningful performance

improvements programs, managers and executives must adopt more systematic and objective performance evaluation procedures, ones which they may not be comfortable with at first. While this may require an extended period of change, training is an area where early and demonstrable improvements are often possible. Many times a company's training commitment has effectively been to the training itself, rather than to carefully linking training interventions to strategically significant business needs.

3. *Piecemeal improvements must often precede wholesale restructuring.* Many companies have found the transition to human resources management to be among the most significant and far reaching changes in their experience, requiring a readjustment of attitudes and behavior throughout the organization. A strategy which emphasizes fixing the most troublesome individual aspects of the current personnel system first, delaying any attempt to integrate a restructured system until substantial individual gains are made, may facilitate the ultimate reorganization. When a system is making such basic errors as confusing performance evaluation with the assessment of individual potential, or failing to ask if a form is really needed before attempting to develop an improvement, trying to bite off too much at first is likely to be a more serious hazard than that of creating the impression of business as usual.

4. *Human Resources staff skills must be upgraded.* Traditional personnel organizations often harbour talented people who have been inhibited by conservative management and lack of executive support. In the worst situation are those companies who have used the department as a final resting place for worn out managers. Most staff, in either case, are likely to need some new skills and perspectives. While some changes in key personnel are usually made, an early assessment of staff development needs is important. The retraining of personnel staff can often be used as a pilot test of new approaches of training and employee development for use throughout the company.

5. *Human Resources Management is likely to require a considerable reorganizing of the personnel staff to achieve measurable results.* Inertia, inappropriate division of functions, the lack of performance measures to gauge their own performance and a shortage of useful information are organizational issues which will need to be addressed. In addition to the assessment of the key tasks involved, a reorganization is most likely to be successful if considerable thought is given to the end results sought for the entire corporation. For example, lack of information often appears to be a key reason for the lack of horizontal movement between functions, particularly in

vertically integrated firms, If more horizontal movement is an important stragetic issue for the company, information flows should be reorganized to reflect that objective.

The problems involved in the implementation of a Human Resources Management approach will, of course, vary considerably from one firm to the next. The common thread appears to be the issue of transforming a function often run without much reference to what the business is about, to one which is responsive to strategic and operating priorities. Even though enlarging and sharpening the strategic perspectives of the traditional personnel department can be painful for the people involved, and for the entire organization, such a transformation can also be one of the greatest keys to the future success of the business.

Human Resource Planning: Managerial Concerns and Practices
James W. Walker

Managers today are taking a greater interest in human resource planning and are supporting practical changes in long-standing personnel management practices. They are concerned with such basic problems as: the planning and control of staffing requirements; the succession and development of talent for key positions; improving job matching; and improving on-the-job performance. These problems are not new—they have been fundamental to human resource planning during the past decade. However, some new approaches have been developed in response to management's heightened concern.

A CHANGING BUSINESS CONTEXT

Management's interest in human resource problems has been prompted by the increased intervention of the government through Equal

"Human Resource Planning: Managerial Concerns and Practices" by James W. Walker, *Business Horizons*, June 1976. Copyright 1976 by the Foundation for the School of Business at Indiana University. Reprinted by permission.

James W. Walker is a Principal of Towers, Perrin, Forster & Crosby, Inc., Boston, Massachusetts.

Employment Opportunity and affirmative action programs and other regulations. The net impact of this expanding government intervention has been an increase in the attention given to human resource planning in all of the above problem areas. In response, managements are developing more rational career systems with explicit career paths and job requirements, and more objective procedures for matching a candidate with a job. To achieve necessary targets for employee utilization, new systems and practices are being adopted in recruitment, selection and placement; and career development and training programs are being expanded.

Because business profits are squeezed by inflation and a weakened economy, management is also concerned with personnel costs and is seeking to achieve increased output with the same or fewer staff. Therefore, pressure for control over staffing extends into the professional and managerial levels. In many instances this control is being achieved through closer attention to the actual nature of the work, through analysis and planning of activities and job requirements.

A third important factor is a continuing short supply of competent talent and a need to assure a return on investments in recruitment and development of talented people. Retention of employees, not recruitment and selection, is where emphasis is being placed. And this means greater attention to long-range career development, individual counseling, work structure and other nonpay aspects of employment.

PLANNING STAFFING REQUIREMENTS

A fundamental management concern is the staffing of the organization, particularly managerial, professional and technical positions. Management must ask the following questions:

> Are the right numbers and kinds of people doing the things we need to have done?
> Are we properly utilizing our people?
> Do we have the people we need to satisfy our future needs?

The common approach to the problem of staffing is the planning and budgeting process, which involves participation by successive levels of management. Proper planning and budgeting yields estimates of supply, demand and specified net needs accepted as reasonable by the managers.

To improve the objectivity of staffing plans, companies are providing basic computer-generated listings of personnel complement, attrition, movement and projected staffing requirements. The analysis of job activities and skill requirements identifies ways to better utilize available talent. Actual activities performed, examined in relation to current and projected business factors, provide a basis for planning improved staffing, organization and work assignment. The management planning process itself may be strengthened by the use of this more specific format for considering human resource requirements.

For example, an international government agency in Washington reviewed its staffing levels and mix and established an ongoing planning process for staffing. A task checklist was developed and used to gather data on work activities. The data were aggregated by types of activities and examined both by occupational groups and by organizational units. With additional interview data, guidelines were developed for possible adjustments in time allocations for each type of activity, and thereby in overall staffing requirements. The results were applied in the budget formulation process, and were extended and refined for use in future annual planning cycles.

A major commercial bank introduced a similar planning method which involved analysis of officer time allocated to bank products and services. The time was analyzed in relation to business results such as transactions and volumes, which then provided statistical guidelines for decisions regarding staffing levels in branches and other organizational units.

Thus, planning and control over staffing requires detailed information on the activities performed in relation to changing business needs. Yet few companies have this basic information available; most will have to generate it to permit the level of planning and control now required.

Management Succession and Development
Continuity of management is another concern, particularly with earlier retirements and high turnover among talented management candidates. Management must ask, "Do we have qualified backups for our key positions?"

The answer has traditionally been provided through a backup chart which identifies successors for each executive position. The charts present appraisal, age, length of service, and other data on the incumbent and one or more designated backup candidates for each position. Then the charts, usually prepared by unit managers with staff assistance, are submitted to senior management for review. This approach suffers from several shortcomings:

There is little consideration of the actual requirements of the position or of the prospective changes in the job when the present incumbent is succeeded.

Identification of backups is largely subjective, based on personal knowledge of the nominating manager. Rarely are there any objective indicators of performance, individual capabilities, or past achievements. Often, even basic biographical data is not considered.

A high-potential candidate may be qualified for more than one position, but may be boxed in by the succession planning, or if named for several positions, may give a false impression of management depth.

The planning is fragmented; rarely is there a provision for bridging among organization units.

There is rarely any input from the individuals themselves regarding their own self-assessments and career interests.

Most significantly, the charts rarely result in job assignments or training experiences. The process tends to be a static, annual, paperwork exercise.

To overcome these shortcomings and make management succession planning more meaningful, companies are replacing the simple charting technique with more intensive executive review meetings, with discussion of:

job requirements and the dynamics of positions in relation to changing organization and management needs
candidate information (skills, experience, interests)
candidate appraisal information
specific assignment and development decisions.

This new process is reduced in scope to cover only 30 to 50 key executive positions and 100 to 200 candidates, which provide corporate management with a talent pool. Additional groups of positions at the next level, in which many of the corporate candidates are typically incumbents, represent key positions in each organizational unit. The focus on substantial data regarding job requirements, staffing needs and individual development plans promotes active management involvement in the succession planning process and typically results in concrete, practical actions and planned succession decisions.

An oil company introduced this process as a supplement and ultimate replacement for its established backup procedure. In the initial application, twenty-five positions and seventy candidates were discussed by a senior management group comprised of the fourteen vice-presidents. The results of two days' discussion included specific decisions regarding ten anticipated position vacancies during the year and a number of planned developmental steps, many involving cross-functional moves.

IMPROVING JOB MATCHING

Because of affirmative action program requirements and increased employee interest in career development, managers today are concerned with job assignment and career progression. As a result, organizations are adopting more formal, and presumably more objective, systems for appraising individual capabilities and potential, identifying candidates for position vacancies and guiding individual development.

Among the tools used are appraisal programs, assessment centers, job posting, skills inventories and career planning techniques. Emphasis in recent years has been upon improving assessments of individual skills, knowledge, aptitudes and interests. Tools such as assessment centers and skills inventories have been limited in their usefulness, however, because of the lack of relevant job requirements. In turn, the individual data gathered are frequently incomplete or not fully relevant to the jobs, and the system ends up providing "garbage in, garbage out."

To improve the usefulness of candidate identification, appraisal, development, training and related practices, many organizations are recognizing the importance of the job requirements side of the match. Through analysis of actual job behaviors and related qualifications requirements, career progression possibilities are being made more explicit.

Various individual characteristics such as age, sex, work experience, educational level or national origin are evaluated as to their job relatedness. An essential step towards removing discriminatory employment practices, this also results in improved assessment of the employee's potential performance on other jobs.

Further, positions with similar requirements are being clustered as job families, and paths among these families are designed to represent incremental skill and knowledge requirements. This "career opportunities map" makes individual appraisals, career counseling and training more job related. Assignment of employees across organizational and geographic lines is also facilitated.

The management of a forest products company, for example, was concerned that employees were not being given opportunities across regional and functional boundaries, even in cases where jobs were similar. The company's adoption of a job coding scheme that groups its salaried positions now provides a basis for identifying career progression possibilities. The system is used for both job matching and staffing analysis and planning purposes.

A manufacturing firm supplemented its skills inventory with a system of "target development positions" based on defined career paths and job requirements. This provides a realistic basis for individual development planning.

Managers and employees are asking that promotions and transfers be logical and rationally determined. Numerous organizations have demonstrated that it is possible to identify the best candidates for positions and to change long-established perceptions of job requirements ("We need a younger man," or "A woman can't do the job"). This improvement may be accomplished without major systems changes or a tedious process of rewriting job descriptions. It is not a radical departure from current practice, but it is a step in evolution of career management in an organization.

IMPROVING ON-THE-JOB PERFORMANCE

The call for improved productivity from managerial, professional and technical positions ultimately translates into improved individual performance. In some instances individuals are simply not properly matched with their jobs, and so their perfomance is constrained. In most instances, however, individuals could be more productive if job performance priorities, standards and objectives were established and skill and knowledge requirements were more clearly defined and training provided to bridge the gaps.

For many years, managers have relied on job descriptions and trait-oriented employee appraisals as the basic tools of managing performance. But job descriptions are commonly outdated and not descriptive of the work actually performed on the jobs, and appraisals are often too general and unrelated to the work.

As a result, in recent years supervisors have appraised subordinate performance in terms of results. Implicit in this approach are the following:

agreement on performance standards and objectives and the activities and resources necessary to achieve these
review of achievements, with measures or indicators of results.

The individual's participation in both the planning of the work and the review of accomplishments is held as an important principle. In practice, the approach doesn't always work out well. Performance planning and review is often perfunctory personnel paperwork and doesn't significantly influence individual productivity. The reasons include the following:

Managers are not accustomed to a mutual planning and review procedure.
It involves paperwork and by nature becomes routine.

Many jobs are difficult to define and performance standards or objectives are elusive.

Many jobs are fluid, rapidly changing.

Many jobs overlap, and individual performance is hard to define.

Performance shortcomings are often rooted in skill or knowledge gaps or in broader organizational or staffing problems.

To overcome these obstacles, and thereby have an impact on job performance, organizations are taking the following steps:

providing managers and subordinates with data on their actual activities—how they spend their time

clarifying job requirements and performance expectations

providing assistance to supervisors in performance planning, review and counseling

providing training to employees to bridge gaps in specific skills or knowledge

providing incentive to individuals to make it work, through merit pay that reflects performance levels.

For example, many banks have adopted incentive compensation plans based on performance targets. Performance areas are defined for each type of job on a standardized basis and then specific achievements or "important aspects" and a rating of overall accomplishment are noted when performance is reviewed. Individual allocations of incentive awards are determined by this process.

Managers' concerns today are "back to the basics." Advanced applications and models, skills inventories and elaborate goal-setting or organizational change programs simply don't "fly" in the pragmatic world of most businesses. Rather, practices in human resource planning today are responding to the need for practical, job-related actions that can bring visible results to the managers who make human resource planning happen.

Manpower Planning at National and Company Level
Joan Cox

Admittedly there must be differences of approach between manpower planning at National and Company level. 'Redundancy' which may be the concern of personnel departments has a different aura from 'unemployment' which is the parallel concern of the Government planner. Again, the earnings of the company have only a remote connection with the gross domestic product of the country. But these are matters of scale and approach rather than of substance. It is generally recognized that the creation of new job opportunities is a concomitant of a buoyant and growing economy, but, to be itself growing and buoyant, the economy must consist of growing and buoyant companies. Similarly, if companies or public corporations are to expand, then they must also expand their personnel. It makes little difference that, in the national aggregate, it is usual to refer to 'manpower'.

THE COMMON AREA

It is axiomatic that the growth of the economy is no more than the growth in aggregate of public corporations and innumerable private enterprises. Thus (although there are certain differences) national manpower planning is a parallel activity to the company planning (implicit or explicit) of those enterprises that make up the industrial sector. It will be remembered too that national planning is unlikely to be undertaken unless the views of the public and private employers are first obtained.

Company and national planning draw further apart when policy matters are being considered. A company, looking forward 5 or 10 years, must consider the personnel that it must employ to carry out its current short-term programme as well as its more tentative longer-term programme; and it will first draw from the pool of people it already has in its employment. A generously staffed organization may be able simply to re-arrange posts and responsibilities whereas a fast-growing company may be involved in a sizeable recruiting campaign.

Manpower planning at national level, however, has to encompass the whole of the working population or, more precisely, that part of the working population relevant to the plan under consideration. In doing

"Manpower Planning at National and Company Level," by Joan Cox, Long Range Planning, June 1971. Reprinted by permission.

Joan Cox is Head of the Scientific and Technological Statistics Branch, Department of Trade and Industry, London, England.

so it must take into account such factors as the level of unemployment, the availability of personnel outside the working population (such as married women), the extent of mobility between sectors and finally, migration. The national manpower planner must interest himself in the demography of the country's manpower and reflect on the Government's responsibility for manpower as a whole. This makes him see the problem from a different angle. This is not to say that manpower planning at national level has 'full employment' as a primary aim but it does mean that the manpower implications of any particular set of propositions at national level should be understood and communicated to senior officials and Ministers. The manpower planner must be in a position to assess the effects of expansion or retrenchment *on the economy as a whole*. Thus he is concerned with an aggregate of enterprise and public sector plans and must assess whether it is likely to come into balance with the numbers resulting from past demographic trends and activity rates. And, if they do not balance in the first instance, what economic and social consequences can be expected.

It can be seen that there is a very large common area of interest between manpower planning at national and company level—planners are concerned with the same people, in the same age groups and in the same posts. It is only at the final stages of the analysis that the interests tend to diverge; while the national planner is assessing the balance between supply and demand for manpower as a whole or in broad categories, the company personnel planner is checking whether his recruitment plans are consistent with manpower costs and are providing an acceptable age and promotion structure. Economic and social considerations are, of course, of interest to both sides; it is just that the impact on their responsibilities is somewhat different.

Having identified what are the essential differences, we can now see the extent of these similarities and can study the desirability of an interchange of ideas between national and company planners in their common areas.

DECISION MAKING

Management literature rightly puts the emphasis on decision making. It is axiomatic that the sequences of forward planning must follow a decision and it is immaterial whether this decision to commit resources is taken by the Director of a company or the Government of a country. Again, while there is no conceptual difference between the decision to commit resources by Government or by an enterprise, the scale of the operation and the chain of command by which the results are obtained can be very different. Furthermore, the *direct* action taken by the company contrasts with the *indirect* action normally taken by Government—with its much longer time span.

The decision to commit resources is the starting point for planning. It is sometimes supposed that planning can take place in a vacuum but this is clearly unrealistic; such a view confuses planning with the monitoring or appraisal of events already occurring. It is equally true that the initial decision to commit resources for a particular objective is followed by a sequence of secondary decisions usually at lower levels of command and it is the appreciation of the sequence of decision-making that provides, so to speak, the chart that will guide the manpower planner.

Before going into the sequence of logical steps needed to implement a decision it is worthwhile looking at the differences and similarities between these procedures as they present themselves at national and company level. Figure 1 makes a first comparison between the sequence of decisions as they will be taken.

Figure 1. Manpower Planning at National and Company Level.

National level	Company level
National objective. ↓	Company objective. ↓
Identification of activities and function(s). Construction R & D. ↓	Identification of function(s) within which company must operate (R & D, production etc.). ↓
Translation into posts to work within function(s). ↓	Translation into posts to work within function(s). ↓
Identification of broad group of skills required in such posts. ↓	Identification of job skills required in posts. ↓
Using cross-analyses of job skill/subject of qualification, assess subjects likely to be called for by employers.	Translation into subject of qualification (or job experience) required in posts.

As already observed, in practice national manpower planning tends to operate through indirect processes. Whereas the company can bear directly on the problem by moving people within the company or by recruiting from the market, at any point in time, the Government must operate with a working population of a given size and with a distribution of qualification and experience. If, for instance, the decision is to launch a new road building programme, it is only a limited help if universities transfer resources to their civil engineering departments. By the time the additional graduates are leaving the universities, the civil engineering contractors who are responsible for the programme will have completed their recruitment.

Up to this point we have ignored one of the biggest differences between company and national planning: the speed at which plans are brought into effect. The company can act promptly; if it is prepared to raise its price, it can obtain the necessary personnel in competition with home-based or even with overseas-based employers. The achievement of its immediate needs is a matter of economics but, except in very rare circumstances, the achievement of Government plans is a matter of time and persuasion as well as money. This factor of the time lag may well prove to be the main difference between the environment of the company and the national planners. Nevertheless, there is still a considerable degree of similarity and Figure 2 indicates the main points of comparison.

Figure 2. Matters to be Considered.

Who are already in the country and available for employment?	Who are already in the company?
Data from census of population.	Planning requires that a full register of posts is made and of the people in them.
Periodic surveys of manpower.	You cannot plan ahead without full knowledge of the posts in the company at any date.
Compare numbers required overall with number in stock.	Compare number in each category required with people already employed.

PLANNING IN THE ORGANIZATION

Planning is an activity which is initiated by a decision to commit resources to a given objective or goal.[1] The resources which now come under the scrutiny of the corporate planners comprise finance, capital facilities and people. Personnel planning concentrates on the last of these but the investigation of interplay with the investment programme and with cash flow is part of the planning process.

The personnel planning part of the total or corporate planning falls into four stages:

1. The examination of the objective.
2. The resources to be allocated to personnel.
3. The analysis of the jobs required:
   (a) in which functions
   (b) the authority of posts within these functions
   (c) the skills required and

(d) the identification of the level at which the skills must be performed.
4. The matching of posts and people.

Before this last stage, the finding of the people, personnel planners
must ask a number of questions:

First question. Who do we have in the company who could be
shifted? What is their age? Qualification? Experience?
Second question. Who shall we have to recruit?
Third question. What does this imply for other posts in the company?

It will be appreciated that these questions cannot be answered
without information. All these questions:

Who do we have?
Which posts should they fill?
How many shall we have to recruit?
What does this imply for other posts in the company?

require precise and, equally important, *immediately retrievable* information.
This indicates the first rule of planning, the requirement of adequate
information. This must comprise:

1. Posts in the company at the date the planning starts,
2. Information about the individuals who fill these posts; and if
possible,
3. The situation as it has changed over the last few years, so that wastage
and promotion rates can be studied.

In view of its importance—why are organizations so slow to collect
and retrieve information of this type?
It is an odd thing that, while we can produce the necessary 'systems'
to send men to the moon, the equivalent 'system' to do what has just been
described is evolving very slowly. Why is this? Two things stand in the
way of proper information:

1. The sheer cost of holding, updating and sorting files on individuals
and the posts that they fill.
2. The difficulty of even attempting this until we had a consistent
system of defining and describing posts—so that these could be

recognized for what they are, and not be hidden behind different job titles.

A project to explore such a system for defining and describing posts, so deceptively simple in concept but so fiendishly difficult in practice, brought industry and Government together.

INFLUENCE OF THE COMPUTER

As companies grow and become more complex, more information is needed about the men employed and the posts they fill. But by the laws of arithmetic the larger the number of records the harder it is to extract information from them. Five hundred punch cards need skilled handling—what if there are 10,000 or 24,000 as in a large Government Department? How can 20 people be found with the required characteristics for a new research team from such a number? It is almost impossible. This simple frustration—the absence of time, systems and resources explains why so little is known about posts and manpower utilization in organizations.

Undoubtedly the reason that job classification came to the forefront of manpower thinking around 1964 was the intrusion of the computer into personnel work and manpower analysis. Personnel administrators saw clearly that, within a few years, they would be keeping the posts record for their company on magnetic tape. This would involve systematic description and coding of the posts that men were occupying or were to occupy. And systematic description of posts means that the main characteristics must be identified and set into a list of descriptors. The job can then be identified by the selection of the appropriate descriptor for each characteristic.

As has already been seen from the first diagram, manpower planning at company and at national level is a parallel and not dissimilar activity. A number of companies who provided manpower data to Government also recognized that national and company planning were not mutually exclusive exercises but were entities that were involved one with the other. They argued that the data collected for essential personnel planning *by companies* should be so designed that it would link directly with that used by Government Departments for national planning. Perhaps the most surprising thing about this statement of the obvious was that it had not been actively explored before.

As yet, no complete solution to the problem has been found, but discussions between Government and industry are going forward. These centre round the characteristics which derive from the processes of decision making—and involve distinguishing the job skill, the *basic criteria* of each post, from the *associated factors*. The underlying principles of the proposed classification are derived from the planning stages 1 and 2 set out above.

Planning properly follows a sequence of decisions, thus the information to be stored and retrieved for planning should depend on a system of descriptors which, itself, is based on the logical processes of decision making and committal of resources. Again, since the approach to job classification accepts that top level decisions must impose their characteristic on the post being described, it follows that the information can most usefully be interpreted in a corresponding form. For instance, an initial decision to increase the R & D effort can be monitored by retrieving the number of posts (and costs) reflecting the current effort in the R & D function.

MANPOWER PLANNING BY GOVERNMENT

A brief description of manpower planning at national level was given above. We can now look at two further aspects of the complexities of planning by a central authority.

The first aspect which is of importance for manpower planning is the cumulative build-up of stock. Large manpower aggregates such as the whole of the working population will change only slowly whatever the economic climate—for instance, the number employed in manufacturing in the year 2000 is expected to be little different to what is now. However, in small occupational groups the situation can be very different—this is because the inputs to the group from the educational system can be very large in comparison with the size of the stock. It follows that abrupt changes in flows can bring quite dramatic results.

It will be remembered that, at the height of the Apollo programme in the United States, the number of emigrants with engineering qualifications, over 6000, was equivalent to 50 per cent of the new supply.[1] Looking at this another way, if there had been neither natural wastage nor migrations, the number in employment would have risen by 8 per cent each year. This is a sobering thought for planners.

It can thus be seen that in certain circumstances, changes in flows can bring very marked changes in stock. It follows that the manpower planner must pay *even more attention* to this 'cumulation factor' where the body of people is small and specialized; and where the economic rewards are high, attracting even more entrants to training.

From time to time the economy experiences a very sharp increase in the number of job opportunities in a new specialism or technology; nuclear science and computers are two such examples. It is very much the responsibility of the national manpower planner to assess whether the upsurge in training that follows is meeting a long-term need or whether, sometime later, the number of new job opportunities will be below the numbers that are trained each year.

This brings us to a second important factor, the dynamic characteristics of the organization. Organizations are invariably subject to a feature of growth that might be described a the 'S curve'. They start slowly, experience a period of fast growth in employment and then tend to level off. In recent times we have seen this phenomenon occur in aviation, in atomic energy, even in the staffing of the universities following the Robbins expansion. As the growth occurs, universities and other educational institutions do their utmost to fill the gap between demand and supply; and employers, who in such situations face an inflation of salaries, will be critical if the trained people do not become available.[2]'

It is in this situation that the manpower planner has his heaviest responsibility. There is invariably a disinclination to look far enough into the future. Infrequently the extent of the shortage is exaggerated, even to the point where demand would be met by stock accumulation with no further action taken. The danger is that the new supply becomes available just when the creation of new posts requiring such skills is tailing off.

The phenomenon of the 'S curve' growth, and its effect on the provision of new job opportunities can best be illustrated by an example. Figure 3 represents a sector which is introducing a new technology over a period of years, let us say 1958-1972. As a result, there is very fast growth in employment around the second quarter of the period shown and slightly less growth in the third quarter. In the fourth quarter employment levels off and finally declines as international competition restricts its market. The pattern of recruitment for that sector is shown in the bar chart below the line representing employment. It will be seen that the recruitment would be highest in the second quarter—corresponding to the period of fastest growth. By the fourth quarter, recruitment would be required only for the replacement of these who died or resigned[2]; without any further growth this may level out at about 3½ per cent, even less. (See Table 1 for calculation of necessary recruitment.)

The characteristics of these inter-related charts suggest that the planner must pay special attention to two things:

(a) Pressure for raising the output of specialists can be expected to be most intense around the second quarter of any growth period: the period when advertisements for the period when advertisements for posts are most numerous and salaries are high relative to other specializms.

Figure 3. Employment in Sector Adopting a New Technology over 15 years Simulated Example.

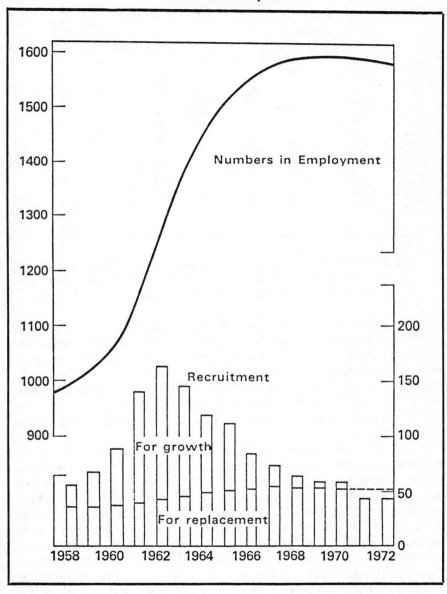

Table 1. Simulated Example of a Sector Adopting a New Technology over 15 years.

	Employment				Recruitment		
	At January	Change in year %	Total	For growth	Total	To replace losses from Normal mobility	Wastage
1958	980	2.0	57	+ 20	37	20	17
1959	1000	3.0	67	+ 30	37	20	17
1960	1030	4.9	88	+ 50	38	21	17
1961	1080	9.3	140	+100	40	22	18
1962	1180	10.2	163	+120	43	24	19
1963	1300	7.7	146	+100	46	26	20
1964	1400	5.0	119	+ 70	49	28	21
1965	1470	4.1	111	+ 60	51	29	22
1966	1530	2.0	83	+ 30	53	31	22
1967	1560	1.3	73	+ 20	53	31	22
1968	1580	0.6	63	+ 10	53	32	21
1969	1590	0.3	58	+ 5	53	32	21
1970	1595	0.3	58	+ 5	53	32	21
1971	1600	− 0.6	43	−	43	22	21
1972	1590	− 0.6	43	−	43	22	21
1973	1580						

(b) The initiation of additional training places at this point on the growth curve almost ensures that the additional graduates present themselves just as the market weakens.

The lower bar chart also suggests that longer-term courses for specialized technologies should be planned with care: possibly restricted to no more than 5 per cent stock replacement. This would leave the peak demand to be met by overseas graduates or by 'crash' courses. To achieve this, some estimate must be made of the level at which employment will level off—the top of the 'S curve'—but experience has shown that economic assessments of this type can be made and are good enough to set the limits.

This task, though exacting, is not one that can be side-stepped by the national manpower planner. The risk of disappointment and frustration among young people who graduate and then find the job opportunities are not there is very considerable. At the present time the overall position for highly qualified people is such that the ability for sideways transfer between one occupational group and another is already being restricted. In the past this has largely been avoided because the number of highly educated people in the economy has been well below demand. The situation now arising suggests that some ground rules should be observed by any planner (or advisory committee) who is seeking the correct response to a rising demand for specialized graduates.

1. Such a decision, of course, will be preceded by a review of alternative goals— but this is not strictly part of the planning stage.

2. In situation of declining employment employees leaving for posts in other sectors will not be replaced.
   For discussion of natural wastage and normal mobility see Sections 11 and 22 of *Persons with Qualifications in Engineering, Technology and Science, 1959-1968*.

REFERENCES

(1) Statistics of emigration and new supply are taken from Table 28 of *Persons with Qualification in Engineering, Technology and Science 1959-1968* HMSO (March 1971).

(2) For discussion of flows see Section 22 of *Persons with Qualifications in Engineering, Technology and Science 1959-1968* HMSO (March 1971).

CHAPTER 2
TOTAL ORGANIZATIONAL STRATEGIC MANAGEMENT PLANNING

The State of Practice in Planning Systems
H. Igor Ansoff

Introduction

This article is concerned with *formal management systems* which are the explicit arrangements for guiding and controlling the work or complex goal-seeking organizations. Within the U.S., the prime inventor and developer of management systems has been the business firm. These inventions have occurred in response to both the growing size and complexity of internal operations and the growing turbulence of the firm's environment.

Since 1900, the challenges confronting the firm have become more numerous and complex, the scope of the relevant enviroment has expanded, and the rate of change has accelerated. From the simple task of "giving it to them in any color so long as it is (cheap and) black," defined by Henry Ford, management tasks have expanded to include global diversification, mastering the "R&D monster," coping with external socio-political pressures, and responding to growing demands for redesign of the working environment within the firm.

In order to cope with these problems, leading firms have invented systems and other firms have followed by adopting these inventions. The resultant of this process is an accumulation of one hundred years' worth of management technology. Since each generation of systems was designed to respond to immediate and pressing problems, the overall development has appeared to lack logical continuity. Successive systems were usually advertised as inventions superior to and superseding all previous approaches. Thus, long-range planning replaced

"The State of Practice in Planning Systems," H. Igor Ansoff, *Sloan Management Review*, vol. 18, no. 2, Winter 1977, pp. 1-24. Reprinted by permission.

H. Igor Ansoff is on the faculty at Vanderbilt University.

budgeting, in turn to be replaced by profit planning, only to be succeeded by strategic planning. Then, the latter was claimed to have become old-fashioned when PPBS (Planning-Programming-Budgeting System) was introduced.

In the perspective of history two facts seem clear:

1. Systems development has followed a coherent logic dictated by the growing complexity of the problems which needed solving.
2. The succeeding systems usually were not replacements, but were enlargements and enrichments of the preceding efforts.

These facts permit us now to treat the accumulated systems know-how not as a collection of unrelated problem-solutions, but as a coherent body of design technology which can be used to custom-make the system needed by a particular firm.

The rest of this article is devoted to two objectives:

1. To trace the historical logic of systems development and to predict some key characteristics of future systems.
2. To briefly describe an approach to custom designing a system to meet the needs of a firm. Information will be provided to enable the reader to initiate a diagnosis of his firm and to begin to determine the needed improvements.

Evolution of Managerial Problem Space

The activity of the firm can be subdivided into different classes:

- The *logistic* or productive activity devoted to the acquisition, conversion, and distribution of resources. This class is typically further subdivided into functions of R&D, manufacturing, distribution, selling, purchasing, advertising, and promotion.
- The *management* activity which designs the logistic activity, sets objectives, creates plans, and guides the execution of plans.

The logistic process is very complex, involving the use and conversion of many inputs: raw materials, partially fabricated products, facilities, equipment, energy, financial resources, human beings, and information. At first glance, the management process appears simpler because it handles only information and because, until recently, it was essentially a "manual" process involving little labor-saving technology and virtually no capital labor substitution. In response to the growing challenges to the firm, the job of management has become ever larger and increasingly complex. The advent of management technology and the electronic computer has recently begun a transformation of management from an essentially labor intensive into a capital intensive process. Already, the quality of management has become more critical to the success of a firm than the quality of its logistic work.

Until the early 1950s, analysis of management activity had typically followed the *functional* structure of the logistic process (e.g. sales management or production management). Overseeing these functional managers was *general management*, which was seen primarily as a process of "adding things up," coordination and integration of the functional activities. In recent years, these traditional classifications have become increasingly inadequate for understanding and analyzing the drastically changing agenda of managerial problems. As a result, new classification schemes have emerged.

Figure 1 shows an approach for describing the three hierarchically related managerial activities which guide the logistic process.

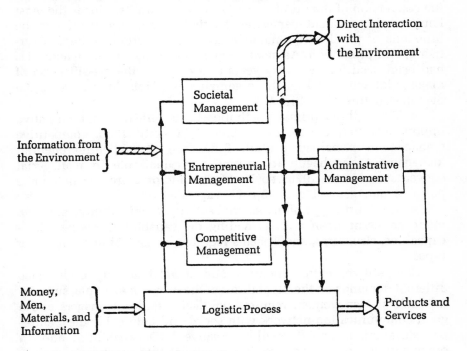

Figure 1. Principal Managerial Activities

● At the highest level, *societal or politcal management* determines the legitimacy and viability of the firm in society. It concerns itself with the firm's noncommercial environment: legislative, judicial, and regulatory governmental bodies, as well as social groups which have a "stake" in the firm: labor unions, consumers, shareholders, ecologists, and others.

The end products of societal management are the freedoms, constraints, and the "rules of the game" under which the firm operate within society. For the past one hundred years in the U.S. and Western Europe, societal management has remained a minor activity, but it is now emerging as a puzzling and probably the most important problem management will face over the next fifteen years.

● At the second highest level, *entrepreneurial management* concerns itself with creating the profit *potential* for the firm: identifying areas of opportunity, creating and developing products for these areas, and introducing the products to the markets. When the potential of an area is exhausted, or the products become obsolete, entrepreneurial management concerns itself with divestment.

● At the third level, *competitive management* concerns itself with the conversion of the profit potential into real profits. This is the most familiar and prevalent management activity. It concerns itself with the functions of purchasing, manufacturing, distribution, selling, advertising, and promotion. As mentioned above, these operating activities had been used for the many years as a basis for the classification of managerial work and as the organizing principle in designing the overall structure of the firm.[1]

● These three primary activities have shifted in their relative importance. In the U.S. from about 1890 until 1950, competitive management remained central. Since the 1950s, entrepreneurial management has begun to assume a coequal role in managerial concerns; and in the 1970s, societal forces and pressures began to force political management to the top of the agenda.

● The fourth type of managerial activity, *administrative management*, concerns itself with providing the capabilities: values, skills capacities, structures, and systems required by each of the three other types.

Competitive, entrepreneurial, and societal activity each place different demands on the capabilities of the firm. For example, successful societal management requires politically skilled managers and a good communication network with social and political bodies; entrepreneurial management requires creative R&D capabilities and an organization capable of converting inventions into commercial reality; successful competition depends on a fine balance between internal cost controls and external responsiveness to customer needs and wants. As priorities shifted from competitive to entrepreneurial to societal management, new demands were placed on administrative managements to provide the requisite capabilities.

The historical evolution of systems can be seen as a response to these changing managerial priorities. However, a perspective on systems is likely to be distorted, unless we keep in mind that changing priorities did not mean that the previously important activity "faded away." Rather, the changes expanded the scope of managerial work. Today, good competitive management is no less critical to the survival of the firm than it was fifty years ago, but increasingly, it has to share the limelight with entrepreneurial and societal management.

Static and Dynamic Management Systems

The constantly changing nature of managerial work generated a comparably changing need for formal arrangements to cope with and control the new complexities. In addition, the study of American business history shows that, besides the environmental pressures, there has always been a persistent, internally generated drive to do things better and more efficiently. The result of these two drives has been a continual flow of new ways and approaches for doing managerial work.

The earliest systematic arrangements of the managerial work originated in the second half of the nineteenth century, when the shape of the modern firm was emerging. One of the first systems developed was *standing policies and procedures*, which was typically embodied in a manual with this name and which is still found in all firms today. The manual collects rules for decision making (policies) and steps to be followed (procedures) for a wide variety of repetitive and contingent activities of the firm ranging from hours of work to leaves of absence and union negotiations.

Another early development was a formal grouping of the firm's logistic and managerial activities which became known as the *organizational structure*. The first formal structure to receive almost universal application grouped "like logistic activities" in ways which permitted maximum economies of scale and specialization.[2] In this form, the managerial structure was made to follow the same logic, except for addition of the general management functions on top. During the following sixty years, this structure, which emerged around 1910 under the name of *functional structure*, was followed by a rich proliferation of replacement alternatives, such as *divisional structure, multinational structure, matrix structure,* and *innovative structure.*

Until very recently, all of these replacement alternatives shared with the functional form two important features which characterize each of them as *static systems:*

- They specified the responsibility, authority, and tasks assigned to organizational subgroups — but did not specify the dynamics of interactions or the transfers among them.
- A structure once put in place was supposed to be "permanent," not to be changed in the foreseeable future. A change typically

came after it became evident that the prior structure had outlived its usefulness.

Static systems were a major step in systematizing the administrative concerns of management. They provided an overall conception of relationships throughout the firm which were easily communicated. Also, like the trunk of a tree, they can be elaborated with various branches. A number of important branches addressed to systematizing administrative management have evolved in the past fifty years. Some of these are sketched in the left-hand stem of Figure 2.[3]

The concerns of this article direct our attention to the right-hand stem which traces the history of systems first for competitive, and then, for entrepreneurial management. Most of these are *dynamic systems* in two senses of the word:

- They concern themselves with flows of informaton, influence, and decision making within the structure.
- They are explicitly concerned with the timing of the flows.

Before focusing on these action systems, we need to recognize that their relationship to organizational structure has been a close one. Historically, dynamic systems have developed with the framework of structure. Structure provided the static network of relationships, the "plumbing" of the firm, the dynamic systems defined the flows of information and decision making within the "pipes."

It was not until the 1960s that dynamic systems such as PPBS found themselves so much at cross purposes with structure that a formal technique, called the "crosswalk," was invented to assure coordination of system and structure. The trend in the future, undoubtedly, will be toward a gradual disappearance of the distinction between static and dynamic systems and toward the emergence of integrated systems and concepts.

Evolution of Dynamic Systems

The currently available inventory of dynamic systems is shown in Table 1. Included are the purposes which each system serves, the environmental and external conditions under which it applies, and management objectives and style for which it is best suited.

As can be seen from the right-hand column, contrary to contemporary claims that these systems were mutually preemptive, each expanded and complemented the range of managerial tasks which could be assisted by formal systems. The remaining columns offer an insight into the logic of system evolution. All of the early systems started in an

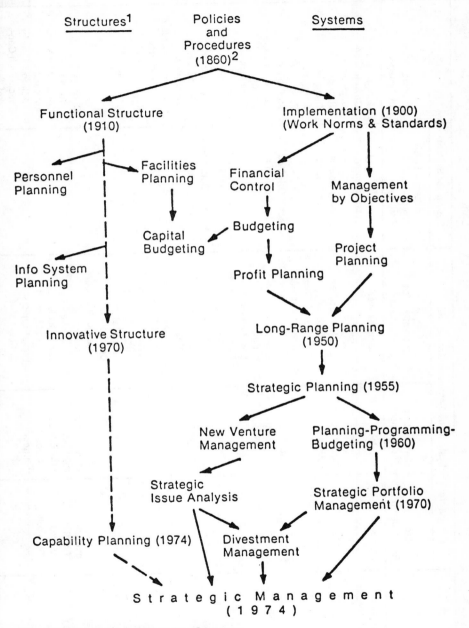

Figure 2. Evolution of Planning Systems.

1 For development of structure see Ansoff and
  Brandenburg [4].

2 The dates show the advent of each form.

| | Pressures for System and Necessary Conditions | | | Desires for System | Contributions of Systems |
System	Strategic Environment	Competitive Environment	Characteristics of Problems	Management Style, Objectives, and Strategy	
Implementation (Work Management)	Stable	Stable	Complex Work	Work Efficiency Management	Assignment Coordination Supervision Recognition
Control	Stable	Smoothly Growing	Stable Resource Allocation Short Lead Times Complex Organiz.	Cost-Conscious Management	Diagnosis Correction Productivity
Management by Objectives	Stable	Smoothly Growing	People Intensity Low Human Productivity Low Morale Demand for Better Conditions	People-Oriented Management	Motivation Human Productivity Teamwork Skills
Budgeting	Stable	Smoothly Growing	Complex Organiz. Scarcity of Resources Long Investment Lead Times Capital Intensity Large Working Capital Competition for Resources	Finance-Conscious Management	Allocation of Resources Anticipate Investment Needs Cost Efficiency Basis for Control
Project Planning	Changing Products Markets Technology	Fluctuating Competitive Alternative Opportunities	Interdependent Activities Large Scale Development Long Projects Critical Paths		Coordination of Activities Control of Actions Anticipation of Action Critical Path Control

				Growth-Oriented Management	Selection of Activities Anticipation of Action Needs
Long-Range Planning/Operations Planning	Stable	Same as Above	Interdependent Operations Complex Tech. Competition for Activities Long Action Lead Times		Selection of Activities Anticipation of Action Needs
Long-Range Planning/Development Planning	Changing Products Markets Technology	Same as Above	Technological Intensity Active p-m Development Short Product Cycles Conflict among Functional Areas	Innovation-Conscious Management	Optimal Selection of Product-Markets Cost-Effective Development Technological Responsiveness Market Responsiveness Shortened Innovation Cycle Timely Divestment
Strategic Planning	Discontinuities New Industry Opportunities New Technology Opportunities	Same as Above	Industry Decline Maturity Strategic Imbalance Discontinuities Threats of Discontinuities Innovation a Major Activity Foreign Competition Same as Above	Innovation Diversification Management Management Objectives Exceed Potential	Anticipation of Threats and Opport. Accelerated Growth Profitability Potential
PPBS (Sum of Strategic and Operations Planning)	Same as Above	Same as Above	Same as Above	Same as Above	Same as Above

Table 1. Determinants of Management Systems.

environment which was at worst, mildly competitively unstable. As the instability grew, the duality of cost-focused systems and performance-focused systems increasingly created situations, where the sides failed to know the other's actions and where they even operated at cross-purposes. For example, on occasion, plant capacities were expanded for products with declining demand!

A synthesis of cost and performance was offered by long-range planning which emerged in the mid-fifties. This was the first "total system" and also was hailed as the first management system which enabled the firm to prepare itself for its long-term future. Since 1950, it has been widely adopted, first in America, and somewhat later, throughout Western Europe.[4]

In the mid-fifties, an increasing number of firms encountered environmental problems which could not be handled by long-range planning. The reasons were not clear at the time, but another system, strategic planning, appeared to remedy these new problems. In the perspective of time, it seems that the "future" projected by long-range planning was not capable of handling strategic discontinuities and was limited to competitive management. Strategic planning, through its systematic analysis of alternative possible futures, turned attention to entrepreneurial management.

However, it alone could not replace long-range planning, because it lacked the mechanism of translating strategies into actions: the stipulated output of the strategic planning process was a set of strategies which were left to be "implemented" in a vaguely specified manner.

Planning-Programming-Budgeting System (PPBS) removed this vagueness by integrating strategic and long-ranging planning to serve both strategic and competitive management. PPBS was more than a simple addition of strategic and long-range planning. It also introduced a perspective on the environment which was previously missing. Earlier systems perceived the environment through the perspective of an organizational structure; each important organizational unit made its own strategic plan. In firms which were functionally organized, this produced an overly aggregated view of the environment; whereas in large divisionalized firms, the perspective of the future was obscured by the multiplicity and interdivisional overlaps of product lines and markets.

To avoid this loss of perspective, PPBS organized its environment into "mission slices" each of which represented a distinctive "product-market" area with distinctive needs, growth characteristics, and risks. The "mission slice" terminology which was developed in the early military use of PPBS has been replaced by the more precise concept of "strategic business area."[5]

The strategic business area perspective gives the firm a much clearer perception of its environment and its future, but it frequently runs contrary to the logic of the firm's organizational structure. In original PPBS applications the contradiction was solved by the "crosswalk" technique: the strategic plan was made by mission slices, and then cross-mapped into implementation. The General Electric Company tried to avoid this "crosswalk" by mapping the independent strategic business areas in which it participates onto the most suitable units within the organization, disregarding both hierarchical level and size. Organization units thus identified were labeled "strategic business units."

A BUILDING BLOCK APPROACH

Table 1 contains considerably greater detail than is needed to illustrate the differences among the nine types of currently used management systems. The extra detail provides a diagnostic tool which the manager can use, either to diagnose the adequacy of his current system, or to determine the system needs of the firm.

The suggested process has four steps:

1. Starting in the right-hand column, circle each aspect of the firm's performance that is either currently deficient, or that can be improved through a systematic approach.
2. Diagnose and circle the appropriate desires for the system (in the second column from the right).
3. Circle the type of strategic and competitive environments facing the firm (in the second and third left-hand columns).
4. Lastly and most important, circle those problems (in column four) which are confronting the firm.

The examination of each line which has been circled will identify the set of systems that are needed by the firm. A comparison of this list with the systems already found in the firm will identify which additional ones are needed.

The systems identified are, of course, not complete in themselves. They represent only isolated steps in a complete cycle of managerial activity and must be related to one another and integrated into a coherent total system configuration. A building block method for integrating the subsystems together is depicted in Figure 3.

The content and procedure of four of the basic blocks are not subject sensitive. The managerial tasks within these blocks are described below:

● The *implementation* or "work-management" block includes the establishment and communication of work norms, monitoring of progress, and correction of the performance of work.

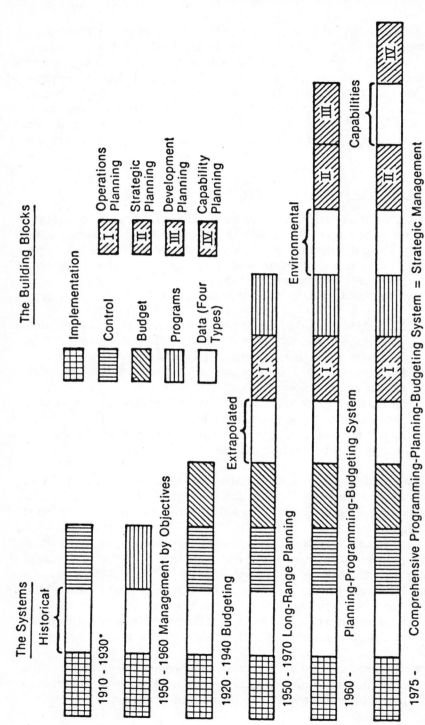

Figure 3. The Building Block Approach to the Design of Total Management Systems.

*The dates span the periods of growing acceptance.

- The *control* block includes the establishment of output norms, performance measurement, and diagnosis and correction of problems.
- The *budgeting* block includes the determination of the future pattern of activities and their costs, resource allocations among activities, scheduling of expenditures, and the establishment of milestones.
- The *programming* block includes determination of performance objectives, analysis of activities, scheduling of activities, and establishment of performance milestones.

These blocks plus historical data compose the earlier, less complicated systems.

There are four different subject sensitive data block types which provide input data for the management systems:

- *Historical* performance data (usually called "information systems") includes the measurement and interpretation of past performance.
- *Extrapolated* data includes forecasted trends in related demand areas, analysis of competitive behavior, and prediction of competitive behavior.
- *Environmental* data includes the results of a surveillance and analysis process which forecasts discontinuities in related trends, forecasts trends in unrelated areas, interprets trends into threats and opportunities, and identifies unfilled social needs.
- *Capabilities* data includes measurement of organizational resources and inventories of skills, capacities, and capabilities.

Also subject sensitive are the four different types of planning blocks which are the decision-making elements in the systems:

- *Operations planning* (I) includes forecasting environmental conditions and future demand, establishing performance objectives, developing growth directions, making comparisons with objectives, and selecting preferred growth directions.
- *Strategic planning* (II) includes the evaluation of environmental trends; determination of opportunities and threats; establishment of corporate philosophy; setting of corporate objectives; generation, evaluation, and choice of strategic alternatives; and the portfolio balancing of alternatives.
- *Development planning* (III) includes the generation of new project proposals, the evaluation of the proposals against objectives and strategies, and the assignment of organizational responsibilities.

- *Capability planning* (IV) includes the evaluation of present capabilities, determination of future capabilities selected by strategy, and determination of the ultimate pattern of capabilities along with priorities in the transition.

The descriptions of the procedures and contents of these building blocks provide the manager with another diagnostic opportunity. Having identified which of these systems are now in place in his company, he can proceed using this information as a checklist to determine how well each of his subsystems is elaborated and executed.[6]

Returning to Figure 3, the left-hand side shows the sequence of total system configurations, as they evolved in the U.S. It should be noted that the needs for input data have cumulated progressively—from historical data, to extrapolated perception of the environment, to a perception of the turbulent environment (labeled "environmental data" in PPBS), to data on the internal capabilities and capacities of the firm (commonly called "strengths and weaknesses"). The last system, strategic management, is only now emerging on the scene and will be discussed later in this article.

The building block approach outlined above is a *recent* development. It makes possible selecting subsystems which result in *tailoring* the total system to the needs of the firm. This approach should be contrasted to the practice, used until recently, of imposing a "universal" system on all customers of a given consulting firm.

CONTENT OF THE PLANNING SYSTEMS

An important conceptual break occurred in the planning component of management systems, when the system called long-range planning was enlarged to become PPBS.

In long-range planning, the future was made explicit through environmental forecasts. Given the forecast, the firm's goals were set for the near and long-term future (typically for sales, profits, and return on investment). Next the goals were translated into action programs, then into budgets, and finally into profit plans. Since proposed budgets typically exceeded available resources, feasibility was checked next and the reconciled plans were examined and approved by higher management.

Clearly, the validity of the resulting plan is no better than the validity of its informational input. In long-range planning, the key input is the forecast of the future trends in demand, prices, competitive behavior, economic climate, etc. Invariably, these forecasts are extrapolative—*smooth* projections of historical trends into the future.

The systems which historically preceded Long-Range Planning—Budgeting, MBO, and Control—also explicitly or implicitly assumed that the future would be a smooth extrapolation of the past. The systems differed from each other depending on whether the future was forecast explicitly or implicitly and on how comprehensively future profits, programs, and budgets were specified.

When the environment became turbulent, reliance on an extrapolation of the past became unwise. A new type of planning system, capable of coping with discontinuities, was developed. This approach which is called *entrepreneurial planning* is shown in Figure 4. It is a decision-making logic which is common to the modern systems, including strategic planning, new venture planning, PPBS, strategic management, strategic portfolio management, strategic issue analysis, and real-time strategic planning.

Entrepreneurial planning makes two fundamental departures from the earlier extrapolative planning techniques:

- It treats the environment in a much broader perspective. The forecasts of the future seek to discern likely significant discontinuities and changes in directions. The field of search for these discontinuities and changes goes beyond the traditional boundaries of the firm's environment to encompass technological, political, sociological, and economic trends which are relevant to the firm's future.
- It differs in the manner by which information is processed. If the evaluation of the firm's prospects makes it evident that the future of the firm's current business is unattractive (See box "Extrapolate or Change?"), a search for new alternatives is instituted, their consequences are analyzed, and the best orientation is selected.

This enlarged environmental awareness necessitates enlarged *internal* awareness. If the firm is to consider alternatives to its past activities, it needs to know its capabilities and capacities ("Strengths and Weaknesses") for undertaking new departures.

Similarly, the problem of the firm's objectives is considered. Whereas extrapolation typically projects *past goals* into the future, the entrepreneurial openness of outlook raises questions about both a possible *discontinuity in goals* and a *shift of emphasis of the objectives* of the firm.

The results of the planning process are usually incorporated into a planning document. The typical chapters include mission, key environmental assumptions, key competitor assumptions, constraints,

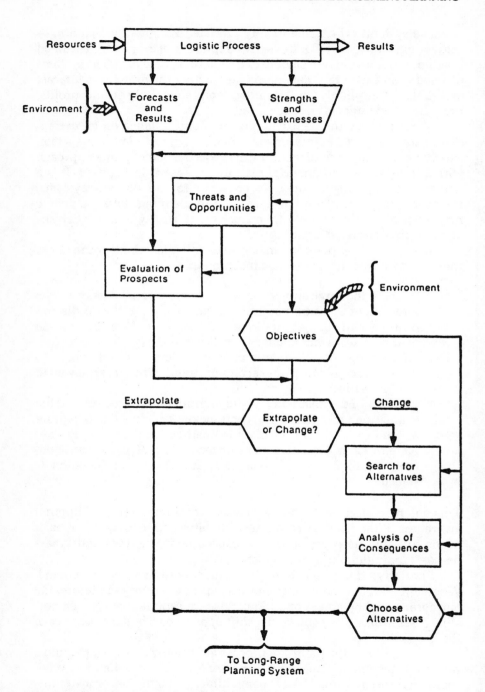

Figure 4. An Entrepreneurial Planning System.

objectives, goals, strategies, programs, budgets, contingencies, and a long-range forecast. The early systems lacked most of these sections; budgeting has only budgets and management by objectives has only goals. PPBS has all of these chapters, while long-range planning looks only at competitors, goals, budgets, programs, and a long-range forecast. Strategic planning, as described in this article, lacks only the budgets, programs, and competitor information found in the full-scale plans of PPBS. The comparison of these chapter listings with the chapters found in the manager's current planning documents provides another diagnostic opportunity.

INDIVIDUAL ROLES AND RESPONSIBILITIES IN DESIGN AND USE OF SYSTEMS.

During the era of long-range planning when extrapolation was the base for viewing the future, the principal function of the planner was to design and to install the system, to monitor its operations, to coordinate and to integrate plans prepared by working managers. Thus, the working manager planned while the staff planner tried to make the planning process work. Today, although process management has remained important, the advent of the higher forms of planning has substantially expanded the repertoire of the planner's work. Usually neither the capacity nor capabilities for the new tasks were to be found inside the firm. As a result, the planning and control staff had to be expanded in size, scope of responsibilities, and the range of competence and skills. Table 2 presents an up-to-date listing of the planning work required in a sophisticated entrepreneurial planning system.

This broad scope of activities suggests that it is no longer helpful to characterize "the planner" in the singular, since there is more planning work than an individual can handle. Also, the new range of work requires a variety of knowledge and skills rarely found in a single individual. The traditional systems designer-expediter is still needed, but also required are the entrepreneurially-minded new venture analyst, the analytic diagnostician-controller, a skilled forecaster-analyst, and the computer model builder.

Nevertheless, there is still an important distinction to be made between this group of planning workers and the line managers. The responsibilities of the latter as found in practice are to:

- Assure that planning is integrated with implementation and control;
- Make the necessary decisions, choices, and commitments in the course of the planning process.

Capability Development	Information Base	Process Control	Performance Control	New Venture Management
Design of Organizational Structure	Environmental Surveillance	Coordination of Planning	Measurement of Performance	Identification of Opportunities
Design of Planning Systems & Procedures	Forecasting	Integration of Plans	Diagnosis of Deficiency	Analysis of Opportunities
Management Development	Threats and Opportunities	Evaluation of Planning Systems	Generate Corrective Actions	Acquisition and Development of Opportunities
Modeling	Capability Analysis	Evaluation of Plans	Analyze Corrective Actions	
Revision of Planning Systems	Generation of Alternatives		Monitor Corrective Actions	
Implementation of Planning Support Systems	Analysis of Alternatives			
Introduction of Planning Systems				

Table 2. Functions of a Planning and Control Staff.

ORGANIZATIONAL FLOW OF PLANNING

In the early days of planning, it appeared that the advent of formal planning would lead to the centralization of decision power. Early system designers visualized that, eventually, all important planning decisions would be made in the corporate office, with the aid of high speed computers. Very quickly this solution proved unworkable in practice. When centralized planning was attempted, the planning process became separated from the realities of day-to-day action; plans were neglected and disregarded by managers responsible for carrying them out; planning became largely an academic exercise. A decentralized planning concept emerged which directed that plans should be prepared by individuals responsible for executing them. This produced much better results and has been adopted in general practice.

Application of this principle made it necessary that system decision points be matched to the organizational responsibility points. But another problem arose: In what direction should planning flow—from the top of the firm down or from the bottom up?

Since the entrepreneurial and societal decisions are the higher level decisions within which competitive planning must take place, the flow must be arranged to take care of strategic planning first and competitive planning second. Applying this answer to the divisional form of organization structure, we obtain a sequential flow of planning which is neither top down nor bottom up, but which combines the two flows to enable a constructive interaction of integrating guidelines from the top and local initiatives from below. Flows of this type are to be found today in a majority of firms practicing planning.[7]

A new dimension of complexity occurs in the multinational structure where the concept of divisions is typically replaced by "product-groups" and a new structural dimension of "countries" is added.[8] The directional flows of planning can be modified easily enough to add the country dimension, but the location of the strategic decision responsibility becomes unclear: both "countries" and "product-groups" have responsibility as well as important inputs to the strategic decision process.

At the present time three approaches to resolving the responsibility complex are found in practice:

1. Responsibility for strategic decisions is assigned to "product groups"; the countries contribute and consult.
2. Strategic responsibility is shared and strategic plans are arrived at through negotiation.
3. Responsibility is assigned according to the relative size and importance of the country market. When the latter becomes large enough to justify a separate product-line strategy, the responsibility is shifted to the country.

THE HUMAN DIMENSIONS OF SYSTEMS

Early applications of long-range planning ran into "resistance to planning" from both line and staff managers. As systems became more sophisticated, the resistance to planning persisted as seen in the dramatic example of Mr. McNamara's struggle with the U.S. defense establishment over the introduction of PPBS.[9]

The solution for overcoming resistance to planning, offered in the literature, was to secure an enthusiastic support for the system from top management. Given the high degree of technological sophistication in modern planning, this is a strangely naive prescription: "If managers do not plan willingly, threaten them with the displeasure of the big boss and tell them that he loves planning."

As a result of success and failure experiences, and thanks to the monumental work of A. Chandler, an understanding of the causes of the resistance and more sophisticated ways of coping with it is available.[10] These concepts recognize the profound social, psychological, and political ramifications of introduction of planning into a firm. When successful, formal planning brings about no less than a basic change in the way the firm perceives the environment and conducts its business.

The readiness of a firm to accept the changes inherent with the introduction of planning is key to the success of the effort. Failures frequently result in firms where:

- The managers do not understand the nature and purpose of planning.
- The line managers lack planning skills.
- They are not motivated to plan, because planning interferes with work which yields recognition and rewards.
- The new data base needed for planning is not available and managers are forced to invent unrealistic numbers to put in their plans.
- The responsibilities for plans and the authorities to carry them out are not clearly identified.
- The managers feel threatened with a loss of personal power and a loss of control over resources through the process of making public their private knowledge.
- Some managers fear that planning will expose their incompetence.
- Some managers fear the uncertainty and ambiguity which planning brings into their lives.

This list of eight shortcomings appears to be contradicted by the already impressive spread of corporate planning and its growing applications, but a closer look explains the contradiction.

Typically, introduction of firm-wide planning is a traumatic, turbulent experience. It does require focus of top management attention; it does take three to five years to arrive at a satisfactory planning process. The process is accompanied with latent, if not overt, organizational resistance. If top management support lapses too soon, then planning is either rejected or becomes an annual exercise in managerial frustration.

Often, firms which start with strategic planning "slide back" after a period to the more acceptable and more easily understood extrapolative long-range planning, which does not incur the third and fourth shortcomings in the previous listing. As a result, in spite of almost twenty years of existence of strategic planning technology, a majority of firms today engage in the far less threatening and perturbing extrapolative long-range planning.

Today in anticipation of the previously noted shortcomings and sources of resistance, introduction of planning is increasingly preceded by diagnosis of the *planning readiness* of the firm.

- The first and the most important step is to assure that the proposed system is capable of treating the problems and challenges that management wishes to address. (This step of system selection was discussed earlier in the article.)
- The second step is to rate the firm in terms of the eight shortcomings. The rating process should also consider the planning formats and procedures, top management commitment, linkages to both control and implementation, staff support, and the procedures available for managing the system improvement. This process generates an organizational profile which is used to develop a coordinated program of organizational and cultural change which culminates with the introduction of formal planning.[11]

Future Management Systems

This discussion so far has dealt with systems used in current practice. The systems up to and including long-range planning are widely used; formal strategic planning is still to be found only in a handful of progressive firms. As has happened in the past, the existing systems are already becoming obsolete in an environment growing more turbulent and complex. In response to these changes several systems are currently emerging or can be expected to emerge. Each system is briefly discussed below.

- *Strategic portfolio management* is more a method of analysis than a system; it provides techniques for planning a firm's long-range strategy. The initial applications of this approach are within large firms whose market position is diversified among several turbulent industries which are subject to both "breakthrough" discontinuities and frequent changes in basic technology. Such firms need to pay special attention to balancing their long-term versus short-term growth prospects. They also need to balance their industry "portfolio" against catastrophic breakthroughs. Strategic portfolio management accomplishes both of these tasks.[12]

• Historically, whenever environments changed, firms have adapted their strategies. If the degree of adaptation was major, the internal capability of the firm was unable to support the strategic change. Typically, this "strategy-structure" gap was discovered through trial and error. This process caused structural adaptation to lag substantially behind a change in strategy.

Today, in a number of industries, major strategic shifts have become so frequent that a trial and error adaptation of the capability puts a firm in danger of never having an up-to-date "structure." The concept of *strategic management* has emerged in response to this danger. Briefly described, it puts the planning and management of the firm's capability on an equal footing and in a similar time frame with the planning of strategy.[13]

• Current formal planning systems deal predominantly with the technological-economic environment of the firm. As previously mentioned, both the internal and the external socio-political problems are becoming priority concerns of management.

The major response to date has been development of a "social audit" technology which seeks to do for the socio-political problem what "strengths and weaknesses" analysis did for commercial ones. Given the growing interconnection of the socio-political and commercial problems, it is safe to predict that strategic planning and strategic management will be expanded to accommodate socio-political issues.[14]

• A *strategic issue management system* provides a simple and quick way for responding to both socio-political and commercial trends and to potential discontinuities in the environment. The need for strategic issue management arises from a conflict between the acceleration of environmental change and the slowing response rate of the firm. Company-wide planning systems such as strategic planning, long-range planning, and PPBS, while comprehensive, are also cumbersome and unwieldy. The planning cycles often last from three to six months, involve all parts of the firm, and incur large direct and indirect costs. In an environment where a six-month period can yield a fundamental change in the firm's perspective, this slow response time is in danger of producing obsolete and irrelevant plans. Beyond the sluggishness problems lies an equally difficult cost problem: if the entire firm is to be exercised on each new major strategic issue, it can soon find itself in a perpetual planning turmoil, with little time left to attend to implementation.

Strategic issue management is a "real-time" management system which permits rapid strategic responses, even in large and complex firms. This is made possible by two major features: the system scans the environment for *weak signals,* and it responds to them through ad hoc team-work, which cuts across organizational boundaries.[15]

● The recent "energy (petroleum) crisis" forcefully called attention to a phenomenon which had been observable for many years before. Despite their best efforts, firms are increasingly subject to *strategic surprises:* changes which appear suddenly which have a major impact on the firm, and which must be treated urgently. I predict that in response to the growing incidence of strategic surprises, a *surprise readiness system* will be installed in the business firm. The system will employ strategic surprise readiness techniques used today by military and para-military organizations.[16]

Summary

This article has used an analytical framework to trace the historical evolution of practical management systems in the United States. While each new system appeared to supersede its predecessor, the actual process was one of *enlargement* of the overall systems repertoire. The result is the impressive array of systems which are available today to assist management in a large range of its activities. Several new systems are on the horizon and the building block technology is already available for tailoring systems to the particular needs of a firm.

The emerging systems appear to signal a reversal of an underlying philosophy of management systems design. The progress from the early days of financial control to PPBS was seen by many as a movement toward a *fully integrated and comprehensive* management system (in a manner very similar to the early conceptions of the "ultimate" management information system). The goal was to handle within a single framework, all of the planning problems of the firm. However, even as the trend toward comprehensiveness continues, the requirement for integration and for monolithic frequent exercise of the entire system is slackening off. Instead, there appears to be a shift towards *comprehensive, fully interconnected, but loosely coupled systems* in which:

● "Comprehensive" means a design which encompasses all the important concerns of management which lend themselves to systematic approach, not only *planning* aspects of the process but *planning and implementation and control.* Thus, the term "planning systems" will be replaced by "management systems."
● "Fully interconnected" means that all subsystems within the total system which affect operations of one another are properly interconnected through informational and influence linkages.

- "Loosely coupled" means that each system is designed primarily to meet the needs of the particular managerial problem and a particular management level, and secondarily to meet the needs of integration-coordination with other systems. (This is precisely the reverse of the currently practiced design philosophy.) This means, for example, that the "time clocks" on which the subsystems operate are allowed to be different, so long as they are coordinated. This also implies a freedom for ad hoc exercise of a system in one part of an organization without involving other parts.

The underlying assumption in the preceding predictions is that progressive management will remain true to its historical tradition. As the problems become more complex and the world more turbulent, management will continue to devise new systems for reducing complexity and solving unfamiliar problems. In all fairness, it should be recognized that some observers of the same scene arrive at a different conclusion: when the environment becomes turbulent, managment will abandon its systems and return to managing by intuition and experience.[17]

NOTES

1. See Ansoff [1] and Ansoff and Brandenburg [4].
2. See Chandler [8].
3. For a further discussion see Ansoff and Brandenburg [4].
4. See Ringbaack [11].
5. See Ansoff and Leontiades [6].
6. For a detailed procedure for management systems diagnosis and design see Ansoff [3].
7. See Ansoff [3].
8. See Ansoff and Brandenburg [4].
9. See Schick [12].
10. See Chandler [8].
11. See Ansoff, Hayes, and Declerck [5].
12. See Ansoff and Leontiades [6].
13. See Ansoff, Hayes, and Declerck [5].
14. See Ansoff and Nelson [7].
15. See [9].
16. See Ansoff [2].

REFERENCES

Ansoff, H. I. "Corporate Structure, Present and Future." *La Structure de L'Enterprise, Aujourd'hui et Demain.* Switzerland: Foundation Nationale Pour L'Enseignement de la Gestion, no. 9, October 1974.

Ansoff, H. I. "Planned Management of Turbulent Change." *Encyclopedia of Professional Management.* New York: McGraw-Hill, forthcoming.

Ansoff, H. I. "The State of Practice in Management Systems." Brussels Belgium: European Institute of Advanced Studies in Management Working Paper 75-11.

Ansoff, H. I., and Brandenburg, R. G. "A Language for Organizational Design." *Management Science,* vol. 17 no. 12, August 1971.

Ansoff, H. I.; Hayes, R. L; and Declerck, R. P.; eds. *From Strategic Planning to Strategic Management.* New York: John Wiley & Sons, 1976.

Ansoff, H. I., and Leontiades, J. C. "Strategic Portfolio Management." Milan, Italy: *l'Inustria 1,* first semester, 1976, and *The Journal of General Management,* in press.

Ansoff, H. I., and Nelson, O. T. "Societal Strategy for the Business Firm." Forthcoming.

Chandler, A. D., Jr. *Strategy and Structure.* Cambridge, Mass.: The MIT Press, 1962.

"Managing Strategic Surprise by Response to Weak Signals." *California Management Review,* Winter 1976.

Mintzberg, H. "Planning on the Left Side and Managing on the Right." *Harvard Business Review,* July-August 1976.

Ringbaack. "Studies of U.S. and European Planning Products."

Schick, A. "Systems Politics and Systems Budgeting." *Public Administration Review,* vol. 29 no. 2, March-April 1969.

Linking Human Resource Planning and Strategic Planning
James W. Walker

Planning is generally regarded today as vital to the effective management of large organizations. During the past several decades, most companies have adopted systematic processes for deciding on objectives, on the resources needed, and the manner of operations that

Reprinted with permission from *Human Resource Planning,* Spring 1978. Copyright © 1978 by the Human Resource Planning Society.

James W. Walker is a Principal of Towers, Perrin, Forster & Crosby, Inc., Boston, Massachusetts.

will be applied to use these resources to attain these objectives. In many instances, this planning is *strategic* in nature. That is, the planning addresses prospective changes in business objectives and the forces affecting the business. Drucker notes that it is necessary in strategic planning to ask: What is the business? What will it be? and What should it be? With respect to the last question, the usual assumption is that the business will become different in one or more ways (Drucker, 1974).

Natural resources, technological capacities, patents and products, market share and position, and financial capital are all given close consideration in strategic planning. However, consideration of human resource needs is usually limited to annual budgeting and planning, or to analysis and planning conducted by personnel specialists for the planning of personnel programs such as training and recruiting. Often, human resource planning is viewed as a necessary, but subordinate, process of assuring that adequate numbers and types of people are available to staff planned operations. Published discussions of human resource planning practices indicate that generally ignore the possibility that human resources may affect business plans (Steiner, 1969; Vetter, 1967; Burack, 1972; Keys, Thompson and Heath, 1971; Ettelstein, 1970).

Companies often give lip service to the importance of human resources in achievement of business objectives, but rarely is detailed, thoughtful analysis performed. Executives are confident that necessary personnel can always be recruited in the marketplace to meet future needs, should the internal supply prove inadequate. Business planners tend to focus on financial and marketing aspects of planning, often the functional specializations in which they were primarily educated. Personnel professionals, even human resource planning specialists, often are not well informed regarding business planning processes (and rarely have any direct contact with business planners) and are thus ill-equipped to introduce linkages between human resource planning and business strategic planning.

Yet the risks of neglecting this important link are great. A consumer products company developed a plan to consolidate product lines and assumed that the same sales personnel could represent all lines. The assumption turned out to be wrong and previously profitable lines turned sour and were ultimately divested. As another example, a chemicals company rapidly added new production facilities and expanded existing plants to meet demand without planning for the grooming of necessary managers. As a result, startups were sometimes delayed and problems were encountered due to inadequate experience and training of key personnel.

On the positive side, a major lumber and paper products company anticipated its requirements for new mill managers and senior technical personnel and systematically rotated prospective candidates among mills and pertinent headquarters and regional staff positions to satisfy the projected needs. As another example, a bank staffs its offices to satisfy workload demands as projected in its business plans and develops banking office managers according to plans for long-range banking expansion. Positions are authorized in the offices (branches) to support specific business plans such as a new business "call" program desired as part of a specific marketing program.

This article presents the concepts and techniques necessary for linking human resource planning with business planning. The author has worked with numerous corporations in developing human resource planning processes. The approach described in this article reflects the experience of these companies in attempting to forge this important link that is so often missing in practice and neglected in the published literature on both business planning and human resource planning.

Objectives and Benefits

Companies commonly prepare annual forecasts of staffing needs as a basis for external recruitment, personnel reassignments and promotions, and annual training program planning. But the one-year planning horizon fails to take into consideration longer-range business plans and needs, such as new facilities, new products, retrenchment, expansion, or gradually changing talent requirements of a qualitative nature. Effective human resource planning involves longer-range development of talent and longer-range planning for the utilization and control over human resources in an organization.

The need for a strategic perspective in human resource planning was stated in one manufacturing company as follows: "As our Company grows larger and more complex, we recognize a need to plan more systematically for the people needed to staff the business. A lack of adequate talent may be the single major constraint in our ability to sustain future Company growth. This (process) is a practical step towards more comprehensive employee planning and development."

The company expected the following benefits from longer-range human resource planning:

- an improved understanding of the human resource implications of business strategies;
- recruiting talent well in advance of needs, both from campuses and from the market for experienced people;
- improved planning of assignments and other employee developmental actions such as lateral moves to permit longer-range broadening of managerial perspective; and

- improved analysis and control over personnel-related costs, by providing more objective criteria concerning payroll, turnover, relocation, training, and other costs.

These benefits were perceived by the company executives as extensions of benefits resulting from shorter-range planning. The link with strategic planning was seen as the logical next step in human resource planning in this company.

What Is Strategic Planning?

Strategic planning is the process of setting organizationl objectives and deciding on comprehensive programs of action which will achieve these objectives. As an example, strategic planning in one major oil company includes:

- formulating corporate and regional company objectives and operating charters (statements of identity or purpose);
- choosing the mix of business which will make up the operating entity and will reflect that entity's objectives and its concepts of its own identity;
- the organization structure, processes, and interrelationships appropriate for managing a chosen mix of businesses;
- developing appropriate strategies for carrying out the objectives and directing the evolution of the chosen mix of businesses within the organizational structures thus established; and
- devising the programs which are the vehicle for implementing the strategies.

Strategic planning should not be confused with shorter-range operational or tactical planning. Strategic planning is concerned with decisions aimed at achieving a major change in direction or velocity of growth. For example, a company may review its various product lines or component businesses and conclude that one or more should be discontinued because they no longer fit the company's overall objectives and plans. New business may be sought, new investments made, or new management approaches adopted (Ackoff, 1970; Drucker, 1974; Lorange and Vancil, 1976). Operational or tactical planning deals with the normal ongoing growth of current operations or with specific problems, generated either internally or externally which temporarily knock the pace of normal growth off the track.

Strategic planning decisions involve major commitments of resources, resulting in either a quantum jump in the business along the path it is progressing, or a change in the fundamental direction itself.

Because assumptions must be made about an unpredictable future (and resources committed could be lost), strategic planning involves a significant amount of uncertainty. As a result, strategic planning is more complex, more conceptual, and less precise than shorter-range operational planning. Typically, it involves consideration of not just one, but several possible scenarios about the future business environment and consideration of several alternative courses of action for the enterprise.

Operational planning, on the other hand, generally assumes a fairly constant business environment and considers changes only concerning such factors as immediate tactics, production efficiency, fine-tuning of ongoing systems and practices, adjustment of levels of business activity, responding to customer or other demands, and modification of products, advertising, services, or other business processes. The central difference is the degree of change resulting from the planning, hence the degree of impact on human resource planning.

New directions in management do not come about easily. Strategic planning, therefore, involves a series of steps, each of which may involve considerable data collection, analysis, and iterative management review. The important elements of strategic planning and their potential effects on human resource planning are as follows:

1. *Define the corporate philosophy.* As a first step, fundamental questions regarding the nature of the corporation are addressed including: "Why does the business exist? What is the unique contribution it makes or can make? What are the underlying motives or values of the owners or key managers?" In a large electronic equipment manufacturing firm, for example, providing employment and promotional opportunities for employees is held as an important purpose of being in business and therefore for guiding future growth and change. The dependence of the community on the company is an overriding factor in the minds of the key executives.

2. *Scan the environmental conditions.* "What economic, social, technological, and political changes are occurring which represent opportunities or threats?" Labor supply, increasing legal demands governing human resource policies and practices, and rapidly changing technology may, for example, have significant impact on a business. Additonally, the question is asked "What are the competitors' strengths, strategies, etc.? Even human resource strategies of other companies may affect the future direction of a business (e.g., ability to attract and retain the best available talent.

3. *Evaluate the corporation's strengths and weaknesses.* "What factors may enhance/limit the choice of future courses of action?" Human resource factors such as an aging workforce, overspecialization (immobility) of key managers, a lack of promotable "high-potential"

talent, and past failure to develop broadly-experienced general management talent, and past failure to develop broadly-experienced general
management talent are common problems that may constrain strategic
planning.

4. *Develop objectives and goals.* "What are the sales, profit, and
return on investment objectives? What specific time-based point of
measurement are to be met in achieving these objectives?" Frequently,
managers fail to set and stick to specific objectives and goals. Where
commitment to objective and goals is difficult to attain, strategies suffer.
Also, important qualitative goals give way to more easily defined and
measured quantitative objectives even though strategic objectives
frequently involve commitment to changes in quality of service, quality
of management, quality of research and development, etc.

5. *Develop strategies.* "What courses of action should the
corporation follow to achieve its objectives, while meeting specific
operational goals along the way? What types of action programs are
required in the pursuit of these strategies? What changes in organization
strucuture, management processes, and personnel are required?" Here
the focus is sharply on human resource planning and the acquisition,
assignment, development, utilization, and (frequently) termination of
employees to properly staff the organization. It is at this point that
human resource planning most directly links to the strategic planning
process.

Three Levels of Planning

The different levels of planning suggested in the above discussion are
illustrated in Figure One. As shown, strategic planning deals with a
long-range perspective and flows into operational planning. This level
of planning has a mid-term perspective and is concerned with the
specific programs planned. The kinds and amounts of resource required,
the organization structure, and management succession and development, as well as specific plans for implementing the strategic plans.
Finally, an annual budgeting process provides specific timetables,
assignments, allocations of resources, and standards for implementation
of actions. Simply, the detail in planning moves into sharper focus as the
time frame telescopes into the shorter term.

Human resource planning logically parallels the business planning
process. Some companies hold that the annual budget is all they need,
particularly for human resource planning. In practice, their "strategic
planning" is really vague operational planning. "Any people we need
we can hire when the time comes from outside," they state. And in some
instances, such as construction, retailing, or project-oriented
engineering (or aerospace) firms, the lead time for planning is

necessarily short. But even in these kinds of organizations, engineering talent, managerial talent, and specialized skills required in support of strategic objectives may not be readily available on the market and require lead time for recruitment and/or development.

Figure 1. Links Between Business Planning and Human Resource Planning

	Strategic Planning: Long Range Perspective	Operational Planning: Middle-Range Perspective	Budgeting: Annual Perspective
Business Planning Process	Corporate Philosophy Environmental Scan Strengths and Constraints Objectives and Goals Strategies	Planned Programs Resources Required Organizational Strategies Plans for Entry into New Businesses, Acquisitions, Divestitures	Budgets Unit, Individual Performance Goals Program Scheduling and Assignment Monitoring and Control of Results
	Issues Analysis	Forecasting Requirements	Action Plans
Human Resource Planning Process	Business Needs External Factors Internal Supply Analysis Management Implications	Staffing Levels Staffing Mix (Qualitative) Organization and Job Design Available/Projected Resources Net Requirements	Staffing Authorizations Recruitment Promotions and Transfers Organizational Changes Training and Development Compensation and Benefits Labor Relations

College recruitment plans, for example, are not always accurate if they are developed solely on an annual basis. Rather, they are found more effective when based on a rolling plan involving a multiple-year forecast of needs as part of operational planning, which, in turn, is based on strategic planning. Similarly, training and development activities are often budgeted and scheduled on a short-term basis without a long-range context defining the needs that are to be satisfied. As a result, training programs often represent a smorgasbord for employees with little assurance of cost-effectiveness for the business or of career relevance for the employees.

Linking human resource planning with strategic planning, therefore, involves a focusing on major changes planned in the business–critical issues:"What are the implications of proposed business strategies? What are the possible external constraints and requirements?

What are the implications for management practices, organization structure, managerial development and succession? What can be done in the short-term to prepare for longer-term needs?"

THE IMPACT OF HUMAN RESOURCES

The capacity of an organization to achieve its strategic objectives is influenced by human resources in three fundamental ways:

- cost economics
- capacity to operate effectively
- capacity to undertake new enterprises and change operations.

The factors contributing to these three impact areas are listed in Figure Two. The factors identified are useful as a basis for helping business planners and executives think about the relevance of human resource planning. They also serve as the basic elements comprising the approaches commonly used to bridge the two planning processes.

Personnel costs are significant in many organizations, frequently ranking just below the cost of financial capital or the cost of goods and materials. Costs of capital, equipment, and materials are increasingly difficult to control due to their scarcity and to inflation. Accordingly, control over staffing levels, compensation and benefits, and staffing mix are important focal points of management attention. In one instance, a midwestern manufacturing firm established a plant in Europe as a step towards increasing its penetration of that market. But after start-up operations, it found that local managers with the necessary expertise could not be found, or at least corporate management back home felt more comfortable having individuals personally known to them managing the foreign operations. As a result, the costs of maintaining U.S. expatriates were extremely high. Additionally, the individuals were not as effective as they needed to be because they did not adequately understand the market, language or customs. After five years, the plant was sold to a European company, with management problems cited as a principal factor.

This suggests the importance of the second group of factors – the positive benefits human resources may have on business plans. The talents and efforts of employees do have tangible effects on productivity, organizational effectiveness, management competencies, organizational stability, external relations, adaptivity to changes, and other changes supportive of a company's strategic objectives. Such effects are often taken for granted, but companies that fail to grow and change are frequently characterized by an absence of such positive support by their employees. An electronics company holds that its phenomenal record of

Figure 2. The Strategic Impact of Human Resources Factors

growth and technological innovations is due, in large part, to the quality and motivation of its employees.

The assumption of positive "people impact" is used in one oil company as a way to stimulate management thinking about human resource issues in relation to business plans. In this technology, capital, and natural resource-oriented company, the impact of human resources was identified through "zero-base analysis". "We assume there is no impact at all in any area of human resource management, and then through the strategic planning process examine each potential cost and benefit factor on its actual merits. If human resource planning is found to have no relevance to strategic planning, we won't require any further management attention to the subject." This null hypothesis worked well in getting the attention of the managers, and now a procedure of considering human resource needs is an integral aspect of the company's strategic planning.

Application of an Approach

Air Products and Chemicals, Inc. a major producer, distributor and marketer of industrial gases, chemicals and cryogenic processes and equipment, guided its division managers through an analysis of the human resource issues through the use of a "human resource planning guide". Exhibit One presents the essential pages of this guidebook consisting of a series of questions regarding human resource factors relating to strategic plans. The information presented in the exhibit is indicative of the type of responses received from the sales and marketing function of an operating entity of the company, and is provided for illustrative purposes only.

The approach called for each division's management to analyze and plan its human resource needs, organizational changes, and other programs and actions. Assistance was provided by the human resource planning staff assigned to work with the divisions. Responsibility for the process was given to the division managers for several reasons:

- The division managers are most familiar with their own unit's strategic plans and related human resource circumstances – they were the best source of reliable information.
- This focused the attention of line managers on important human resource issues, increasing their appreciation for them and potentially influencing their judgment in business planning.
- The process focused attention on the continuing emphasis on employee development as an ongoing process.

Also, the process was viewed as a way to present to managers the full gamut of human resource functions as a single, unified system. As illustrated in the diagram below, Air Products' various personnel programs and the process of human resource planning fit together logically with the ongoing business and financial planning cycles.

Each of the sections of the "human resource planning guide" lists a series of questions relating to issues affecting business strategies. The four sections are:

EXHIBIT ONE

Identify below those strategic plans having human resource implications.	Possible areas for action. What could be done?	Objectives: what will be accomplished in the year ahead?	What specific programs or actions are planned?
A. BUSINESS NEEDS			
1. Expansion of existing business activities?		1. Geographic expansion into new markets.	1. Initial staffing will be internally sourced with back up recruiting as necessary at the entry-level.
2. Addition of new capacity (new plants, distribution facilities, etc.)?	• Recruiting	2. Addition of a new plant and associated distribution and support facilities as specified in the Strategic Plan.	2. Key employees (i.e., Plant Manager, Dispatchers) will be internally sourced. Operators will be regionally hired from external sources.
3. Deemphasis or discontinuance of any business activities. Not at the present time.	• Employee Communications • Training and Development		
4. Ventures, acquisitions, or divestitures?	• Organization/Position Changes	4. Possible acquisition to augment our existing capabilities.	4. Management audit of any company under serious consideration.

5. New products or services?	• New Specializations	5. Business analysis, testing and possible commercialization of a project currently in development.	5. If commercialization occurs, sales and operating personnel with experience will be required.
			  a. Internal recruiting/training
			  b. External recruiting

6. New technologies or applications?	• Retraining		
7. Changes in operating methods or productivity improvements?	• Lateral Transfers		

Identify below those strategic plans having human resource implications.	Possible areas for action. What could be done?	Objectives: what will be accomplished in the year ahead?	What specific programs or actions are planned?
None with major human resources impact anticipated.	• Terminations		
8. Changes in administrative, information or control systems? None with major human impact anticipated.	• Reassignments • •		
9. Changes in management or organizational structure (matrix management)?		9. Create a greater operating interface among sales, marketing, applications and technical support activities	9. Lateral transfers among functions.
10. Other.			
B. EXTERNAL FACTORS			
1. Are qualified (competent) recruits available in the market?	• Modify Recruiting • Training/Development	1. A minimum of three individuals experienced in related technology will be required for the new project.	1. Possible utilization of personnel agencies/internal or external training programs for current employees.
2. Are you able to recruit competitively the desired talent?		2. Staff for new market expansion.	2. Establish relationships with regional recruiting agencies to provide staffing assistance at the entry-level.
3. Are there changes in the personnel relations climate? Not presently.	• Management Orientation/Training • Modify Compensation/Job Evaluation		

4. Are there new EEO/Affirmative Action requirements?	• Fact Finding • Modify Staffing Requirements	4. Increase minority representation in the middle and upper levels of represented job groups.	4. a) Reevaluate job requirements for product manager positions b) Investigate internal training program c) Increase participation at regional minority career conferences.
5. Are there new OSHA or other regulatory requirements affecting human resources? Not presently.	• Performance Appraisals • Modify Job Requirements		
6. Are there new international business demands?	• Employee Communications • New Systems/Procedures	6. Increase the technical marketing support provided to (Department) in Europe.	6. Possible transfer of (Name) to foreign assignment. a) Will require experienced replacement
7. Other:	• Additional Staffing • •		
C. INTERNAL ANALYSIS 1. Do we have excessive turnover in any group?	• Modify Recruitment/Selection	1. Decrease employee turnover across all regions.	1. a) Redesign and expand the individual sales representatives' responsibilities to include more technical customer assistance following the sale. b) Selectively reassign product line responsibility.

Identify below the human resource issues pertinent to the strategic plans.	Possible areas for action. What could be done?	Objectives: what will be accomplished in the year ahead?	What specific programs or actions are planned?
2. Is there adequate to movement within groups?	● Reassignments/ Lateral Moves	2. Increase internal movement opportunities for developmental purposes.	2. Devise longer term approach to movement through career path planning.
3. Are age patterns imbalanced in any group, suggesting high future attrition or career path blockage? The organization is quite young but adequate movement and career opportunities should be supported by the forecasted growth.	● Improved Employee Appraisals		
4. Is there a proper balance (employee mix) of managerial, professional/ technical and supporting personnel in each group? Yes, sufficient for near term strategic objectives.	● Career Counseling		
	● Terminations		
5. Are there noteworthy performance problems in any group (or appraisal results signalling significant problems)? No.	● Organization/Position Changes		
6. In what areas are levels of technical competency potential short-comings?	● Accelerate Career Advancement	6. Greater technical support will be required if the new project is commercialized.	6. If required, internal transfers from other departments.

7. Is the employee mix desired for EEO/AA being achieved? (women and minorities)

- Modify Job Requirements

7. Increase the number of qualified females and minorities at all levels in the organization.

7. Increase recruiting activity at minority career conferences.

8. Other:

- Reassignment of Work
-
-

D. MANAGEMENT IMPLICATONS

1. Are there enough employees who could become general managers? (pool of successors)

- Organization/Position Changes
- Recruitment of Managerial Talent

1. Increase the experience base key middle managers.

1. Increase individual responsibilities in related functions.

2. Do the present managers have adequate technical competence in the face of changing demands?

Presently, yes. If the new project is commercialized, however, our needs will change.

- Communication/Orientation

- Compensation Changes

2. Increase general expertise in related technology.

2. Internal training programs augmented by selected academic courses and professional seminars/conferences.

3. Do they have adequate managerial skills to meet the changing demands of a growing company? (leading, planning, decision-making, etc.)

Yes.

- Evaluation of Successors

- Study of Strategy Implications

Identify below the human resource issues pertinent to the strategic plans.	Possible areas for action. What could be done?	Objectives which will be accomplished in the year ahead?	What specific programs or actions are planned?
4. Do key managers and successors have adequate management experience (multiple function exposure)?	• Accelerate Management Development	4. Increase varied functional exposure of field managers.	4. Restructure position responsibilities to include some functions normally performed at Corporate Headquarters.
5. Is the management structure and staffing appropriate for the achievement of our business objectives?	• Job Rotation Among Functions	5. Increase total staffing at all field locations in consonance with the Staffing Plan.	5. Involve field managers to a greater extent in the normal recruiting activity.
6. Other:	• Modify Recruitment/ Selection • Training/Development • Change Staffing Levels • • •		

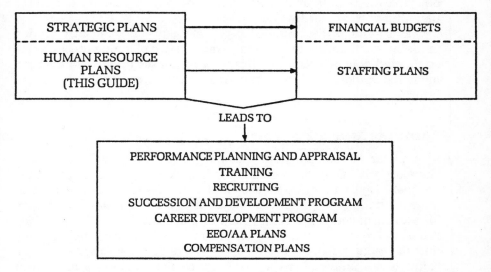

A. Business needs — the human resource implications of planned expansion, contraction, or other changes indicated in the strategic plans.
B. External factors — the business impact of governmental regulations, and human resource availability.
C. Internal analysis — the implications of professional turnover, employee mix, and performance patterns.
D. Management implications — the changing managerial staffing needs and management skills required.

Finally, a format for forecasting exempt manpower levels is included on the last page. This calls for a projection of staffing levels planned for a five-year peciod, by year, for departmental and functional groups. This long-range forecast reflects the general parameters suggested by strategic and operational plans. The first two years of the five-year forecast also serve as the basis for planning specific manpower requirements (Staffing Plans) in the annual financial budgeting process.

The managers are asked to consider each question and briefly note pertinent facts, observations, or assumptions. Questions that are not considered pertinent are deleted and additional questions may be added where appropriate. The guide is intended to be a workbook to direct and stimulate management thinking, and not a rigid procedure.

The second column lists possible responses to stimulate thinking about the human resource implications of each question. Other possible actions may be considered practical depending upon the circumstances as known to the managers. The third and fourth columns call for a translation of the long-range strategy-related needs into near-term objectives and programs is an important step to making the whole planning process worthwhile.

This guide is disseminated as part of the overall strategic planning guidelines and instructions. In this way, the two planning processes are conducted concurrently. The resulting responses indicate to management the important human resource issues to be considered in the future.

Alternative Approaches

In a major oil company, the manpower planning staff provided a summary analysis of the previous year's strategic plan, highlighting the pertinent facts and issues for each division. These summaries, together with tabulations of present employment, past and projected attrition (due to turnover, retirements, etc.), and appraisal statistics provided "substantive starters" to the divisions for use in considering pertinent human resource issues. The anlaysis of strategic issues was termed a "situational analysis", as a first step in the company's manpower planning cycle. Questions similar to those presented in Exhibit One were posed in four areas:

- impact of people on the growth or profitability of the business;
- personnel-related costs having a substantial impact on the profitability of the business;
- avoidable people-related problems that require inordinate time and attention by management; and
- management values requiring emphasis on certain human resource programs.

In this case, employee relations staff in the divisions performed much of the necessary analysis and completed the planning submissions. The quality of the responses varied, therefore, with the experience, skills, and time availability of these staff, and with their access to the line executives in their divisions for purposes of discussing the human resource analysis.

In a packaging company, simple guidelines were included as a section in the annual one-to-three year planning process. The request for information was minimal, but in this first cycle, the response was positive and "the seed was planted from which a full-size human resource planning process can grow." Each division in this company was able to pinpoint one or two issues that were important and that needed attention which had not been explicitly considered before.

In other organizations, human resource issues are studied solely by staff personnel, who present their findings to management or to the business planning staff as inputs to strategic or operational planning. In several instances, committees or task forces have been appointed to consider long-range human resource issues and needs, usually on a one-time basis. Particularly in the tasks of scanning the environment to identify emerging legal, competitive, labor supply, and other constraints, such a study group has proven a useful tool. Of course, some companies rely on consultants or outside experts to advise on trends, issues, and needs warranting company attention.

Perhaps the most common approach applied, however, is the informal planning process. While not always thorough or systematic, informal management thinking about business strategies often leads to recognition of human resource issues. Planning for the management of corporate resources, including human resources, is a process inherent in the role of a manager. And few managers would admit that they do not consider human resource issues in strategic or operational planning.

However, the process is more likely to be effective if it is systematic, rational, organized, and based on knowledge, not merely assumptions. As Drucker observes, "the systematic organization of the planning job and the supply of knowledge to it strengthen the manager's judgment, leadership, and vision" (Drucker, 1974, p. 129).

REFERENCES

Ackoff, R.L., *Concept of Corporate Planning* (New York: John Wiley & Sons, 1978).

Burack, Elmer H., *Strategies for Manpower Planning and Programming*, (Morristown, New Jersey: General Learning Press, 1972).

Ettelstein, Morton S., "Integrating the Manpower Factor into Planning, Programming, Budgeting," *Public Personnel Review*, Vol. 31, No. 1 (January, 1970), pp. 51-54.

Drucker, Peter F., "Strategic Planning: The Entrepreneurial Skill," *Management: Tasks, Responsibilities, Practices*, (New York: Harper & Row, 1974).

Keys, B.A., Thompson, F.G., and Heath, M., *Meeting Managerial Manpower Needs*, (Ottawa: Economic Council of Canada, 1971), pp.9-12.

Lorange, Peter and Vancil, Richard F., "How to Design a Strategic Planning System,"*Harvard Business Review*, Vol. 54, No. 5 (September-October, 1976), pp. 75-81.

Milkovich, George T. and Mahoney, Thomas A., "Human Resource Planning and Policy," *ASPA Handbook of Personnel and Industrial Relations*, Vol. IV (Washington, D.C.: Bureau of National Affairs, 1976), pp. 1-30.

Novick, David, "Long Range Planning Through Program Budgeting," *Business Horizons*, Vol. 12 (February, 1969), pp. 54-65.

Steiner, George A., (ed.), *Managerial Long-Range Planning*, (New York: Macmillan & Co., 1969).

Vetter, Eric W., *Manpower Planning for High Talent Personnel*, (Ann Arbor: Bureau of Industrial Relations, 1967).

CHAPTER 3
STRATEGIES FOR HUMAN RESOURCE PLANNING: AN OVERVIEW

Human Resource Planning
W. H. Hoffman and L. L. Wyatt

The long-term success of any business depends on effective resource planning. Many companies are quite good at planning raw materials, finances, technology and markets. However, the human resource often gets far too little attention. Perhaps the nature of people makes planning this resource appear less critical. People, though not always predictable, are available almost everywhere; they can perform a variety of tasks and can adapt to changing conditions without outside intervention. Yet, the human resource is undoubtedly the most important element because it links all the others. Clearly, it demands some kind of formal planning. And clearly, some kind of formal planning can contribute significantly to the improved utilization of human resources and the success of the business.

We do not mean to suggest that human resource planning is a totally untilled field. On the contrary, a considerable amount of work has been done in government, industry and academe. Much of the work, however, has focused on skills inventories, replacement charting and training or management development. This article will discuss a different approach modeled along the lines of cash management.

By approaching human resource planning with the "cash flow" model in mind, overall boundaries are established first. Detailed plans concentrating on deployment of resources can then be formulated. The system described here is intended to supplement management judgments and to function as a *businessman's* plan rather than a *planner's* plan.

"Human Resource Planning" by W. H. Hoffman and L. L. Wyatt, The Personnel Administrator, January 1977. Reprinted by permission.

W. H. Hoffman is Manager, Organization Planning for the Aluminum Company of America and L. L. Wyatt is an Organization Analyst for the same company.

The first step concentrates on the total personnel resources and planning for the whole organization. Work can thereafter be directed toward more precise planning for segments of the organization and eventually for individuals.

We have used this approach primarily for the management cadre because this group is normally the most critical to the long-range success of the business. Management people are the most highly-skilled employees; they require the longest time to develop; and they are individually the highest paid. Their loss can have a most severe impact on the business.

Prerequisites

Human resource planning cannot be put into effect overnight. Certain prerequisties must be met. Without these, human resource planning becomes an intellectual exercise rather than a useful management tool. The two essential building blocks for human resource planning are:

- A comprehensive personnel information system.
- A basic business plan.

The human resource planning process is like selecting the route for a trip. The personnel information system shows you where you are. The business plan tells you where you want to go.

The personnel information system must provide comprehensive data about each individual in the organization. The system must not only be able to provide static data, but must also be able to store historical data and analyze the information so that changes can be tracked. The minimum requirements for the stage of planning described here are:

- Age of individuals
- Length of service of individuals
- Population additions
- Population losses

Later detail planning and analysis require:

- Identification of job requirements
- Education, training and experience of individuals
- Current job performance evaluation
- Potential job performance evaluation

A general personnel information system used for salary and benefit administration usually contains the necessary information. For most companies only a little reorganization of this data is required for a human resource planning system.

The other building block is a business planning system which provides information on:

- Anticipated changes in size of the company
- Anticipated changes in the nature of the company's business
- The desired rate of these changes

As with the personnel information system, historical, current and projected information are needed to tell where the business has been and where it is going.

Assembling the System

Using these two building blocks, a human resource plan begins to take shape. The first step is to link these blocks by determining what personnel resources are required by the business. Historical analyses are necessary to define indicators and trends. Normally, good correlation can be established between business activity level and human resource requirements. Results of these correlations may be expressed in terms of production or sales units and numbers of people.

Next, attrition must be analyzed. Normally the two principal indicators of attrition are length of service and age. The attached charts, Figures I and II, illustrate typical attrition characteristics of a population according to service and age. Figure I shows the percentage of an original group of employees remaining after each year of service; losses are heaviest in the first few years after hiring. Figure II shows the percentage of an original group of employees remaining each year after age 50; losses are light in the first few years but increase rapidly near the normal retirement age of 65. A mathematical model utilizing these criteria can be applied to anticipate what will happen to the population in the future so as to forecast the replacement needs.

The model should be capable of:

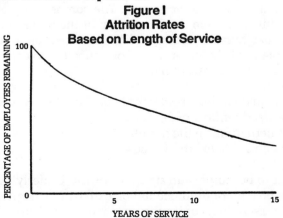

Figure I
Attrition Rates
Based on Length of Service

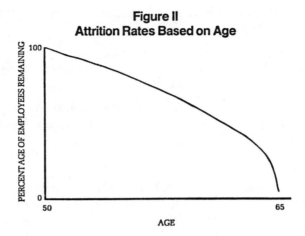

Figure II
Attrition Rates Based on Age

- Examining each individual.
- Applying the proper predictor to determine the probability of attrition.
- Accumulating expected-attrition for the total population.

The model also should be flexible enough to accept changes based on managerial judgment. In addition, the model must be able to store historical data so that adjustments can be made in the probability based on current experience. Recent economic conditions provide a case in point. Voluntary terminations may be fewer because there are fewer job opportunities available in a recession. Because of inflation, fewer employees may retire early because of the uncertainty of the cost of living and its impact on a fixed retirement income. Judgment must be applied to temper the model's predictions in light of such conditions.

Taking this approach, planning is first concentrated on the management of gains and losses of personnel. The company's goals and objectives within them become the foundation of the program. This further emphasizes that human resource planning must relate to the overall long range plans of the enterprise. Four specific objectives are easily identified for most organizations:

1. Assure adequate human resources to perform the required work.
2. Provide a steady inflow of new talent.
3. Manage fluctuations in the population.
4. Maintain control of manpower costs.

These appear to be simple and straightforward. Underlying them, however, should be a more fundamental objective of managing for productivity. This is essential if continuity, profitability and growth goals are to be met. From our earliest work in human resource planning we have determined that an overall strategy is the key to making the planning activity useful. When a clear sense of objectives specifically related to the company's business activity is missing, planning activities can't have the desired impact.

To arrive at realistic objectives, historical data on business and population levels must be analyzed. Past trends can be identified and extrapolated for future business plans. However, management judgment should be applied to determine if a continuation of past performance is a satisfactory objective for the future. Figure III illustrates the productivity improvement achieved in one area of study and projections of alternative strategies.

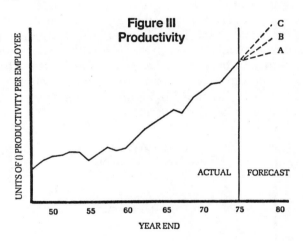

STRATEGIES

One useful strategy is to try to hold salary costs per unit constant over an extended period. If the normal pattern of salary increases is granted, this goal can only be achieved by improved productivity. In other than double digit inflation periods this is quite a proper goal.

A particularly effective technique in examining and establishing the human resource strategy is to identify gains which arise primarily from improved process or facility productivity. To do this, the population requirements for proposed facilities can be added to the population requirements for existing operations which use current staffing practices. This total population matched against projected business levels will indicate the future productivity base. This projection indicates the change in productivity that would be available simply because the new facilities are more productive than the existing ones. The projections can be compared with what has been achieved historically and what objectives seem appropriate for the future. In Figure III, curve A is equivalent to the projection of productivity due to facility efficiency. Curves B and C represent extrapolations of different time period trends. This shows that improvements greater than those due to facilities alone have been made in the past.

Identifying facility-related improvement separately from total productivity focuses on the need to do something other than merely build more efficient facilities. It encourages the careful examination and improved utilization of human resources through better job design and organization structures. Moreover, it highlights the interaction of growth of the business and improvement of human resource productivity.

Analysis of the population reveals other perspectives on strategy. A particularly useful analysis can be developed utilizing attrition data. If the assumption is made that all employees are hired when they complete their education and work their entire careers with the company, an ideal age distribution can be plotted based on anticipated attrition. This smooth curve superimposed over the actual population distribution found in one study is illustrated in Figure IV. Shortages and overages of certain age groups are readily apparent.

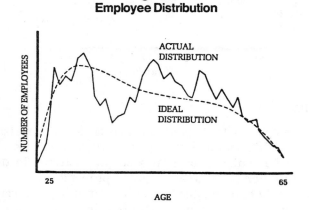

Figure IV
Employee Distribution

Analysis of this particular age distribution subsequently helped to set the objectives of our human resource planning program. Because recruiting had tended to follow the business cycles, age gaps developed in the population. This meant that sometimes training had to be accelerated or that inexperienced people had to be placed in positions when more seasoned employees were not available. At other times, progress was blocked for younger employees because older employees stayed in their jobs longer. Both conditions are disruptive.

If age gaps are recognized as a potential problem, planning can help develop a reasonably balanced population by minimizing year-to-year fluctuations in hiring. However, this is only useful if long-range plans are available to guide the direction and magnitude of change in the total population.

The development of a strategy is not a one-time activity. It must be repeated over and over again. Tentative objectives must be tested for their impact on the business plan and it, in turn, tested against the human resources required to achieve the business goals.

TACTICAL PROGRAMS

Two major tactical programs are required for this human resource plan. The first is an acquisition program. Using data from the human resource plan, the total population requirement can be determined. When this is matched against the attrition projections, the total requirements can be established. Specific skills can be identified within this framework to meet business demands.

A more effective job can be done if the acquisition of people is viewed as a continuing activity rather than a start and stop process. Most organizations can assimilate only a limited number of people at a time and, therefore, a steady influx will allow better training and greater employee satisfaction. Also, better relations can be established with universities which increases the opportunities to attract better talent.

A major tactical program for attrition also is essential to the overall management of human resources. A recognized attrition program is far less common than an acquisition program. But it is no less essential if control is to be maintained. Figure V illustrates the program concept. In this the overall strategy of reducing the population by 25 is one of the factors balancing the acquisition and attrition programs.

A certain amount of attrition will occur naturally through deaths and normal retirements. However, a larger percentage of attrition is the result of voluntary or involuntary terminations both of which are a function of company policies. Many voluntary terminations are the result of dissatisfaction with company policies such as compensation practices, promotional opportunities, or the general managerial atmosphere. If desired, each of these policies, of course, can be changed by management.

Underlying these tactical programs is the need for good analysis of data from the personnel information system. This is essential to everything from identifying the causes of attrition, to testing the effect of changed policies, to establishing a tactical program, to implementing the overall human resource plan.

Figure V
Tactical Program for Population
Control of Management Personnal

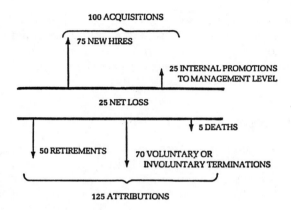

This article has described a model of a human resource plan to control the total population. The basic concept can be applied to individual segments of the population whenever the variables affecting that segment can be identified. Within the management group, specific disciplines may warrant particular attention. For example, the engineering disciplines can be critical if the business is growing and new facilities must be designed and built. Marketing skills might be particularly critical in a consumer-oriented business. The interchangeability of skills between areas of the business will provide guidance on how the population should be analyzed and whether separate plans can or should be developed within the overall plan.

By using the total resource approach, we have focused attention on the need to integrate human resource planning with other business plans and highlighted the importance of a productivity strategy. The technique produces a plan which is readily related to the rest of the business. This is essential because people are a key resource in the success of any company.

Human Resource Planning: Foundation for a Model

Vincent S. Flowers and Bernard A. Coda

The current demands on the world's material resources and their spiraling cost are building pressure to increase the productivity of human resources. Adding to the strain is society's mounting insistence on a higher quality of life through more meaningful work. In the business environment, response to this dual priority requires decisions that simultaneously meet the goals of organizations and the needs and values of their employees. To make these decisions, information is needed to:

- Improve understanding of the nature and scope of human resource expenditures.
- Improve selection, retention, and motivation of employees.
- Allocate more wisely the money spent on human resources.
- Overhaul the approach to communication among managers, between managers and other employees, and between the organization as a whole and outside parties.
- Expand the scope of internal and external reports to deal with social as well as financial accomplishments.

Sony's former managing director, Shigeru Kobayashi, has remarked that "they [western managers] seem to spend about 10 percent of the time understanding the nature and significance of a problem and about 90 percent of the time attempting to solve it." A first step in developing human resource decision models and information systems is to get a broader view of these resources—to spend a good deal more than 10 percent of the time understanding the nature and significance of the problem. For example, while many recognize the value of strategies such as job enrichment and job enlargement as solutions to some problems, others take them as curealls, assuming that problems are universal and center only in the conditions of the work. Actually, the problems are

Reprinted, by permission of the publisher, from PERSONNEL, January-February 1974, © 1974 by AMACOM, a division of American Management Associations. All right reserved.

Vincent S. Flowers is Administrative Assistant to the Dean of Business at North Texas State University and Bernard A. Coda is Professor of Accounting at North Texas State University.

more individual than general: Not all organizations have the same goals and problems, and individual employees have different needs and values.

With such a diversity in mind, the author's purpose here is to broaden an understanding of the scope and significance of human resource management. At the outset, there are these key questions to be resolved:

- What do employees "need"?
- What are their "values"?
- How do needs and values relate to the "work ethic"?
- What are the attributes of employees (employee assets) that make them valuable to organizations?
- How do needs, values, and assets relate to the money spent on employees?
- Can needs, values, and employee assets be measured?
- What dangers are involved?

HUMAN RESOURCE DIMENSIONS: EMPLOYEE NEEDS

The familiar Herzberg research findings indicate that man has two sets of needs—the need to avoid pain (hygiene) and the need to grow psychologically (motivation). The point is that maintaining hygiene needs at acceptable levels will minimize dissatisfaction, but satisfaction will result only when motivational needs are met. Thus, satisfaction-dissatisfaction are not opposite ends of the same continuum; rather, they represent two separate continua. Some psychologists have attacked this theory, and the discussion of values presented later in this article may help to explain some of their concern.

Using the dual-factor theory, Texas Instruments' M. Scott Myers suggested the following classification of some human resource expenditures:

Expenditures for Motivational Needs

- Growth—educational programs to counteract stagnation and obsolescence
- Achievement—job enrichment programs to provide challenging work
- Responsibility—supervisor training to develop delegation skills
- Recognition—systems of direct feedback related to performance.

Expenditures for Hygiene Needs

- Economic—wages, salaries, and fringe benefits
- Security—grievance systems and tenure rights
- Orientation—company newspapers and bulletins
- Status—special parking privileges and executive dining rooms
- Physical—air-conditioning, parking lots, and cafeterias
- Social—office parties and coffee breaks.

Often, many of these expenditures are not recognized as human resource investments, and such a restricted view can lead to ineffective cash outlays. For example, a manager might invest in training in an effort to remedy productivity decline, but training is at best only a possible solution to his problem. An expanded awareness of the way expenditures relate to employee needs leads to a clearer view of the range of potential solutions and the kinds of problems they relate to. With a broader view of human resources, expenditures for parking lots, company newspapers, safety shoes, cafeterias, on-site police protection, and even restrooms take on new meaning. It becomes apparent, for instance, that installing a company cafeteria involves not only the nutritional needs of employees but also their social, status, and economic needs, all of which have something to do with performance.

Herzberg's motivation/hygiene model provides insights about human drives but by itself offers only limited assistance in deciding how to make specific human resource expenditures. Suppose an organization decides to invest in a supervisor training program to improve leadership abilities. If so, it first needs to determine the leadership style that will appeal to its employees. Do they want a boss who:

- Tells them exactly what to do and how to do it and encourages them by doing it with them?
- Is tough but allows them to be tough, too?
- Calls the shots and isn't always changing his mind, and sees to it that everyone follows the rules?
- Doesn't ask questions as long as they get the job done?
- Gets them working together in close harmony by being more a friendly person than a boss?
- Gives them access to the information they need and lets them do their job in their own way?

To answer the question of which kind of boss the employees want, an understanding of the heterogeneous value systems of employees is essential.

HUMAN RESOURCE DIMENSIONS: EMPLOYEE VALUES

Here, we recommend Clare W. Graves' model of "levels of psychological existence," a relatively new concept but perhaps the best theory of values available in the current literature. Graves' ideas add a dimension to the process of thinking through investment strategies for human resources. Those ideas were described in some detail last year in *Personnel* (March-April); briefly, this is an adaptation of the Graves theory to the world of work:

Employees' Value System 1—Reactive

It is unlikely that any employees have this value system, because for the most part, it applies to infants, people with serious brain deterioration, and certain psychopathic conditions. The reactive person, in effect, has no value system; he just responds to feelings of pain, hunger, warmth, cold, and the like, so for our purposes, this system can be disregarded.

Employees' Value System 2—Tribalistic

Tribalistic employees prefer easy work, friendly people, fair play, and above all, a "good" boss. A tribalistic individual ordinarily believes that he may not have the best job in the world, but that he does as well as others with jobs like his. He feels deeply that he has not had much of a chance to better himself; therefore, doing well simply means having a steady job where he can follow orders given by a good boss. The less responsibility he has the better he likes it; he likes a boss who tells him exactly what to do and how to do it, and encourages him by doing it with him. Money is important to him because it pays for groceries, rent, and other basics. He sees a merit increase as a lucky break, usually obtained because he has a good boss.

Employees' Value System 3—Egocentric

A system 3 employee wants to receive good pay and have people keep off his back. He doesn't like any work that ties him down, but will do it to get some money; when he gets the money he needs, he may either quit or take off from work and do what he wants. This employee needs a boss who is tough but allows him to be tough, too. Money is most important to the system 3 employee because it allows him to buy things like cars and clothes that make him feel important. Base pay is always too low, in his view; merit pay is rarely worth the effort—it usually goes to the boss's pet.

Employees' Value System 4—Conformist

This type of employee likes a job that is secure and has well-defined rules to preclude favoritism. He feels that he has worked hard for what he has and thinks he deserves some good breaks. He likes a boss who calls the shots, rarely changes his mind, and sees to it that everyone follows the rules. Money allows him to save for a rainy day, to aid the less fortunate, and to have a decent standard of living. He believes his base pay is fairly set by management. Saving and spending are carefully planned. A merit pay increase says that he has done a good job and his boss has rewarded him fairly.

Employees' Value System 5—Manipulative
The ideal job for a manipulative employee is full of variety and allows some wheeling and dealing. Compensation, he thinks, should be based on results. He feels responsibile for his own success and likes to play all the angles in his ceaseless effort for higher positions and greater financial rewards. A good boss doesn't ask questions as long as the job gets done. This employee responds to hard bargaining and respects mastery and power. Money signifies success and is the means of maintaining an attractive home, club memberships, and the respect of important people. Base pay is O.K., but he wants ample opportunity to earn extra money; merit increases are a strong incentive to do good work.

Employees' Value System 6—Sociocentric
A job that allows for development of friendly relationships with supervisors and others in the work group appeals to a sociocentric employee. Working with people toward a common goal is more important than getting caught up in the materialistic rat race. A good career is one that permits him to be a "good" person, to have many friends, and to contribute to society. A good boss gets people to work in close harmony by being a friendly person. Money enables him to enjoy many friendships and puts him into a position to support worthwhile causes. The problem with base pay is the injustice in permitting some people to make so much more money than others. The same goes for merit pay—it can cause hard feelings and destroy harmony.

Employees' Value System 7—Existential
The employee prefers work of his own choosing that provides continuing challenge and requires imagination and initiative. A good career is one that allows him to be himself and to be involved in responsibilities that are important to him and to society. A good boss gives him access to the information he needs and lets him do the job on his own—the task is to accomplish objectives, but not in a predetermined or fixed way. Money is important because it can buy freedom and independence; base pay is important, too, but the kind of work a man does is more important. A merit pay increase is personally satisfying, but only if he has truly done something to earn it.

Human Resource Dimensions: Employee Assets

It is evident that employees bring differing needs and values to their jobs and expect that their needs will be met, but there is a human effectiveness side of the coin as well as a human dignity side. The organization has needs and values, too. It needs productive resources, contributive attributes on the part of its employees. The five attributes that enable employees to contribute to organization needs are knowledge, skills, health, availability, and attitudes. Here, attention is focused on what the organization is spending its money on, not how it spends it. More effective investments in people are made possible by directly considering which of these attributes the organization needs and in what degree and then determining the best way to get them.

Knowledge, Skills, and Health

Recruiting and hiring typically involve medical examinations and testing for aptitudes and skills, and after an employee is on board the organization may continue its investment program through expenditures for orientation and on-the-job training. Primarily, these investments provide specific job knowledge and specific skills to enable new employees to become more valuable contributors; professional seminars, educational programs, and annual medical examinations also relate to knowledge, skills, and health. These three factors have such an obvious relationship to job performance that investing in them is taken for granted. Linking them with availability and attitudes, however, opens up fresh perspectives about turnover, productivity, and morale.

Availability and Attitudes

Temporary loss of employee availability means tardiness, absenteeism, or short-term nonproductive time off; permanent loss is, of course, termination. Most companies measure availability negatively by calculating turnover ratios. Moreover, through exit interviews they find out the reason that employees leave, yet most employers were at a loss for words when the authors asked, "Why do your employees stay?"

To explore "availability" further, we asked 400 employees in three manufacturing organizations to complete a 60-item questionnaire on "Why do you stay with your company?" The results suggested that employees stay simply because of inertia, the tendency to remain with an organization until some force pulls or pushes them into a change. The amount of force required depends on the strength of inertia, which, in turn, is influenced by conditions inside the company—job satisfaction (motivation) and work environment (hygiene)—and outside job opportunities and factors unrelated to the work itself.

The research showed that employees in the sample stayed for

varying combinations of job satisfaction and environmental reasons (hygiene factors within the company plus external ones), but there were identifiable profiles. (For a detailed analysis, see Vincent S. Flowers and Charles L. Hughes, "Why Employees Stay," *Harvard Business Review*, July—August, 1973.) Going well beyond the findings provided by traditional turnover analysis, our findings made it possible to divide the employees into four groups:

Turn-overs are those who are actively seeking alternative employment, are not satisfied with their jobs, don't like the benefits, have few outside pressures to keep them in the company, and will soon terminate. *Turn-ons* have jobs that meet their motivational needs but they may leave if job satisfaction declines for even a short time span, because their inertia is not significantly strengthened by environmental factors. *Turn-ons-plus* are most likely to stay in the long run because their inertia is strengthened by both job satisfaction and environmental factors. *Turn-offs* stay only because they are locked in by environmental factors. We will have more to say about the importance of identifying these four groups of employees later on.

Determining why employees stay relates to both availability and attitudes. For this reason, an "inertia survey" is a more powerful managerial tool than a conventional attitude survey. Typically, an attitude survey ignores environmental factors outside an organization, but the research indicated that they have a significant and previously under-rated effect on inertia. This is especially true in situations where a firm is a dominant employer in a particular locale. In one case, 72 percent of the employees sampled responded positively to the "I enjoy my job here" statement and thus suggested that the job itself was among their reasons for staying. This firm is a dominant employer in its locale, so a follow-up survey could supply valuable information. Suppose that within a year the percentage declined to 42 percent even though the turnover rate remained constant or even improved. Such a shift could indicate that the firm had employees moving from *turn-on* and *turn-on-plus* categories to *turn-off* and *turn-over* categories, and this information could alert the organization to a need to changes while there was still time to act.

MERGING THE HUMAN RESOURCE DIMENSIONS

We have presented and discussed the following broad dimensions of human resources:

Employee Needs		*Employee Values*	*Employee Assets*
Growth	Security	Tribalistic (2)	Knowledge
Achievement	Orientation	Egocentric (3)	Skills

Employee Needs		Employee Values	Employee Assets
Responsibility	Status	Conformist (4)	Health
Recognition	Social	Manipulative (5)	Availability
Economic	Physical	Sociocentric (6)	Attitudes
		Existential (7)	

These three dimensions, along with the many investments made in human resources, serve as the major components of a human resource planning model. (See pages 94 and 95.)

Inputs
The model acknowledges that employees bring differing systems of values into an organization, which have an important bearing on their motivation and hygiene needs. For example, achievement for a tribalistic employee means "doing as well as others with jobs like mine." To a sociocentric employee achievement means "doing something that benefits people." A reasonably accurate description could be written for each of the 60 elements in the values/needs matrix (ten needs, six value systems).

Typically, an organization invests in the five employee assets— knowledge, skills, health, availability, and attitude. Investments may be directed at individual employees (on-the-job-training, educational supplements, and so on) or groups of employees (benefits programs, a company cafeteria, and so on). Ordinarily, an investment will affect more than one of the five attributes.

Outputs
Job satisfaction.

This is an indicator of how well expenditures on people are meeting the needs and values of employees; it can be measured with a well-designed attitude survey.

"Why Employees Stay."

This is determined by the degree of job satisfaction and external factors. A questionnaire can be used to determine what factors influence an employee's inertia.

"Why Employees Perform."

Although we have no concrete proof, we believe performance is significantly affected by the reasons employees stay, if not in the short-run, then in the long-run, and if the effect is not overt, then it is concealed.

As we have said, understanding changes in *why* employees stay and *why* they perform, instead of relying only on turnover and productivity figures, can alert an organization to the need for human resource investment before a crisis occurs. For example, a firm may be able to skimp on expenditures for motivation and morale with little or no immediate effect on the traditional turnover or productivity measures. But what if this kind of economy converts a significant portion of the workforce from turn-ons-plus to turn-offs? This situation is like walking up to the edge of a cliff—the ground is still solid but you now run a greater risk of falling off. A company could unknowingly be on the verge of a Lordstown incident. Investments for motivation and morale might be cheap insurance against such disaster.

GROUNDWORK FOR APPLICATIONS

Up to this point, we have been developing a conceptual foundation for a broader view of human resources. Now let's consider the application of these concepts, which requires measurement—we need measurements to select alternatives, evaluate results, and communicate more effectively.

Daniel Yankelovich has summarized what he calls the "McNamara Fallacy" this way:

> The first step is to measure whatever can be easily measured. This is okay as far as it goes. The second step is to disregard that which can't be easily measured or give it an arbitrary quantitative value. This is artificial and misleading. The third step is to presume that what can't be measured easily really isn't important. This is blindness. The fourth step is to say that what can't be easily measured really doesn't exist. This is suicide.

Obviously, we want to avoid the kind of syndrome Yankelovich describes. To use all the power of mathematics to improve planning and control of human resources expenditures, we eventually need very precise measurements, but the experimental measurements and instruments described in this section are qualitative comparisons.

Values for Working Survey

This instrument was developed by Scott and Susan Myers. It is based on Graves' theory and is designed to help an organization determine the extent to which various values and needs systems are represented in its workforce. The instrument contains 18 questions about supervision, benefits programs, pay, corporate profits, company loyalty, and so on. The following is an example of the kind of questions included in the survey:

EMPLOYEE ASSETS					COMPANY INVESTMENTS
Know-ledge	Skills	Health	Avail-ability	Attitudes	
					• Instruction
					• Policies
					• Training
					• Development
					• First Aid
	THESE ARE WHAT THE ORGANIZATION NEEDS				• Job Safety
					• Job Design
					• Placement
					• Working Conditions
					• Benefits
					• Rest Rooms
					• Cafeteria
					• Etc.
					• Etc.

How well these two match influences

EMPLOYEE NEEDS	EMPLOYEE VALUES					
	2	3	4	5	6	7
• Growth						
• Achievement						
• Responsibility						
• Recognition	THESE ARE WHAT THE EMPLOYEES NEED					
• Economic						
• Security						
• Orientation						
• Status						
• Social						
• Physical						

- Job Satisfaction
- Why Employees Stay
- Why Employees Perform

TURN-OFFS	TURN-ONS	TURN-ONS-PLUS	TURN-OVERS
These employees don't enjoy their job, but are locked-in by environmental factors. They stay and perform primarily because they have to.	These employees enjoy what they are doing, and stay and perform because they want to.	These employees enjoy their jobs, and stay and perform primarily because they want to. However, they are also locked-in by environmental factors.	These employees don't like their job and are in the process of looking for another. They will continue to perform because they don't want to— • Upset the "Tribe" • Get fired • Do the "wrong" thing • "Burn any bridges" • Hurt any feelings • Shun self responsibility
STIFLED BEHAVIOR	ENRICHED BEHAVIOR		TRANSITORY BEHAVIOR

The kind of job I like is one:

A. That allows some free-wheeling and dealing and pays off as long as I get good results.
B. That pays well and keeps people off my back.
C. Where rules are followed and no favoritism is shown.
D. That allows me to develop friendly relationships with my supervisor and others in my group.
E. Where the goals and problems are more important than the money, prestige, or how it should be done.
F. That has steady work, fair play, and, above all, a good boss.

Respondents allocate 12 points among these statements based on the degree to which they agree with each. The results show which value system or systems are dominant for a given individual and thus enable an organization to learn more about the work ethic of its employees.

Checklists for Employee Attributes

The following shows a simplified job knowledge checklist designed to relate an employee's contributive attribute, or human resource asset, to jobs:

	Present Job	Other Job
4. Meets all knowledge requirements		X
3. Meets most knowledge requirements		
2. Meets minimal knowledge requirements	X	
1. Does not meet knowledge requirements		
0. Knowledge level unknown		

In the example the employee meets only minimal knowledge requirements for his present job but meets all requirements for another job. A checklist to include skills and health requirements in the manner illustrated for knowledge requirements could be used. These checklists would be helpful in matching employees with jobs and in discovering the need for training or educational programs. Information about the other employee assets, attitudes and availability, gathered from other sources would also affect investment priorities.

An Attitude Survey

One such instrument is a 20-item questionnaire (reduced from 95 original questions by statistical factor analysis) that measures job motivation and inside-the-company hygiene factors. Raw results are quantified, subjectively weighted by job grade and company tenure, and then used to construct an "attitude index." One firm plans to use the index or one similar to it in its internal reporting systems, with the implication that supervisors are responsible for both employee attitudes and employee productivity.

"Why Employees Stay" (Inertia) Survey

This survey is a powerful tool in determining the extent of stifled, enriched, and transitory behavior within an organization. An organization may be structured to permit all employees (without regard to value system or position in the managerial hierarchy) to maximize their effectiveness both in contributing to the financial success of the organization and in attaining personal objectives; other organizations may be concerned with personal objectives only as a means of achieving overall financial success. In either case, an instrument that helps identify and understand the differences between turn-ons, turn-ons-plus, turn-offs, and turn-overs will enable managers to select alternatives that reinforce what they believe are positive reasons for staying with a company and to avoid encouraging employees to stay for reasons that in the long run are detrimental all around.

KEEPING AN EYE OUT FOR PITFALLS

It is easy to do just the opposite of what Daniel Yankelovich warned against—to be too eager to measure the unmeasurable. We should guard against this just as much as against the temptation to ignore important factors we are unable to measure. Valid measurements are better than intuition, but the intuition of an experienced manager is better than pseudo-measurements.

Problems of measurement, however, are not the only sources of trouble in any effort to use the concepts developed in this article. For one thing, value systems, needs, and the contributive attributes of employees are deceptively complex.

To begin with value systems, Graves' ideas are of considerable immediate benefit: They point up the futility of trying to understand someone else's behavior with our own value system, add a new dimension to Herzberg's dual-factor theory of needs, and also explain why it is impossible to make all of the people happy all of the time. Our research does not disprove Herzberg's two factor theory, but it does suggest that the dichotomy of motivation and maintenance depends on the value system of the employee—what motivates a tribalistic employee may simply maintain an existential one.

On the negative side, however, is one of the more important potential dangers in any effort to use Graves' model. Stereotyping—predicting an individual's behavior by tagging him with a particular value system—is risky, because most individuals show elements of at least two, and possibly more of the six operative systems. And, for a variety of reasons, value systems change over time. Moreover, even a clear-cut adherence to a particular value system couldn't guarantee predictability; ordinarily, an individual's on-the-job behavior will be influenced by his work ethic, but the way he is approached, his mood on a particular day, and countless other factors will also affect his actions.

As opposed to individual stereotyping, there is also group stereo-typing. For example, a manager who hires professional employees and deals primarily with young college graduates might well decide that value systems 6 and 7 are widespread within his organization, and a production supervisor may, in his entirely different situation, find value systems 2 and 3 dominant. Obviously, overreacting to an erroneous belief that certain value systems pervade an organization can lead to counterproductive actions.

The value systems/needs matrix is a tool, and like most tools it can be abused as well as used, just as a hammer can be used to build a house or as a lethal weapon. An awareness of the relationship between value systems and needs can be directed to responsiveness to employee needs or to manipulate employees. The best interests of employers and employees will not always coincide, and some organizations may attempt to change (in their eyes, improve) employees' value systems. Does anyone have a moral right to do this?

A number of social issues are intertwined with the moral issues. It may be economically more efficient from a company point of view to terminate turned-off employees, rather than spend money to convert them to turn-ons, or turn-ons-plus. But companies that adopt policies that turn off employees, leave them with health problems and negative attitudes, and then hand the problem over to someone else are ignoring others' costs—they are polluting the national workforce in the same way that air or water is polluted. Perhaps satisfaction of employees' needs will someday be a goal in itself, not just a means of improving economic performance.

The interrelations among knowledge, skill, health, attitude, and availability are too complex to detail in a single article, even if we knew how. These attributes, or employees assets, bear a factorial relationship to one another: If one attribute is below an adequate level, it will destroy the effectiveness of the others. For example, if an employee is well qualified in terms of knowledge, skills, and health but has an extremely poor attitude, he probably contributes little to the organization and may even be destructive. In such a situation a company should obviously make expenditures to improve attitude before spending resources on the other attributes. To further illustrate the complexity, consider the effect of an expediture to send an executive through an M.B.A. educational program. The firm will expect improvement in knowledge and skills and probably a favorable effect on attitude, but at the same time, this expenditure reduces availability, both during the period of study and afterward, when, with his M.B.A. degree, the manager's inertia diminishes because he has more alternative job opportunities. In this case, the employer may find it necessary to make concurrent expenditures in job satisfaction that strengthen this executive's inertia in order to get the expected benefits from the expenditures for the educational program.

To sum up, the merger of concepts represented by the model suggests new management strategies for increasing human effectiveness and improving the quality of human life, explicitly recognizing and stressing the differing value systems of employees. The model is complex, but so are human resources.

Further, the qualitative measurements provided by the instruments can provide insight into the disparate work ethics that evolve from the interaction of employee needs and values and also into the relative importance of job satisfaction and environmental factors in determining the strength of inertia.

The primary purpose of the model is to help with the development of a realistic human resource planning system that would include both financial and behavioral feedback measures. There are, however, some immediate benefits. The comprehensiveness of the model (needs, values, employee assets) can be useful in improving planning and control decisions, and these decisions involve considerable sums of corporate money. The quality of these decisions determines whether the money spent will eventually become a productive investment, or simply money down the drain.

Institutional Manpower Planning: Rhetoric Versus Reality
Elmer H. Burack and Thomas G. Gutteridge

Since the early 1960s numerous articles, books, and monographs have been written asserting that the personnel function within contemporary organizations is undergoing a radical transformation. According to this literature, many of the traditional practices and specialist roles included under the rubric of personnel adminstration are being replaced by a comprehensive, future-oriented, integrative approach which focuses on the effective utilization and development of human resources. This new concept, which is supposedly superseding personnel management, is referred to by several different names, including manpower planning, human resource planning, human resources management (or administration), and others. Not too surprisingly, this new process has been defined in a variety of different ways, and there is only minimal consensus regarding the personnel-related activities it encompasses.

The authors are frankly skeptical of the claims or inferences of recent survey research which suggest that manpower planning or human resources management is currently or is about to become a pervasive endeavor in a great many business organizations. It is our contention that, at the present time, considerable misunderstanding and disagreement exists as to what constitutes "manpower planning" (MP) and, likewise, there is a great diversity in the human resource management programs espoused by various organizations. Further, the MP system actually adopted by many organizations often—in direct contrast to the institutions, professed intentions—displays only marginal progress beyond traditional personnel activities and falls far short of a comprehensive design.

The purpose of this article, therefore, is to raise a number of critical issues about the current state of practice in human resource planning and, in so doing, to suggest some important directions for the improvement of manpower management systems as well as some priorities for future research.

© 1978 by the Regent of the University of California. Reprinted from *California Management Review*, volume XX, number 3, pp. 13-20 by permission of the Regents.

Elmer H. Burack is Management Head and Professor of Management in the College of Business Administration, University of Illinois at Chicago Circle. Thomas G. Gutteridge is Associate Professor of Human Resources and Director of the Human Resources Institute, School of Management, State University of New York at Buffalo.

THE GROWING INTEREST IN MANPOWER PLANNING

According to the literature, there are several external pressures which are supposedly motivating institutions to adopt a new role model for personnel management. First, as a consequence of the more rigorous enforcement of Equal Employment Opportunity (EEO) legislation, many organizations are having to prepare affirmative action plans for the recruitment and development of minorities and women. This requirement, in turn, is forcing firms to modify their recruitment, selection, management development, career planning, compensation, performance appraisal, and related personnel practices. Likewise, such laws as the Occupational Safety and Health Act (OSHA) and the Pension Reform Law are perceived by employers as having significant implications for their personnel policies and procedures.

In a related area, the weak legislative commitment to maximum employment, as expressed in the Employment Act of 1946, has given way to a series of federal manpower programs, such as the Manpower Development and Training Act of 1962 and the Economic Opportunity Act of 1964. Now under the "New Federalism" approach espoused by Washington, these categorical programs have, in turn, been superseded by the Comprehensive Employment and Training Act of 1973 (CETA), which allows city, county, and state prime sponsors to develop their own mix of manpower programs to serve the employment needs of their resident citizens. Regardless of the fate of CETA, it is evident that employers will, as under the previous categorical programs, continue to be asked to give hiring priorities to such diverse groups as unskilled Vietnam veterans, the economically disadvantaged, welfare recipients, ex-offenders, and the physically and mentally handicapped. Presumably, this continued emphasis on the employment of the marginal worker to those with special employment problems provides an added dimension to the role of the personnel department and the objectives of manpower planning, especially in view of low profit or recessionary conditions that currently characterize many organizations.

The impact of this manpower and EEO legislative base has been exacerbated by an environment of sociological and technological change. For instance, many new hirees as well as their more established colleagues are seriously questioning the quality of work life and are reluctant to adhere to the traditional concept of the "organization man."[1] Further, many employees, particularly those engaged in exempt managerial and professional positions, are becoming insistent that their employers implement meaningful career planning programs, create improved work climates, and consider their individual needs and desires when personnel decisions are made. Also, shifts in the age distribution of the labor force and the higher educational attainment of the population must be reckoned with by an organization in terms of their import for staffing and development patterns.

Many corporate executives are concluding that insufficient or unqualified manpower is at least as serious a production bottleneck as a scarcity of capital and that manpower investments are as important a factor in company planning as the acquisition of plants, equipment, or materials. In fact, some firms have had to postpone their expansion plans because they were unable to procure the requisite human resources.

Other companies have experienced unusually high error rates, decreased product or service quality, and lower levels of efficiency because they failed to accurately anticipate their manpower requirements. They are looking toward a planned human resource approach to provide cost savings by reducing the expenses associated with excessive turnover and absenteeism, low productivity, an inefficient internal labor market, unproductive training programs, and other problems of the work force.

DEFINITION OF MANPOWER PLANNING

As previously indicated, the term *manpower planning* suffers from a surplus of meanings. This definitional problem has been heightened by the utilization of such related words as human resources management, manpower administration, human resource planning, manpower management and other variations on the same theme. Some claim "manpower" has sexual overtones. And, finally, some observers contend that manpower planning is nothing more than a synonym for a more enlightened style of personnel management.

At the "macro" or societal level, manpower planning is concerned with the national labor force and includes projections of labor supply and forecasts of occupational industrial, and total labor force requirements.[2] "Micro" manpower planning has been construed to cover a wide range of activities, from the statistical forecasting of personnel needs through the full range of traditional personnel functions.[3] Likewise, some manpower planning approaches have focused on specific employee groups such as managers and professional,[4] while others have encompassed the entire work force.[5]

Hughes has suggested that there cannot be one standard avenue for MP.[6] Rather, he contends that there must be a highly flexible approach whereby the manpower planning programs can be tailored to the specific needs of each individual firm. Cassell views manpower planning as a mechanism for resolving a set of simultaneous decisions concerning recruiting and screening methods, hiring standards, job structure and mobility, quantity and quality of training, compensation, and related personnel factors which have traditionally been considered to be a series of separate, unrelated decisions.[7]

Probably the most commonly accepted definition of MP is "a process concerned with providing the right number and kinds of people, at the right place at the right time doing things which help to fulfill organizational as well as individual objectives."[8] Figure 1 presents the authors' concept of what is entailed in a comprehensive human resources management approach.

As Figure 1 depicts, the authors do not consider human resources management and manpower planning to be equivalent terms. Rather, human resources management is viewed as being a systematic effort to insure an effective interface between an organization's human resources and its internal and external environment. An "effective interface" is one that maximizes organizational and individual goal attainment subject to the constraints imposed by each one upon the other.

As envisioned by the authors in the schematic diagram, human resources management is comprised of four distinct subsystems which are antecedents to one another, namely: organizational design, manpower (human resource) planning, career management and, finally,

Figure 1. Human Resource Concepts.

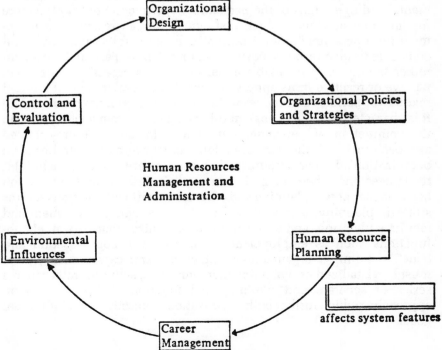

a control and evaluation phase. Organizational design (planning) is the process through which organizational structures or patterns are created and the resultant employee role prescriptions are established. As previously suggested, manpower planning is the process by which the need for and internal availability of human resources, for some future time period, is estimated. It also includes the personnel action plans required to fulfill the net manpower requirements and to achieve the organization's manpower objectives. Career management, in turn, is a process whereby employers endeavor to match individual interests and capabilities with organizational requirements through a planned program encompassing such activities as the recruitment and placement of new personnel, performance and potential evaluation, a flexible compensation and benefits package, design of effective internal career systems, and establishment of a personalized career development plan. Finally, a set of control procedures and an evaluation system are needed to assess the effectiveness of the other human resource management functions in terms of their impact on both the organization and the individual. Based upon this evaluation, the human resources management cycle can be retraced, as needed, to take corrective action when deviations from planned performance arise.

In the authors' opinion, therefore, human resources management is not simply a new label to be attached to the traditional and compartmentalized operations of the personnel department. Some of the more fundamental attributes which distinguish human resources management from personnel administration include the following ones. (1) It considers human resource costs to be, for the most part, an investment rather than an uncontrollable expense. (2) It is proactive rather than passive or reactive in its approach toward the development of internal manpower policies and the resolution of human resource problems. (3) It is characterized by a change in role perspective from an emphasis on the completion of personnel transactions toward a future-oriented approach in which the personnel department acts as a controller of an organization's human resources, that is, a stewardship approach. (4) It recognizes that there must be an explicit linkage and integration between manpower planning and other organizational functions such as strategic planning, economic and market forecasting, investment and facilities planning, and so forth. (5) It recognizes that personnel subfunctions such as employment, labor relations, compensation and benefits, training, organizational planning, and career management must be visualized as dynamic, interconnecting activities rather than a series of separate and nonintegrated functions. (6) It focuses on approaches which further both organizational objectives and individual goals.

RESEARCH ON MANPOWER PLANNING APPROACHES

During the last decade, several studies of the state-of-the-art development of manpower planning practices have been conducted by professional associations, governmental agencies, and individual researchers. Typically, these studies have involved mailed questionnaire surveys of specific target groups and have related to the surveyed organization's general experience with human resource planning and the extent to which each has implemented various manpower planning techniques such as an employee information system.

For example, a 1967 study by Geisler, which encompassed fifty-three companies from the 1966 edition of *Fortune's* 500 directory, attempted to establish a precise definition of manpower planning and to identify the scope of personnel-related activities this process did and did not include.[9] An extensive research study of human resource planning was the 1971 study of 220 large U.S. corporations conducted by Towers, Perrin, Forster and Crosby (TPF&C), a personnel-human resource management consulting firm.[10] This research provided a good picture of organizational endeavors in manpower planning including their accomplishments in implementing effective human resource information systems and manpower forecasting procedures, the development of manpower action programs and their priorities for future undertakings in this area. In 1972, the American Society for Personnel Administration, in cooperation with the Bureau of National Affairs, published a report on the composition and scope of the employee information systems and manpower forecasting programs utilized by some 87 organizations.[11] Finally, a comparatively recent description of the current status of manpower planning systems design and implementation among a sample of 354 local and state governments, federal agencies and private corporations was published in 1973 by the U.S. Civil Service Commission.[12]

The research studies outlined above have given impetus to some provocative questions about the state of the art in the development of human resource planning systems. The authors conducted a pilot field study of the personnel-manpower planning process existent in a sample of thirty-four firms in an effort to further crystallize the questions and speculations arising from these other studies. (All were firms that had an active interest in this topic.) This field study included personnel specialists from primarily larger firms, though it reflected a diversity of business activities. The median employment of the parent organization of the respondents to the survey questionnaire was in excess of 10,000 people; while the median establishment (immediate employer) size was

5,000 individuals. About one-fourth of the establishments employed more than 10,000 persons and about the same percentage had fewer than 1,000 employees. Fourteen firms were in the service sector (such as banking and insurance), four were utilities, and the balance were engaged in manufacturing industrial and consumer products.

Conditions for Considering Manpower Planning Undertakings. The respondents in this survey confirmed the widely understood importance of such factors as the persisting shortage of manpower in selected occupations and the rapid rate of technological change as a catalyst encouraging the development of human resource planning systems. Several other considerations, however, were also identified as having a significant positive impact on the decision to establish a manpower planning program, including:

a. The relative poor quality of the available manpower, such as absence of relevant job skills, negative work attitudes, unrealistic career expectations.
b. General expansion and diversification in the firm, including a trend towards multinational operations.
c. Support of affirmative action.
d. Strengthen management development and reserve programs for high-level positions.
e. The need to increase worker productivity and managerial efficiency.
f. The presence of a strong personality, typically a senior officer or the president, who is committed to the concept of human resource planning.

Interestingly, these latter two factors were perceived by the respondents as being the two most important influences for engaging in manpower planning.

Finally, strong considerations exist for greatly reducing the speed at which firms move toward human resource designs:

1. Past success—"We've been successful—why change now?"
2. Line versus staff authority—"The line operations have functioned in an autonomous fashion and the personnel department is centralized; there's been nobody around to spearhead the MP effort."
3. Corporate capability—"We've been awaiting the start up of corporate planning. Also, we've lacked the staff, necessary skills, and even the budget. Besides, we've been too busy."

4. Cost benefit—"We're heavily profit-oriented and it's pretty hard to relate people development to bottomline profits."
5. Resistance to change—"It's a business-as-usual environment. We don't have a commitment to learning. Corporate knows; regional unsure; district's don't want."
6. Budget stability—"Our activity is heavily tied to government contracts, and this business is too uncertain to make long-term manpower commitments."

Concepts of Manpower Planning. As expected, the company personnel expressed widely different ideas regarding "their" definition of manpower human resource planning. For some, MP was essentially a numbers game to facilitate reserve and replacement planning. Other managers equated manpower planning with human resources development. A few firms even equated human resources planning with the creation of a personnel data base and others with the existence of a capability to deal with "manpower acts" (such as MDTA) or with minority problems through an EEO program. Given the widely divergent notions of MP employed by the practitioners, ꞓompanied by the general absence of an understanding regarding what a comprehensive human resource plan for their organization should include, it is little wonder that a majority of firms have only achieved limited progress in this area.

An interesting sidelight to this issue was an interindustry difference in the level of staff support for the MP process. In particular, consumer products manufacturers and insurance companies had a strong commitment to human resources planning, which suggests an important question: Are there basic institutional features related to product line, clientele, or the nature of the organization's work which influence MP concerns?

Bases for Human Resource Planning. Over 85 percent of the firms indicated that they considered community factors, state and national conditions, and general trends (such as the quality of work life issue) to be important variables in the development of their corporate plans. Surprisingly, however, almost 30 percent of the respondents suggested that they accorded little or no attention to these external factors in establishing their human resource plans. In a related question, the personnel managers were asked to indicate the importance and availability of specific types of external and internal information for manpower planning purposes. According to Figure 2, these practitioners considered internally generated information to be the most

Figure 2. Manpower Planning Information Needs: Priorities and Accessibility.

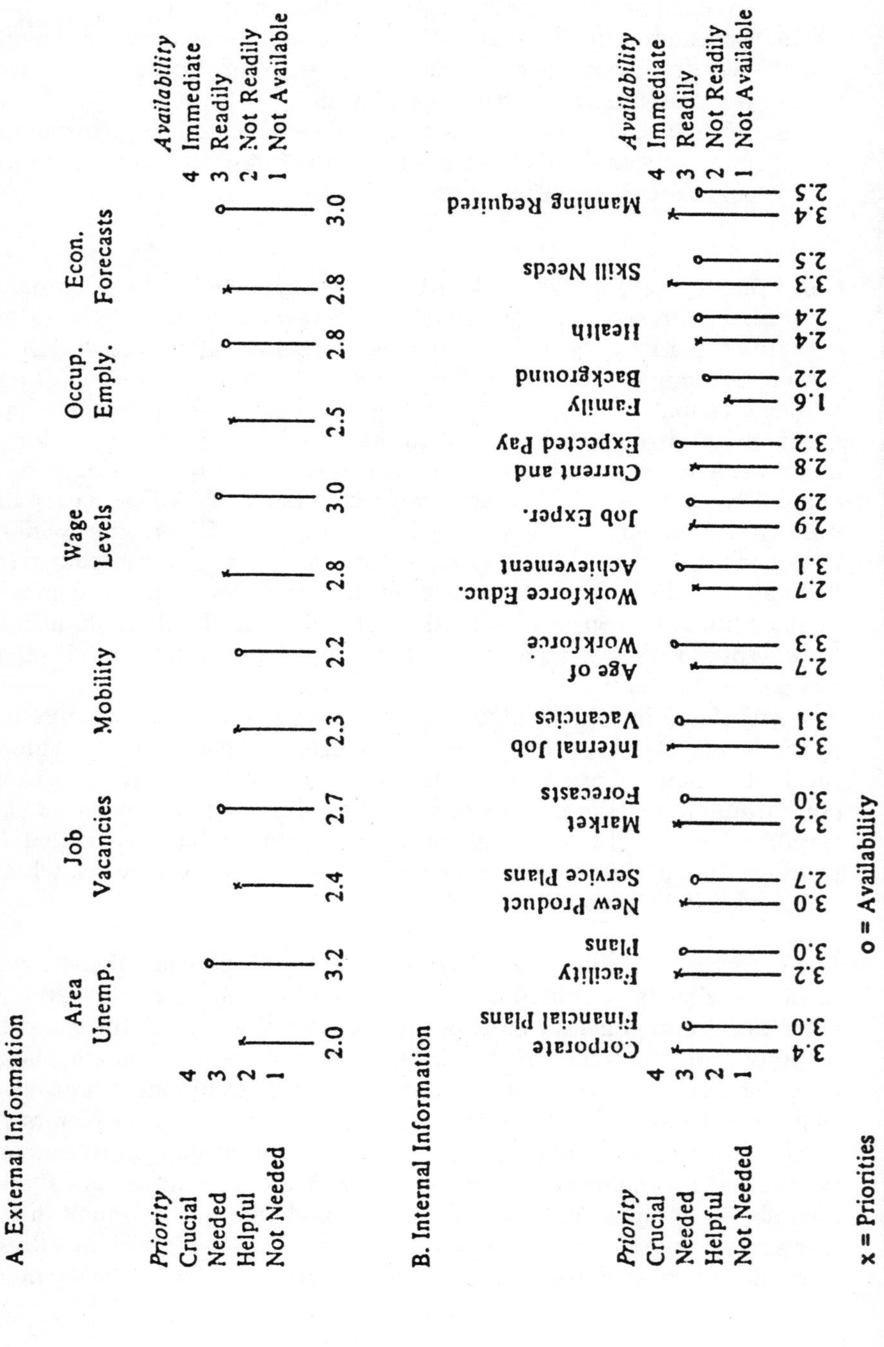

A. External Information

Priority
4 Crucial
3 Needed
2 Helpful
1 Not Needed

Availability
4 Immediate
3 Readily
2 Not Readily
1 Not Available

Information	Priorities (x)	Availability (o)
Area Unemp.	2.0	3.2
Job Vacancies	2.4	2.7
Mobility	2.3	2.2
Wage Levels	2.8	3.0
Occup. Empl.	2.5	2.8
Econ. Forecasts	2.8	3.0

B. Internal Information

Priority
4 Crucial
3 Needed
2 Helpful
1 Not Needed

Availability
4 Immediate
3 Readily
2 Not Readily
1 Not Available

Information	Priorities (x)	Availability (o)
Corporate Financial Plans	3.4	3.0
Facility Plans	3.2	3.0
New Product Service Plans	3.0	2.7
Market Forecasts	3.2	3.0
Internal Job Vacancies	3.5	3.1
Age of Workforce	2.7	3.3
Workforce Educ. Achievement	2.7	3.1
Job Exper.	2.9	2.9
Current and Expected Pay	2.8	3.2
Family Background	1.6	2.2
Health	2.4	2.4
Skill Needs	3.3	2.5
Manning Required	3.4	2.5

x = Priorities   o = Availability

important, and the most accessible; and attached only modest importance to the utilization of externally derived information.

Relation of General Institutional Planning to Manpower Planning. Finally, only one-quarter of the organizations in the sample had achieved a substantial link between their general institutional planning and their manpower planning. An additional 45 percent reported some link, 20 percent had little association, and 10 percent had none. These findings raise two important questions. (1) Are personnel and manpower specialists typically only paying lip service to MP concepts, but in daily action are most responsive to internal pressures (job vacancies) and the needs of the day (EEO and affirmative action)? (2) To what extent are MP designs practicable in the absence of any articulation between the general organizational planning process and human resource planning?

Returning briefly to Figure 2, the most important external data for MP appear to be the existing area wage levels and their rates of change as well as economic forecasts. According to the respondents, these data are generally available. In terms of internal data, manning requirements by function, information regarding internal job vacancies, and the skill requirements of the technology appear to be fairly crucial to MP. Not surprisingly, data on the firm's business plans and forecasts (financial, facilities, products, and markets) were considered to be a needed, although less important, input to human resource planning. The major gap between needed and available internally generated information appears to be related to the lack of specificity on manning and skill requirements. This, too, raises important questions. (1) Do serious gaps exist in the job analysis technology in terms of the ability to translate labor demand forecasts into specific occupational (skills and knowledge) requirements? (2) To what extent is the seeming absence of adequate internal data on skill and manning requirements because of a lack of understanding of its uses versus the inability to procure and interpret it?

Human Resource Information Systems. A fundamental requirement for a successful MP system is a data base which includes information on the personal, professional, educational, and job-related particulars of the work force. Although the authors' research did not examine the percentage of their sample utilizing a manpower information system (MIS, EIS, or HRIS), the TPF&C study reported that some 85 percent of all the companies in their survey had initiated undertakings in this area.[13] As might be expected, this study as well as others have concluded that the larger the organization the more likely it is to utilize some type of employee information system. It is important to note, however, that according to the TPF&C study about one-third of the manpower information systems are operating at the departmental or divisional level rather than corporate-wide. Further, the most extensive applications of these systems involve payroll processing, personnel listings, job placement and, less frequently, forecasting, and manpower development planning.

Probing a bit deeper into the TPF&C research, although over 80 percent of the companies claimed they utilized their EIS for internal job placement, in about one-half of these instances the usage was admittedly "limited." One-fourth of the organizations made extensive use of their HRIS in manpower development and forecasting, yet over one-half reported the application of their system to this area was limited. Similarly, while half of the companies in the TPF&C study suggested that they employed their MIS in career analysis, about two-thirds of this group admitted this usage was limited. This prompts the question: Is the preponderance of EIS usage still largely geared to conventional information processing, EEO compliance reporting, and other applications which are either mandatory or have a readily demonstrable payoff?

Our results, supported by conclusions from the TPF&C and the Civil Service Commission research, suggest that the answer to this query is yes. In the authors' opinion, a *comprehensive* HRIS should include both employee information and job vacancy data concerning such factors as the following. (1) A profile of the individual's past and present work experiences and the experience requirements of the job. (2) The education, training, and job skills of the individual and the analogous job requirements. (3) Performance and other assessment information. (4) Employee career interests. (5) Job specifications, such as salary level, geographic location, and responsibilities. (6) Descriptive personal data. A data base such as this can facilitate the development of a number of nonroutine MIS applications, including: (a) a computerized employee skills inventory, which can be used to provide lists of candidates for vacancies and promotions, assist in the evaluation of in-house human resource capabilities, and identify employees for appropriate career development opportunities; (b) simulations of internal mobility patterns; (c) human resource investment analysis;[14] (d) computerized models which simulate the impact of changing personnel policies on the flow of internal manpower; and (e) personnel research projects.

Manpower Forecasting. Manpower forecasting is that part of MP concerned with projecting the organization's internal demand for labor and determining whether that supply of talent will be available within the firm at the appropriate time. The ultimate product of this manpower forecast is a projection of net manpower requirements (shortage or surplus) which, in turn, become an input to the development of personnel action plans.

Forecasting for Future Manpower Needs. In this study, about one-third of the firms reported they forecasted manpower demand on a "fairly frequent" (10 percent) or "regular" (20 percent) basis. An additional 40 percent conducted forecasting for manpower needs at times and, overall, some 90 percent had varying commitments in this area.

In a related area, reserve and replacement planning for key positions was conducted on a fairly frequent or regular basis by 40 percent of the companies and "at times" by another 40 percent. Only about 5 percent of the respondents reported that they did not develop succession plans.

The authors' study confirmed that although forecasting is a fairly common MP technique, the emphasis is on short-range projections. Further, relatively simple (such as manpower inventories and counts of job vacancies) rather than more advanced (such as Markov chains and productivity analyses) manpower forecasting techniques are the most widely used. The emphasis in short-range manpower forecasting is on budgeting and controlling manpower costs as well as identifying human resource talent. Over a longer range (five or more years in the future) period manpower forecasts are used in planning corporate strategy, facilities planning, and identifying managerial replacements. As previously suggested, however, long-range manpower forecasting is still very much an undefined art.

THE DEVELOPMENT OF PERSONNEL ACTION PLANS

Both the TPF&C and the Civil Service Commission research suggest that the major problem encountered in manpower forecasting is a general lack of credibility in the projections of manpower requirements. In the authors' research, about one-half of the organizations indicated they utilized a planned program for the development of promotable managers on a "fairly regular" basis. Further, about one-fourth of the companies replied that they held career counseling sessions with their employees on a fairly frequent or regular basis. Conversely, one-third of the respondents stated they did not provide career guidance services and roughly two-thirds undertook very few career planning activities. Not surprisingly, in those organizations that did provide some career planning assistance, there was great disparity in the attention provided to managers and supervisors (the major focus) versus the general employee membership (little or no assistance).

In the Towers study, 80 percent of the firms claimed they provided career guidance assistance in one or more areas (promotional and development opportunities, compensation opportunities). Further, about 40 percent of the firms in the Towers research stated they had implemented a career pathing program. As in the authors' study, however, it is noteworthy that this career planning assistance was, for the most part, limited to a select group of high potential employees embarked on a "fast-track" career path. Also, only one-fifth of the firms in the Towers study had a formalized career guidance program with specially trained staffs and the vast majority considered their existing program to be either totally ineffective (41 percent) or only moderately effective (56 percent). These findings suggest two additional queries: (1) How effective is human resources development planning, given its often tenuous connection with MP, the emphasis on high potential management talent to the exclusion of other employees and the lack of professionally trained career guidance specialists? (2) To what extent do the existing career guidance programs *really* provide individual employees an opportunity for meaningful participation in organizational career decisions as opposed to systematizing and strengthening managerial control over the career development process?

In terms of personnel action plans, as indicated below, the employers in our survey were far more concerned with employee benefits and improving the quality of work life than they were with providing career planning assistance.

Priorities in Personnel Action Plans.

	Low	Medium	High
Employee benefits	12%	18%	70%
Quality of work activity	15%	35%	50%
Managerial career planning	32%	41%	27%
General employee career planning	70%	24%	6%

Yet, even here, dollar restraints or technical considerations were seen as important restraints to the implementation of an effective human resources plan.

Impact of Restraints on Internal Improvements in MP.

Factor	Slight	Some	Considerable
Financial restraints	15%	33%	52%
Technical restraints	27%	46%	27%

CONCLUSIONS AND IMPLICATIONS

It is evident from our research that manpower-human resource planning has at least moved into the consciousness of many institutional policymakers and personnel managers. For some, MP has been a defensive strategy implemented in response to government legislation or a desire to improve productivity and profit performance. For others, the interest in human resource planning stems from a recognition that social necessity and economic security are starting to merge as people become a critical factor in institutional performance, and the human relations programs of the past are an inadequate answer to this phenomenon. Unfortunately, for many firms it appears that MP is a sporadic effort at best, which consists mainly of numbers forecasting.

It is important to point out that significant gaps still exist in the adequacy of the internal human resource data base which, even in the interest of traditional job assignment and personnel practicies, required remedying. It appears that there exists a solid basis for considerable skepticism regarding institutional progress in the design of manpower-human resource planning systems. Admittedly, the progress of large firms in human resource planning is significant, but size itself isn't the only factor. Far more work is indicated regarding human resource-manpower planning, taking considerable care that standardized definitions are used, that activity is separated from intention, and that the state of accomplishments is realistically assessed.

NOTES

1. See Studs Terkel, *Working* (New York: Pantheon Books, 1972); and *Work in America*, Report of a Special Task Force to the Secretary of Health, Education and Welfare (Cambridge, Mass.: The MIT Press, 1973); also see Elmer H. Burack and Robert Smith, *Personnel and Human Resources* (St. Paul, Minn.: West Publishing Co., 1977), Chapters 1-4.
2. See Richard Lester, *Manpower Planning in a Free Society* (Princeton, N.J.: Princeton University Press, 1966).
3. See Walter S. Wikstrom, *Manpower Planning: Evolving Systems* (New York: The Conference Board, Inc., 1971); and Robert E. Cassidy, "Manpower Planning: A Coordinated Approach," *Personnel* (September-October 1963), pp. 35-41.
4. For example, John Hinrichs, *High Talent Personnel: Managing a Critical Resource* (New York: American Management Association, 1966); and Eric W. Vetter, *Manpower Planning for High Talent Personnel* (Ann Arbor, Michigan: Bureau of Industrial Relations, University of Michigan, 1967).
5. See for example, L. F. Moore, *Manpower Planning for Canadians* (Vancouver, B.C.: The Institute of Industrial Relations, University of British Columbia, 1975); and Peter B. Doeringer, et al., "Corporate Manpower Forecasting and Planning," *Conference Board Record* (August 1968), p. 27-35.
6. D. B. Hughes, "Introduction," in D. J. Bartholomew and B. R. Morris (eds.), *Aspects of Manpower Planning* (New York: American Elsevier Publishing Co., 1971). Also, see George T. Milkovich and Thomas A. Mahoney, "Human Resource Planning," in Dale Yoder and Herbert G. Heneman, Jr. (eds), *Planning and Auditing PAIR* (Washington, D.C.: The Bureau of National Affairs, 1976).

7. See Frank H. Cassell, "Manpower Administration: A New Role in Corporate Management," *Personnel Administration* (December 1971), pp. 33-37.
8. The original version of this statement is commonly ascribed to Tom Porter from Standard Oil of Indiana. Probably the first reference to this concept to appear in the literature was Eric W. Vetter, "The Nature of Long-Range Manpower Planning," *Management of Personnel Quarterly* (Summer 1964), pp. 20-37.
9. Edwin Geisler, *Manpower Planning: An Emerging Staff Function* (New York: American Management Association, 1967).
10. A summary of this study, entitled *Corporate Manpower Planning*, is available from James W. Walker, Towers, Perrin, Forster and Crosby, New York, New York.
11. Bureau of National Affairs, Inc., *ASPA-BNA Survey: Manpower Programs*, Bulletin #1192 (Washington, D.C.: Bureau of National Affairs, 1972).
12. District of Columbia Personnel Office on behalf of the U.S. Civil Service Commission, *Manpower Planning: The State of the Art* (Springfield, Virginia: National Technical Information Service, 1973).
13. Towers, Perrin, et al., p. 4. Eighty percent of the organizations in the Civil Service study indicated they were either using or developing a human resource information system. See Civil Service Commission. p. 13.
14. See Richard Traum, "Manpower · Bank and Reward Systems for Professionals," *Personnel* (July-August 1973), pp. 19-29. For aspects of careers, see Lee Dyer (ed.), *Organizational Careers: Research and Practice* (Ithaca, N.Y.: NYSSILR, Cornell University, 1976); and Douglas T. Hall, *Careers in Organizations* (Pacific Palisades: Goodyear Publishing Co., 1976).

PART II

APPLICATIONS OF HUMAN RESOURCE STRATEGIC PLANNING

Part II of this readings book deals with applying the strategic human resource surveillance concepts that have been discussed by various authors up to this point. Their application is an extraordinarily difficult process because of the considerable coordination that is required in the managing of human resources. Consequently, the articles in this section will consider the functional human resource management areas which include, among others, the myriad of activities associated with personnel forecasting, procurement, compensation, maintenance, training, information systems, and effectiveness evaluation.

HUMAN RESOURCE FORECASTING

Based on strategic management decisions relating to organizations' missions and objectives that were described in Figures 1, 2, and 3 in Part I of this book, human resource forecasting becomes the first of the applied areas to be discussed in Part II. Human resource forecasting involves making projections of both the organization's personnel needs and the available supply of qualified and skilled people. To the extent that these projections of demand and supply are not fully compatible, detailed strategies will need to be developed to fill whatever gaps may exist. These potential gaps may be related to some combination of the two interrelated dimensions of human resource quantity or numbers and quality or skills.

ESTABLISHING ORGANIZATIONAL AND
PERSONNEL PARAMETERS

Procurement of human resources includes the normal, although often perplexing, activities of identifying specific job tasks, duties, and responsibilities. This process is referred to as "job analysis" and represents the first of the key elements in establishing organizational and personnel parameters. Job analysis is an investigative process that clearly identifies the work requirements as well as personal skills needed to perform the duties and functions of a job. These duties and functions should necessarily blend with overall organizational objectives. The job analysis process is fraught with such ambiguity, subjectivity, and interpretative difficulties that, unless consciously eliminated, can virtually invalidate the results of the entire process. Accordingly, efficient human resource management requires organizations to pursue objectively a functional and nonbiased job analysis program that will clarify the duties and responsibilities of a particular job as well as identify the skills and expertise an incumbent should possess in order to perform in accordance with prestated standards.

Closely associated with the job analysis process is the burgeoning subject of work design, the second key element in establishing organizational and personnel parameters. Questions that responsible managers need to grapple with include:

(1) Can work be designed so as to achieve maximum employee performance and motivation attained at minimal organizational cost, which at the same time is sufficient to achieve organizational objectives? and

(2) Will the design of a particular job's duties evoke organizational loyalty from the job incumbent, with attendant personnel cost reductions?

A third key element implicit in the procurement function of human resource management concerns those management activities actually associated with attracting individuals into the work environment. These activities include recruiting, selecting, placing, and planning for the growth of individuals within their work context. The human resource manager attempts to obtain the maximum utilization of human resources through career planning and development, which provide broad avenues for enhancement of expertise that coincides with organizational objectives.

The fourth broad human resource management element consists of compensation, personnel maintenance, and training and development activities, which in turn depend on an accurate analysis of the tasks, objectives, and goals of the organization and its people. Human resource managers are obliged to structure plans that will link such work analysis to organizational objectives by means of clear, crisp, and workable compensation plans, personnel maintenance efforts, and training and development programs based upon specific needs identified through personnel performance appraisal.

DEVELOPING HUMAN RESOURCE INFORMATION SYSTEMS

Possibly one of the most intransigent areas for the human resource manager to contend with is the aggregated and disaggregated data associated with the large amounts of information necessary to manage organizational personnel effectively. Irrespective of the level of sophistication of work and job analysis, if data cannot be easily retrieved, human resource managers may never be able to implement all of the elegant strategic human resource plans that evolve from laborious deliberations. It therefore becomes obligatory for a human resource manager to create an effective, efficient, and responsive human resource information system that will allow the carrying out of long-range, intermediate-range, and short-range strategic plans. Any manager's attention should be focused on preventing tomorrow's problems from arising, rather than on reacting to and solving the problems of yesterday and today.

The sophistication inherent in later-generation data retrieval equipment is such that human resource managers now have a capability, an opportunity, and a real challenge to adapt their internal information systems' data to a variety of electronic systems, irrespective of their organization's size. Planning, designing, and implementing a human resource information system are severe tests of a manager's creativity, commitment, and mettle. Of course, dysfunctonal results can be obtained almost as easily as those that are desirable and consistent with the stated objectives of establishing a comprehensive information system. Human resource managers need to have an awareness of the paths and pitfalls of designing and introducing an overall electronic information system, as well as knowledge about such optional arrangements as timesharing of software and hardware from specialized data systems sources. Finally, the human resource planner needs to be able to evaluate the information system benefits vis-a-vis its costs in order to assess its continuation, improvement, or, if necessary, its curtailment.

EVALUATING THE EFFECTIVENESS OF HUMAN RESOURCE PLANNING

Assume that a rational and effective organizational tasking system using workable job analysis techniques is in existence. Further assume that this system can be supported by a comprehensive and responsive human resource information system. It then becomes necessary to introduce evaluative techniques that will assess the effectiveness of human resource planning across the long, intermediate, and short-range time horizons.

Any evaluative technique requires that performance standards be established to which both the organization and its people will subscribe. Measurement of performance standards is implicit in their creation. Such measurement is accomplished through analysis of feedback from various organizational outputs: what is the scrap-rate; what is the turnover rate; what is the amount of machine downtime this month compared to last month; productivity measures; and so on.

Human resource planning is no exception to this evaluation requirement. The primary difference in assessing human resource planning strategies and other operational decision-points in organizations is that people often tend to react in unpredictable ways simply due to the introduction of change. Therefore, a complex variable is introduced into strategic human resource planning that is not prevalent when planning the use of other resources.

A useful measure of the effectiveness of human resource planning is through an analysis of tangible and intangible organizational benefits measured against tangible costs. Cost-benefit analyses are relatively common in assessing the effectiveness of strategic and operational planning that focuses on allocated resources other than people. When human resource planning occurs, however, many organizations have experienced great difficulty in specifying precise programmatic costs and benefits and measuring actual improvement that may occur. If an operational methodology could be discovered that when tested proved successful, systematic cost-benefit analysis would indeed be more widely adopted and employed among many organizations that have seriously attempted to rationalize their human resource planning stratagems.

The articles in Part II which deal with each of the above areas have been written by thoughtful scholars and practitioners in the field of human resource planning. The following chapters contain pointed, relevant, and pertinent writings that address each of these human resource planning topics from a unique perspective. In contrast to Part I, Part II has an "applied" cast to it. Plans must ultimately be translated into action. The responsibilities for implementing human resource strategic plans and evaluating their efficacy must necessarily reside in the hands of operational managers. Part II of this book dramatizes and highlights these applied areas of human resource strategic planning.

Chapter Four deals with the concepts and methodologies of human resource forecasting. A wide variety of conceptual and analytically based models are examined. These models run the full gamut from relatively simple approaches to highly sophisticated quantitative models which rely on computer application.

Chapter Five looks at the analytical foundations associated with describing what are the precise functions of a job within its work context. Additionally, Chapter Five includes discussions on personnel development and how organizations can achieve the maximum utilization of their human resources.

Chapter Six looks at human resource information systems. It describes, in logical fashion, the rationale of creating a personnel planning and information system, its design and implementation, and the problems (with their recommended solutions) of nonacceptance by people who do not wish to be depersonalized by being part of a computer-based system.

Chapter Seven contains articles that examine how to evaluate the effectiveness of various human resource planning strategies. This area of evaluation is dealt with thoughtfully and concludes with a framework to evaluate personnel programs that may be offered.

Chapter 4
HUMAN RESOURCE PLANNING AND FORECASTING METHODOLOGIES

Manpower Planning Models and Techniques: A Descriptive Survey

Don R. Bryant, Michael J. Maggard, and Robert P. Taylor

Businesses today are faced with a tightening supply of high-talent manpower. The Research Institute of America has said that "management is not only the most urgent calling of the future but it will be the most critically short resource of all. By 1980, the nation will have to get along with roughly three potential leaders to do the job that four are doing today."[1] As a result, much of the energy that organizations give to manpower planning today is aimed at management planning and development.

However, management will not be the only skill in short supply. The rate of technological change has increased the demand for people with high levels of technical knowledge. It is now difficult for a qualified professional to keep abreast of his field, and this may result in the obsolescence of technical manpower.

Another factor giving rise to the need for manpower planning is the increasing cost of managing human resources. Costs related to recruiting, hiring, training, and maintaining employees go up along with other costs in the economy. A firm, therefore, has an increasingly large financial investment tied up in its labor pool.

Don R. Bryant is chief of contract administration in procurement at Hamilton Air Force Base, California; Michael J. Maggard is a faculty member in the Graduate School of Business at the University of Texas, Austin; Robert P. Taylor is an M.B.A. from the Graduate School of Business, University of Texas.

The increasing shortage together with the high cost of managerial personnel have forced business to recognize the fact that manpower itself must be considered a resource as important as capital. Therefore, planning is required to insure that full value for each manpower dollar will be realized.

This article will describe an overview of existing manpower planning techniques, then summarize the relative strengths and weaknesses of each of the models or techniques in matrix form. The term "manpower planning" will be used as defined by James Walker.

Manpower planning refers to the rather complex task of forecasting and planning for the right numbers and the right kinds of people at the right places and the right times to perform activities that will benefit both the organization and the individuals in it.[2]

The proper utilization of manpower involves the coordination of numbers, talents, times, places, and objectives. Manpower planning is successful to the extent that it properly matches each of these elements.

MANPOWER PLANNING TECHNIQUES

One of the essential components of a manpower planning system is manpower forecasting—the process of anticipating the future size and nature of the manpower force. At this point we turn our attention to taking an overview of some of the techniques used by organizations in their manpower planning programs. All of the techniques may be applied to the forecasting of manpower requirements. For the sake of brevity the models and techniques will not be discussed in great detail. Rather, the intent in the following sections is to present the general characteristics of each technique. The major techniques of manpower forecasting include judgmental or estimating techniques, matrix models, quantitative techniques, and computer simulation.

Judgmental Techniques

Opinion or informed judgment techniques can be divided into two broad classifications: those making use of supervisor estimates, rules of thumb, or replacement charts, and the Delphi Technique, which has some rather unusual characteristics.

Estimates, Rules, and Charts

Utilizing supervisor estimates is one of the oldest and perhaps most used methods of forecasting manpower requirements. This technique uses the intuition and experience of the man closest to the job, and is a good method to use in making short-run forecasts. It is useful in that it is simple and quick and can produce results in the absence of adequate data. However, the method does have its disadvantages: it is based heavily on opinion, requires costly executive time, and requires an accuracy in estimating that a manager may not be able to provide.

The *rule-of-thumb technique* sets up decision heuristics (rules of thumb for certain environmental conditions) which are used in manpower forecasting. For example, a department may choose to hire one new salesman for each $60,000 increase in sales, or one new production worker whenever overtime costs for a department exceed $1,000 per week for more than four weeks. This technique is, at times, useful. However, it has disadvantages in that the heuristics usually are designed to maintain the *status quo* and may not represent changed influences that may affect future requirements.

A *replacement chart* is a graphic device designed to insure that suitable replacements are ready to move into vacated positions as vacancies occur among incumbent personnel. The device may make use of such data as the incumbent's age, performance level, promotability, and the name and degree of readiness of the incumbent's "backup" man. More sophisticated charts may make use of much more data, such as age, internal historical information, actuarial statistics, and estimates or opinions about where and when vacancies may occur. This technique's chief disadvantage is that constructing such a chart may require a great deal of labor in the assembly and compilation of the data. The chart also presents a static, rather than a dynamic, picture of the organization's structure.[3]

The Delphi Technique

The Delphi Technique is somewhat unique in that it obtains and refines group judgments through the use of formal questionnaires.[4] The results of each questionnaire are processed and used as the basis for another iteration. The primary advantages of this method are the use of anonymous responses, the reduction of irrelevant communications, and the requiring of individual panelists to consider other factors which they may have overlooked when making the original judgments. Two disadvantages are that interest in the technique seems to decline after a few trials and that it requires costly executive time.

Matrix Models

Matrix models provide a means of manpower planning which is meeting with increasing acceptance in the business world. Matrix models do not provide a manager with any new information about his personnel situation, but they do provide him with a new way of viewing and evaluating the available data. Two matrix models which will be discussed here are the matrix model for executive development and the management manpower planning matrix.

Matrix Model for Executive Planning Development

This model makes use of a rather sophisticated data base and is actually composed of five matrices for planning present and future executive manpower needs.[5] These five matrices are (1) job analysis: talent-task relationship, (2) man-job relationship, (3) talent-task composition of the enterprise, (4) executive personnel requirements, and (5) talent flows. These matrices will be briefly described in order to illustrate the type of information that goes into their composition.

The *job analysis: talent-task relationship matrix* is used to determine the talent-task relationship for each executive position. When completed, the matrix provides an overview needed for the job under consideration.

The *man-job relationship matrix* is used either for the purpose of adjusting the personnel through training, testing, and other qualifications, or for changing the job to fit available talents. Neither man nor job has to remain rigid and inflexible.

The *talent-task composition of the enterprise matrix* is used to determine talent requirements for the enterprise as a whole. It provides a summary picture of tasks to be performed and the talents needed to do them. It also provides a frame of reference for planning talent search and development requirements for the firm.

The *executive personnel requirements matrix* provides an analysis of present and anticipated personnel requirements. For future periods the matrix provides forecasts based on the growth and change in the organization itself and on evaluations of future potentials of present executives.

The *talent-flows matrix* depicts the training that is needed for executive development.

The Management Manpower Planning Matrix

Developed by Mason Haire, this matrix is a representation of the characteristics of personnel flow on one axis and the factors in the organization (recruitment, pay, training, and promotion) which may affect personnel flows on the other.[6] Basic to Haire's approach is the assumption that in any organization only five types of moves can take place:

> Some people may move into the system from the outside.
> Some people may move out of the system.
> Some people may move up.

Some people may move over (that is, not change jobs, or move laterally to equivalent jobs).

Some people may change their behavior and potential.

The primary purpose of the matrix is to aid management in determining the probabilities of varying types of personnel movement in the system. The first step is to project how many people are needed, what kind of people they will be, and at what levels they will work as the organization grows or diversifies.

The next step is to assign subjective probabilities to the flow of personnel to fill the projected jobs. This is accomplished by applying past experience and managerial judgment to the jobs being analyzed, to move to other jobs within the system, or even to jobs out of the system altogether.

Finally, one must analyze the portfolio of management policies for influencing rates and direction of personnel flow. Haire states, "By judicious use of management tools, the flows of personnel can be speeded up or slowed down, and the character of people to be siphoned off at various levels can be influenced."

It must be remembered that matrix techniques will suffer or gain from the quality of information that is used to constitute the matrix. The techniques do not provide any new information or guidelines. Their chief advantage is that they can provide aids to logic in comprehending the relationships among the variables. They present data in more readable form. They cannot, however, compensate for information which is in itself faulty.

Quantitative Techniques

Quantitative techniques fall into three categories: statistical methods, operations research methods, and network techniques.

Statistical Methods

The *time series analysis* makes use of trend extrapolation. The basic idea is to project past trends into the future. The method has two principal advantages: it forces the forecaster to consider the underlying trend, cyclic, and seasonal elements, and it takes into account the particular repetitive or continuing patterns exhibited by past manpower-use data. Disadvantages include the need for an established data base, the need for a fairly large labor force in order to make results statistically significant, and the assumption that the future will be a continuation of the past.

Stochastic statistical analysis attempts to account for the uncertainty of future events. Under uncertainty, each decision has a set of consequences, but either there are no probabilities associated with these outcomes or they are not meaningful. The decision, however, may be influenced by past experience or prior performance, for example, the selection of a sales team. The probabilistic technique developed by Wadel and Bush utilizes the success or failure of outstanding contract bids as the factor of uncertainty for which probabilities are required.[7] Packard's technique is an extension of the preceding technique in that the probability of success is also a function of the age of the outstanding bids.[8]

Two advantages of this approach are that results are in terms of expected values and that a series of uncertain events can be accounted for through the use of a decision tree. The primary disadvantages are: (1) the need for historical data and (2) the projects being evaluated must be essentially interchangeable—that is, the personnel, contracts, or projects should be similar enough for the decision maker to be indifferent to which is actually selected.

Operations Research Techniques

Linear programming, an operations research technique, can be used to meet objectives when a set of specified constraints is given. It is useful in that it can test for an optimal solution or mix of manpower resources required to reach a quantifiable objective. It is also possible to test these requirements under a variety of assumptions about future costs and constraints.

The *goal programming model* developed by Charnes, Cooper, Niehaus, and Sholtz, makes use of linear programming to develop manpower requirements which consider salary, budget data, and stipulated manpower floors and ceilings in each relevant period in the forecast horizon.[9] The model does not forecast the manpower requirements of the force as a whole. This is an input to the model and is part of the set of constraints. The model is termed "goal programming" because a goal or set of goals is specified, subject to a set of constraints. Goal programming can handle multiple goals in multiple dimensions which cannot be aggregated into a single objective function. This method provides a guideline for hire-fire decisions in the face of conflicting objectives.

Disadvantages are that certain of the input requirements may be difficult to obtain and that the model loses accuracy when used over short time horizons. Furthermore, it assumes linear objective functions when, in fact, quadratic objective functions may be more appropriate.

Sheridan's Naval Shore Activity Model can be used to calculate a least-cost labor mix required to satisfy capability or output requirements for an organization.[10] The capability constraints for this model are:

- Specified output levels must be maintained.
- Consumption and production of intermediate products must be related.
- Upper and lower bounds on labor inputs must be specified.
- Policy constraints which may arise such as specified minority group ratios must be included.
- All variables must be non-negative.

The problem to be solved is that of cost minimization subject to the capability constraints. If the desired output of the organization at some future date is known, the least-cost labor mix can then be calculated. This mix then becomes the forecasted labor requirements.

The disadvantages of linear programming techniques arise from the requirements they impose:

- It is necessary to set up a quantifiable objective.
- There must be alternative courses of action available to achieve the objective.
- The cost of data collection may be very high.
- The variables used in the program must be interrelated.
- The objectives and the limitations or constraints must be stated in terms of mathematical equations or inequalities.

Minimum Risk Manpower Scheduling Technique

Originated by Jewett, this technique is designed to forecast optimum levels of full-time employment for given time periods in which the total workloads are not known.[11] For the solution of this problem Jewett uses dynamic programming. The steps required to use this technique are as follows:

- Determine the set of mutually exclusive workloads which exist and determine the probabilities of each.
- Calculate the plan for each possible workload which will yield the minimum cost.
- Determine the expected transition cost for changing in later time intervals from a specific manpower level to the minimum cost level appropriate for that time.
- Using the above information, minimize expected transition costs for the set of possible workloads.

The chief advantage of this method over the previously discussed techniques is that it allows for flexibility of forecasting over a period of time covering several possible transition points. The previous probabilistic methods yield a forecast for one point in time. This technique yields a forecast which allows for uncertain changes in requirements after the initial starting point, and it does so at the least cost over the long run. It should be noted, however, that doing the four steps of the technique is not an easy task. Moreover, the cost of data collection and the computation time using dynamic programming are high.

Network Flows Methods

Network flow models can also be used to solve manpower planning problems. The network consists of a set of elements, such as job positions or categories, interconnected by a set of links, which may represent training or crosstraining routes, transfers, and the like.

Gorham has developed a model which deals with forecasting, training, and development activities.[12] In this model, the nodes represent positions or groups of positions, and the links represent all potential training and retraining flows and intraposition movements. The links indicate the amount of time required to move from one position to the other. The model takes into consideration varying lead times, uncertainty, and alternative ways of meeting new or increased skill requirements to determine the set of flows that will be most likely to "near optimize" the solution. The model presents a dynamic picture of the personnel situation and can be used to determine costs through the use of artificial nodes. For small time intervals, however, the network becomes unwieldy.

Computer Simulation

Computer simulation is a useful technique in cases where a mathematical formulation may not be possible or feasible. Simulation is especially useful in manpower forecasting when used to determine the effects of variations in policies, availability of personnel, and the utilization of personnel. Three examples of simulation techniques are described below.

PERSYM

PERSYM is an entity model designed for military use.[13] It is an entity model because the simulated population is introduced and maintained in the form of "individual records of individual people (the entities)." Each entity is described by as many attributes as desired, and some of these attributes can also be used as indices of personnel inventories and manpower requirements. The aggregate reports produced by PERSYM can be used as the basis for forecasting personnel requirements, for example, forecasting that there will be a shortage of 500 individuals in occupation number 1234 in 1975.

The Army's Reserve Manpower Model

This model produces annual projections for a ten-year period of Army Reserve manpower strengths, gains, and losses.[14] The model consists of two modules. The manpower projection module produces annual projections of strengths, gains, and losses for officers and enlisted men in the three main categories (ready reserve units, ready reserve pool, and standby reserve). The personnel cost module projects personnel costs associated with the major costs of procuring, maintaining, and training the Army Reserves. The model allows for experimentation with policy changes, manpower requirements, and budget restrictions, and simulates the effects of these changes on costs and requirements.

The Weber Model

Because of the thoroughness with which the Weber model dissects the simulated firm's personnel situation, it will be discussed in some detail.[15] The model simultaneously considers a large number of tasks, objectives, and interrelationships. It has a distinct advantage over techniques which look at one variable or function at a time while holding the others constant. The model represents the human resource subsystem of a hierarchical organization, encompassing the behavior of individuals, management decisions, and aspects of the organization's environment. In this way, detail and depth of individual considerations are depicted along with the totality of the manpower subsystem's behavior, so that interactions of all variables and functions which appear pertinent may be studied. This approach is an improvement over the simplistic approaches used to deal with the organization as a whole.

Concepts and ideas drawn from the literature of management and behavioral science are used as a framework for the model. In this model, characteristics of both the individual and the organization are taken into consideration. Moreover, those factors external to the individual and the organization are also included in the model, and these factors are expressed in general terms as "job market behavior." The environment is represented as a job market which generates offers of alternative jobs outside the simulated organization. Both visibility and active search increase the probability that an individual will receive a job offer, but the greatest effect by far on that probability is caused by the level of activity in the job market. It also determines the probability that the job offered will be promotion.

Organization policies constitute another major part of the model.

MANPOWER PLANNING MODELS AND TECHNIQUES

PROBLEM AREAS		Supervisor Estimates	Replacements Charts	Delphi Technique	Management MPP Matrix	Matrix Model for Executive Development	Time Series Analysis
Forecasting		G–F	G–F	G	F	G–F	G–F
Scheduling		G–F	P	P	P	F	P
Allocation		G–F	F	P	F–P	F	P
Uncertainty		F	P	G	F–P	F–P	F–P
Costing ability		F	F	F–P	P	P	P
Time horizon	L	P	F	G–F	F–P	F	F–P
	M	F	F	G	G	G	G
	S	G	G	G	F	G	G–F
Aggregate		F	F	G	F	F	G
Individual		G–F	G–F	F	F	F	P
Test policy changes		F	P	F	F	F–P	P
Hierarchy level	U	P	F	G–F	F	F	P
	M	F	G	G	G	F	G
	L	G	P	G	G	G	G
Static versus Dynamic		G–F	G	G	G–F	G–F	F
		F–P	P	G	G–F	F	F

Stochastic Statistical Analysis	Goal Programming Model	Naval Shore Activity Model	Minimum Risk Manpower Scheduling	Network Flow Model	PERSYM	U. S. Army Reserve Simulation Model	Weber Model
G	G	G–F	G	G	G	G	G
G–F	G	G–F	G	G–F	G–F	G–F	F
F	G	G	G–F	G–F	G–F	G–F	G
G	G–F	F	G	F	G	G	G
G–F	G	G	G	F–P	G–F	G	G
P	F	P	P	F–P	F–P	G–F	G
G	G	F	G–F	G	G	G	G
G	G	G	G	G	G	G	G
G	G	F	G	G	G–F	G	G
P	F–P	F–P	F–P	F	F	P	F
F–P	G	F	F–P	F	G–F	G–F	G
P	F	P	P	P	G–F	F	G
G	G	F	G	F	G	F	G
G	G	G	G	G	G	G	G
F	G	G	G–F	G	F	G–F	G
F	G	G–F	G–F	G	G	G–F	G

Examples of the kind of policy studied in the model are recruiting, attribute evaluation, and policies for promotion and salary increases. These policies are subject to managerial discretion in real organizations and represent system control points which would be used to manage human resources subsystems. Organization decisions concerning promotions and salary increases are shown as the outcomes of organizational policies. Outcomes which affect an individual's attributes are also provided. For example, an employee receiving a salary increase this year may now change his expectations (an attribute) and expect a similar increase next year.

Individual attributes and behavior constitute the final major portion of the model. A FORTRAN version of the model describes each entity by a list of 115 attributes, which are divided into the kind of data normally recorded in personnel files as well as the more private, primarily psychological attributes. The individual description serves as a data base for the individual, organizational, and environmental behavior in the model. It also provides information on individual outcomes, which are of primary importance to the individual.

This model has been designed so that it can be used for practical applications. Specifically, it is meant to be useful for evaluating the effects of alternative personnel policies of interest to the organization. It may also be of interest to members of the organization for planning their own careers and to organization theorists for studying organizations. Its primary purpose, however, is to serve as a planning model.

Some disadvantages of computer simulation are: (1) a sophisticated model requires time and money to develop, (2) model validation is difficult, (3) it does not guarantee an optimal solution, and (4) computer time may be expensive.

A COMPARATIVE EVALUATION

The matrix presented here summarizes the characteristics of the models and techniques discussed previously. The matrix facilitates the comparison of the advantages of each of the techniques with those of the others and permits the rapid evaluation of a method's relative merit with respect to each of the selection criteria. The selection criteria are given on the vertical axis of the matrix, and the techniques under consideration are placed on the horizontal axis. The cells of the matrix contain the following code letters: G (Good), F (Fair), P (Poor), G—F (varies Good to Fair), and F—P (varies Fair to Poor).

Each of the models and techniques was evaluated with respect to the following criteria:

Forecasting—Estimation of future manpower needs or the effects of
 some expected manpower problem

Scheduling—Timing of the satisfaction of anticipated manpower
 requirements

Allocation—Determination of manpower assignments to maximize
 utility or minimize costs

Testing Policy changes—Determination of effects of changes in
 organizational policy upon costs or required manpower levels

Uncertainty—Assessment of the uncertainty of future events

Aggregate—Determination of an organization's ability to forecast overall
 manpower needs

Individual—Ability to determine the requirements for an individual job
 or group of jobs

Time horizon—Relevant time spans: L—five years or more; M—one to
 five years; S—less than one year

Hierarchy level—Determination of the type of personnel a method may
 be applied to: U (Upper) to management or executive positions; M
 (Middle) supervisory and middle management positions; L (Lower)
 direct labor such as production, clerical, and sales personnel

Static versus dynamic—Situations at a point in time versus changes and
 effects over a period of time.

An important point must be made here. The evaluations provided
by this matrix are subjective in nature; they may change greatly
according to the evaluator's bias. In addition, the applicability of a
method may change greatly from one company to another. When
attempting to choose a technique for use in an organization, the personnel administrator must not base his final decision on a matrix drawn
up for someone else. He must digest the material available on the various
manpower planning methods and techniques himself, and from his
studies reach a decision.

The matrix, however, serves as a means for summarizing the
manager's conclusions about each method. An evaluator can use such a
device because it enables him to view the results of his research at a
glance and to determine the relative merits of the methods with respect
to the needs of his own organization. The need for and importance of
manpower planning has already been emphasized; the need for proper
application of the methods and correct evaluation of data is also
paramount.

In addition, several miscellaneous considerations should be taken
into account when studying manpower planning problems. These
include the productivity index, which is an adjustment for the increase
or decrease in productivity; the personnel response function, which is

analogous to the marginal utility concept used in economics; learning curves, viewed both in terms of their slopes and their time horizons; and system boundaries, which constitute the maximum and minimum values for which accurate forecasts can be made.

The point to be made is clear. There is a wealth of data generally available when one is seeking to analyze a manpower related situation. One must, however, look not only at the data, but also at the factors that can alter the indications derived from analysis of such data. The ideal manpower model would take into consideration all available data and all modifying considerations. Even in such a case, however, a human manager must still make final decisions.

NOTES

1. Richard B. Peterson, "The Growing Role of Manpower Forecasting in Organizations," *MSU Business Topics* (Summer, 1969), pp. 7-14.

2. James W. Walker, "Trends in Manpower Management Research," *Business Horizons* (August 1968), pp. 36-46.

3. W. R. Dill, D. P. Gaver, and W. L. Weber, "Models and Modelling for Manpower Planning," *Management Science* (December 1966), pp. B-142-67.

4. Robert Kemble, "Delphic Forecasting of Critical Personnel Requirements," *AD 664 803* (Fort Monmouth, N.J.: Army Electronics Command, 1968).

5. J. E. William Crissy, Robert M. Kaplan, and Louis H. Grossman, "Matrix Models for Planning Executive Development," *MSU Business Topics* (Summer, 1969), p. 8.

6. Mason Haire, "Managing Management Manpower," *Business Horizons* (Winter, 1967), pp. 23-28.

7. L. B. Wadel and C. M. Bush, "An Approach to Probabilistic Forecasting of Engineering Manpower Requirements," *IRE Transactions on Engineering Management* (September 1961), pp. 158-59.

8. K. S. Packard, "Probabilistic Forecasting of Manpower Requirements," *IRE Transactions on Engineering Management* (September 1962), pp. 136-38.

9. A. Charnes, W. W. Cooper, R. J. Niehaus, and D. Sholtz, "A Model for Civilian Manpower Management and Planning in the U.S. Navy" in *Models of Manpower Systems* A. R. Smith, ed. (London: The English Universities Press, 1970).

10. Thomas R. Sheridan, *Some Linear Programming Models for Forecasting Manpower Requirements of Naval Shore Activities*, AD 706 608 (Monterrey, Calif.: Naval Postgraduate School, 1969).

11. Roger F. Jewett, "A Minimum Risk Manpower Scheduling Technique," *Management Science* (June 1967), pp. B-578-92.

12. William Gorham, "An Application of a Network Flow Model to Personnel Planning," *IEEE Transactions of Engineering Management* (September 1963), pp. 113-23.

13. Robert O. Groover, "PERSYM: A Generalized Entity-Simulation Model of a Military Personnel System," AD 696 986 (Oporto, Portugal: NATO Conference Paper, 1969).

14. Robert W. Moss and Stephen R. Wax, "A Computerized System for Projecting Reserve Manpower Strengths and Costs," *AD 831 565* (McLean, Va: Research Analysis Corporation, 1967).
15. W. L. Weber, "Manpower Planning in Hierarchical Organizations: A Computer Simulation Approach," Management Science (November, 1971), pp. B-119—B-144.

Human Resource Planning Models: A Perspective

George T. Milkovich and Thomas A. Mahoney

The topic of human resource planning has received considerable attention since the publication of Eric Vetter's book, *Manpower Planning for High Talent Personnel,* in 1967. A variety of approaches to and models of human resource planning have been developed and proposed. Concurrently, most organizations engage in some form of human resource planning whether or not the models proposed in the professional literature are employed. We review here a variety of human resource planning models discussed in the literature and make some observations about these models in terms of organizational applications.

Vetter defined manpower planning as:

> The process by which management determines how the organization should move from its current manpower position to its desired manpower position. Through planning, management strives to have the right number and the right kinds of people, at the right places, at the right time, doing things which result in both the organization and the individual receiving maximum long-run benefit. (Vetter, 1967, p. 15)

It is a process in which all organizations engage with greater or lesser degree of formality. Over the years, most human resource planning has been accomplished by individual managers or supervisors determining staffing needs for their subordinate units, a relatively

---

Reprinted with permission from *Human Resource Planning,* Spring, 1978. Copyright © 1978 by Human Resource Planning Society.

George T. Milkovich and Thomas A. Mahoney are both on the Industrial Relations Center faculty at the University of Minnesota.

informal process. A few plans have been developed within large organizations, each focused upon a specific subsidiary or unit. By contrast, the human resource planning models developed over the past ten years, tend to focus on the development of overall human resource plans for the total organization and relate to corporate planning. Human resource planning by individual supervisors striving to meet production quotas continues in all organizations but is not the focus of the discussion. A wide variety of human resource planning models are available. Some are in use by employers, others are in varying stages of development. To lump them into a single human resource planning category implies that they are all similar; that they address the same issues, have similar, uses and are equally effective. That, of course, would be misleading.

The various human resource planning models available in the literature and observed in organizational practice can be related to the components of planning identified in Vetter's definition (Vetter, 1967):

1. Formulate human resource objectives, usually the numbers and skills required to fulfill the organization's plan.
2. Inventory and forecast the portion of future human resource requirements that will be satisfied by current personnel, and forecast the future budget commitments represented by the current personnel.
3. Design and structure personnel programs and policies that will help balance the behaviors of internal human resources with the objectives. Illustrations include the use of job redesign and/or promotions of employees to meet increased workload requirements or determining break-even levels for hiring new employees versus scheduling overtime or subcontracting.
4. Analyze the potential consequences of proposed changes in personnel programs and policies such as changes in promotion or retirement rates, changes in salaries and benefits, changes in recruitment and staffing patterns, and changes in organization rates of growth.

Since this paper presents a perspective of human resource planning models, a degree of classification is convenient. The general types of models observed in practice and in the literature can be classified as:

- heuristic: to provide organization and direction
- theory-research based: for analysis and strategy development and determination
- technique oriented: for forecasting and simulation.

As with most taxonomies, this one serves principally to highlight several points and some of the models may overlap into more than a

Figure One

**Systems View of the Demand for
and Supply of,
Manpower and Organizational
Positions**

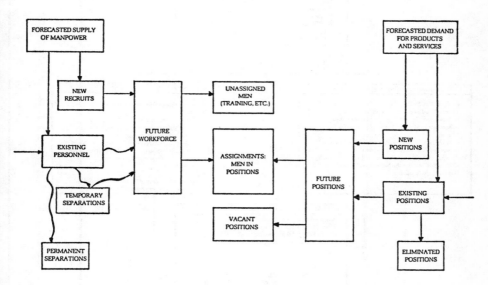

Source: Kenneth R. MacCrimmon, "Improving Decision Making with Manpower Management Systems", The *Business Quarterly*, (Autumn, 1971), p. 31.

single class. The general nature of each of these models and their applications are considered in turn.

HEURISTIC MODELS

When asked to discuss their planning models, many professional human resource planners employed in major corporations will show some variant of the models illustrated in Figures One and Two. These approaches are heuristic in the sense that they are designed to enable the users to organize their thoughts and to approach the issues in a systematic manner. Such models serve in providing aid or direction in the solution of the problem. The literature has several illustrations of these conceptualizations of human resource planning (Burack and Walker, 1972). Generally, the common components of the models reported include:

Figure Two

Human Resource Planning Process (Weyerhauser Corporation)

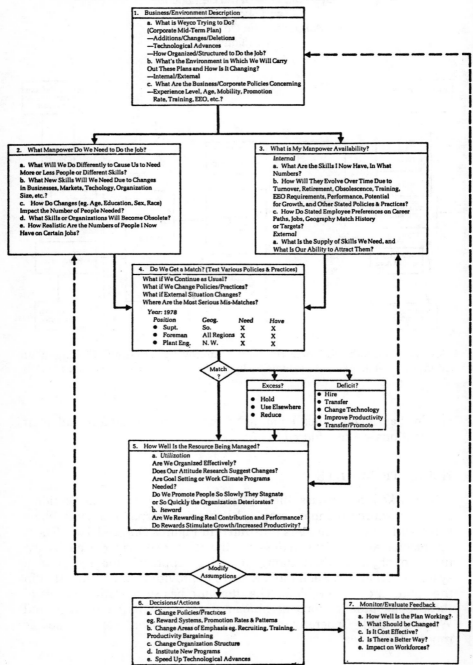

- determining the human resource objectives;
- analyzing the internal labor supplies available and projecting into the future;
- matching the desired human resource position with the estimated actual position and identifying areas of surplus and/or shortage for each period;
- generating and analyzing alternative policies and strategies to achieve the human resource objectives, including alternative staffing, recruiting, job and organization design, and training programs; and
- implementing the programs and reevaluating results against the human resource objectives.

The principal use of this form of human resource planning model seems to be to alert managers to the need for human resource planning and suggest some direction on how to begin. One could speculate over how (or if) heuristic models represent an advance over common sense. However, the explicit identification and determination of key elements and issues involved in the human resource planning process does provide direction and assistance.

These models suggest implicity that much of the content of human resource planning will be organization specific and they merely draw attention to the major factors or questions to be considered in the development of a plan. For example, they guide the search for alternative strategies, rather than specify the content or nature of these strategies. Individuals who apply the models are expected to employ personal judgment in the formulation of human resource plans tailored to their specific situations. Thus, these heuristic models can be quite useful as guides to individual managers and may be more applicable in decentralized planning approaches than are other models discussed below.

THEORETICAL-RESEARCH BASED MODELS

Another major class of manpower models can be labeled as theoretical-research based models. These models are more concerned with the identification of the variables that influence an organization's human resource objectives. Some of the questions theoretical models are designed to answer include:

- What are the specific determinants of unit productivity, employee performance, job satisfaction, or unit labor cost?
- What relationships exist between budget expenditures on manpower programs such as training, and unit productivity?

Figure Three
Towards Total Productivity

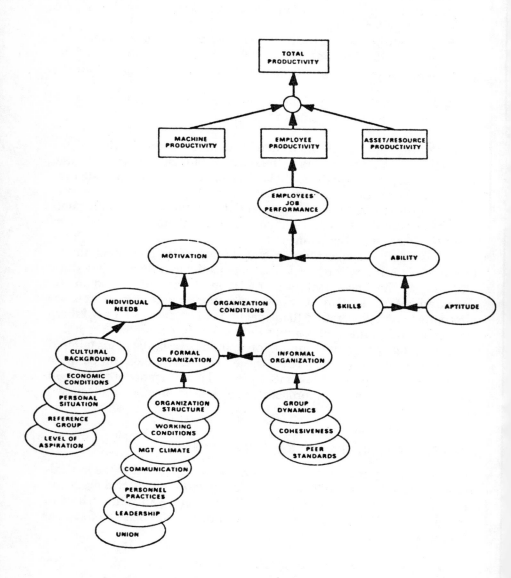

Figure Four

Factors Influencing Employee Performance:
An Illustration of a Human Resource Model with Substance

$$\text{Employee Performance} = f \left(\begin{array}{l} \dfrac{\text{aptitude}}{\text{level}} \times \dfrac{\text{skill}}{\text{level}} \times \dfrac{\text{understanding}}{\text{of task}} \times \dfrac{\text{choice to}}{\text{expend effort}} \times \\[2em] \dfrac{\text{choice of degree}}{\text{of effort to expend}} \times \dfrac{\text{choice to}}{\text{persist}} \times \dfrac{\text{facilitating and inhibiting}}{\begin{array}{c}\text{conditions not under the}\\\text{control of the individual}\end{array}} \end{array} \right)$$

Source: John P. Campbell, "Motivation Theory in Industrial and Organizational Psychology," in M. D. Dunnette (ed.), *Handbook of Industrial and Organizational Psychology* (Chicago: Rand McNally, 1976), p. 65.

● How does a policy of "promotion from within" impact unit productivity, labor costs, or legal compliance with EEO?

The focus is more on the specification of the substance or content of human resource objectives rather than on the issue to be considered for the analytical technique to be used. For example, a heuristic model includes "determine human resource objectives." Whereas, a theoretical model may include, "employee performance is a function of skills, motivation and technology."

Most of these models are derived from behavioral and organizational theory and practice. Two illustrations are shown in Figures Three and Four. They tend to be content rich but devoid of analytical techniques. The emphasis here is on the inclusion of theories and research findings related to human resource management. Most of the heuristic and more technique-oriented models tend to overlook the content, the theory and research related to human resource management.

Some of these models emphasize the critical variables to consider but stop short of specifying relationships necessary to draw specific implications of alternative human resource strategies. This lack of specificity of relationships may reflect the stage of development and knowledge in organizational and social sciences. For example, Sutermeister's model (Sutermeister, 1976) represented in Figure Three, lacks the specifications necessary to determine the nature and direction of the relationships among the variables. To state that the informal organization somehow impacts organizational conditions and motivation doesn't specify the nature of the relationship or provide much guidance to human resource planners and managers to design and develop strategies to achieve the human resource planning objectives.

Campbell's model (Campbell, 1977), represented in Figure Four, was derived from the existing behavioral theory and research related to employee performance. To influence employee performance, a human resource planner using such a model, would, for example, develop and select programs designed to influence such variables as skill level or understanding of the task or the aptitude of the employee.

In sum, these models derived from economic and organizational research and theories can provide critical input for human resource planning. Most managers currently operate with implicit models of the critical factors that will impact their human resources. Concepts and insights drawn from organization-related theory and research such as those found in the Campbell illustration may also prove to be of value.

TECHNIQUE-ORIENTED MODELS

The third area of human resource modeling is the application of mathematical models to human resource issues. Obviously, effective planning doesn't depend necessarily upon the use of sophisticated planning models; however, when properly used, they may enhance the process. There are a wide variety of technique-oriented models that have been applied to various human resource planning elements with reasonable success. However, one caution made here is that in some applications, the main focus seems to be on the technique rather than the content. The common ones are briefly reviewed.

REQUIREMENTS MODELS

Mathematical models are available and often recommended for human resource projections and forecasts as in the forecasting of human resource requirements. The variables most amenable to quantitative analysis are numbers of persons and man-hours and most human resource forecasting models are applied to these variables rather than other variables such as commitment, satisfaction and productive capabilities. While these additional factors might be quantified, forecasting models do not incorporate them. The techniques most commonly used for projecting human resource requirements are time series, correlation/regression, "balancing" equations, stochastic models and work measurement.

Time series models seem to be most useful in predicting seasonal manpower requirements such as in farming, harvesting and food processing industries and retail trades. Since the model assumes that some pattern or combination of patterns of human resource required is recurring over time, (Sullivan and Claycombe, 1977) the principal determinant of requirements is time. Consequently, the model is not particularly useful in analyzing the possible consequences of programmatic and policy manipulation on human resource requirements.

Regression models are most appropriate where the level of required manpower is relatively sensitive to other factors such as production, sales, and unit costs. Generally, the products and services generated by a technology is dependent upon the capital and labor employed. Thus the optimal level of labor to employ is in some manner derived from the goods or services demanded. The practical issue is to identify and quantify the determinants of human resource demand — that is, to determine the empirical relationship between inputs and outputs.

In the most naive regression models, personnel demand depend on estimates of future sales, production and/or services (Drui, 1963). Unfortunately, there seem to be few reported examples of successful application of regression models used to determine required staffing levels. Gascoigne (1968) gives an excellent description of the search for relationships among a wide range of measures of production, sales and services, productivity and manpower levels.

Regression analysis also may be used to determine the appropriate skill mix or proportions of support staff in relation to some skill group most directly related to production or sales. In other words, the personnel requirement for support staff is a function of the requirements of a key skill group. Thus, the level of engineers required is the determinant of the level of clerical, accounting and other support personnel (Shaeffer, 1976). Regression analysis is also used to identify the characteristic time phasing of the various skills utilization projects in a project contract technology (Rudelius, 1966). For example, the level of a particular type of human resources (engineering personnel) on a program in any given one-month period may be correlated to the level of another type of human resources (shop personnel) required one month later.

Balancing equations are similar to regression models in that they include determinants related to manpower levels. However, they do not make explicit use of statistical relations. Two illustrations of this approach are Burton (1958) and Doeringer, et al. (1968). These models are used in a variety of ways including analyzing the impact of a wide range of assumptions reflecting various economic conditions. Thus alternative future levels of productivity, output, sales, and retention are examined and the possible consequences on manpower requirements are considered. Another form of "balancing" model is the breakeven analysis used in determining optimal level of hours to schedule overtime before hiring and/or subcontracting (Fossum, 1969).

Stochastic models are most commonly used in organizations such as government contractors, construction, and management consulting firms in which the demand for the services of a skill/occupational group is derived from several projects. Much of the initial project planning work is done in support of marketing efforts such that the schedules and human resource estimates form a basis for the preparation of cost proposals. The basic issues in determining the human resources required are:

- the varying probabilities of securing each contract;
- uncertainties about the pending project startup date; and
- uncertainties of the required manpower over the life cycle of the project.

These uncertainties are transferred in Bayesian procedures to produce a stochastic demand forecast. The best early illustrations of this approach are found in Wadel and Bush (1962) and a recent application at McDonnell Douglas (Kwah, et al. 1977).

The success in applying mathematical models in the determination of human resource objectives has been limited. There are several reasons for this. One is the nature of the problem, the translation of estimates, projections of business planning, into another set of estimated human resource requirements. In many cases, business plans are not sufficiently precise for detailed modeling. Even in cases where they are, the human resource variables are difficult to define and quantify. Another reason, discussed earlier, is that mathematically based models typically express requirements in terms of staffing levels only. Yet an organization may include other human resource objectives such as improvements in productivity rates and labor costs, desired rates of safety and accidents, and perhaps even employee satisfaction rates.

FORECASTING AND ANALYSIS

The most significant advances in human resource modeling techniques have occurred in the application of Markov chains, renewal, and goal programming models to the human resource stocks and flows processes within the organization. The application of these models include most of the human resource uses discussed earlier. They are used to:

- forecast the future human resource requirements that will be satisfied by the current inventory of personnel, and to forecast the future human resource budget commitments represented by the current stock of personnel:
- analyze the impact of proposed changes in policy and programs; and

- design and structure systems that will balance the flows of internal human resource supplies and requirements and costs and to design human resource information systems suitable for policy analysis and planning.

The most commonly discussed models are briefly reviewed below.

Markov chain models (Vroom and MacCrimmon, 1966; Bartholomew and Smith, 1970: Mahoney and Milkovich, 1970; Forbes, 1971) are most appropriate where the job classes and rates of flow between them are stable and the flows out of a class depends on the class occupied and the number of people in the class. Typically, the data required consist of starting head counts or stocks, historical records on personnel transactions and data on new entrants into the system.

In the simplest form, the rates of movement depend upon the current class which has been defined in terms of organization level, salary grade, function, experience, age, sex or race. The transitional matrices used in Markov analysis have considerable descriptive utility for analyzing the behavior of current and personal movements (Heneman and Sandver, 1977). However, as the model is refined by adding attributes, the complexity increases. Forbes (1976) and Mahoney and Milkovich (1970) investigated the accuracy of forecasts generated with Markov models; both studies raised concerns about the stability of the transitional probabilities over time, and thus the accuracy of forecasts.

An alternative use of Markov models is simulation — that is, to forecast and analyze the potential consequences of alternative staffing policies and procedures. For example, simulation may demonstrate "how the current personnel inventory of an organization will be distributed in future periods if they continue to promote, transfer and hire personnel in some prescribed manner". Markov chain models are beginning to be applied to affirmative action and equal employment issues also. (Ledvinka, 1975; Churchill and Shank, 1976; Milkovich and Krzystofiak, 1977).

Renewal models (Bartholomew and Smith, 1970) are most usefully applied to situations where personnel flows are generated by movement out of one class in response to the pull of vacancy in another class — for example, when promotions in a system are made only to fill jobs that become vacant, or when the level of recruitment is determined to maintain or control the levels in personnel inventory. There are few published applications of renewal models in corporations, though applications in government agencies have been reported (Forbes, 1976).

Most applications of goal programming models to human resource issues consist of embedding a series of Markov process models in a goal programming context. This makes it possible to deal with the dynamics of recruitment and allocation policies in ways that tie directly to objectives or goals stated in terms of manpower levels and/or budgetary dollars (Forbes, 1976). The personnel requirements are accommodated by the goal programming aspects and the transition of recruits and job incumbents from one position to another are dealt with by the stochastic elements of a Markov chain. More complex versions of these models extend over several time periods and across several levels (Charnes, et al. 1972). Most of these models have been developed and applied in military and government settings, and a substantial part of the literature reports demonstration projects. However, a few industrial applications are beginning to appear. Flast (1976) reports the use of goal programming in an equal opportunity application, and Platz (1970) demonstrates its use in a training situation.

The state of knowledge of mathematical manpower modeling far outstrips the actual application. Existing internal supply models discussed above are well in advance of implementation — that is, few organizations make use of them in their planning efforts. Further research is needed, not so much on the development of new and perhaps more complex models, as on the translation of existing models so that they may be used by managers in practical situations.

INTEGRATED HUMAN RESOURCE MODELS

A final class of models attempt to integrate the heuristic, theory-based, and the technique-oriented models. Only three such models have been reported in the literature (Miller and Harie, 1967; Weber, 1971; Mahoney and Milkovich, 1975). These models abstract the human resource subsystems of an organization, including employee behaviors, managerial decisions and characteristics of the organization, and the external environment. For example, factors included in these models are employee decisions to perform, to turnover, to accept an offer, to accept transfers and promotions; managerial decisions to expend budget and resources on a variety of personnel strategies such as skills and supervisory training, job design, wage increases, etc.; and finally, factors such as labor market supplies, product market demand, and rates of inflation. The estimates of variables and relationships among them are derived from existing practice and the state of knowledge based upon research and theory. These models interrelate policies and decisions in one human resource function with those from other functional areas. Consequently, implications of the interactions of human resource variables and functions which appear to be relevant to human resource planning can be examined. This approach attempts to avoid the over-simplification of studying single variables or programs which ignore the complex interaction in the system.

Such models have potential practical applications. Specifically, they can be used to evaluate the potential consequences of alternative personnel policies on performance criteria of the organization. They can also be used to plan and simulate the individual careers. However, the state of development of human resource planning in most corporations and the complexity of these integrated models has precluded their use.

Despite the development of analytical models, human resource planning still remains essentially an art. Part of the reason lies in the fact that the models make demands upon data that cannot be met and they require more quantitative historical data than exists in most organizations. The models also abstract human resource systems of necessity and in the process, discard from consideration some of the more significant influences of human resource performance. The more sophisticated mathematical models abstract to staffing levels and disregard influences of cross-training, job rotation, and personnel backups; they are most applicable to relatively rigid, formalized bureaucracies and less applicable to more dynamic organizations. Also in this context, the more sophisticated planning models are directed toward forecasts, not the formulation of objectives, the generation of strategies or the evaluation of alternative strategies. These models can be usefully applied in the generation of forecasts which may then be analyzed as inputs to the more heuristic process models of manpower planning.

The type of model which appears to offer most potential in the long run is what we termed the integrative model. This type of model integrates the theory-research base of information, employs forecasts as inputs for analysis, and provides outputs aligned with the heuristics of human resource planning. Futher development of this type of model would benefit from more detailed investigation of the application of human resources related theories and research to human resource planning and the identification of critical variables and their inter-relationships. The integrative model might then be developed to take advantage of these factors and to align better with the art of human resource planning.

REFERENCES

Bartholomew, P. J. and Smith. A. R. (ed), *Manpower and Management Science* (London: English University Press: 1970).

Bonini, C. P. *Simulation of Information and Decision Systems in the Firm* (Englewood Cliffs, N. J.: Prentice Hall, 1964).

Burak, E. H. & Walker, J. W., *Manpower Planning and Programming* (Boston: Allyn & Bacon, 1972).

Burton, W. W., "Forecasting Manpower Needs — a Tested Formula" in Ewing, D. W. (ed). *Long Range Planning for Management* (New York: Harper, 1958), pp.

228-236.

Campbell, John P. "Motivation Theory in Industrial and Organizational Psychology," in *Handbook of Industrial and Organizational Psychology*. M.D. Dunnette, (ed). (New York: Rand McNally. 1976).

Charnes, A., Cooper, W. W. and Niehaus, R. J., *Studies in Manpower Planning*. (Washington, D.C.: OCMM, 1972).

Churchill, N. and Shank J., "Affirmative Action and Guilt-Edged Goals," *Harvard Business Review* Vol. 54, No. 2, (1976), pp. 111-116.

Doeringer, P. B., Piore, M. J. and Scoville, J. G., "Corporate Manpower Forecasting and Planning," *The Conference Board Record* (1968, 5, 8), pp. 37-45.

Drui, A. B., "The Use of Regression Equations to Predict Manpower Requirements," *Management Science 9*, (July 1963).

Flast, R., "Manpower Models Applied to Affirmative Action," *Personnel Journal*, (June 1976), pp. 31-39.

Forbes, A., "An Advisory Service on Computer Based Manpower Models" in *Readings in Manpower Planning* (Canadian Operations Research Society, 1976).

Forrester, J. W., *Industrial Dynamics* (New York: Wiley and Sons, 1961).

Fossum, John "Hire or Schedule Overtime? A Formula for Minimizing Labor Costs" *Compensation Review*. Vol. 1, No. 2, (1969), pp. 14-22.

Gascoigne, I. M., "Manpower Forecasting at the Enterprise Level" *British Journal of Industrial Relations* 6, 1, (1968), pp. 94-106.

Heneman, H. G., III and Sandver, M. G. "Markov Analysis in Human Resource Administration" *Academy of Management Review*, (1977).

Ledvinka, J., "Technical Implications of Equal Employment Law for Manpower Planning," *Personnel Psychology*. Vol. 28, (1975), pp. 299-323.

MacCrimmon, K. R., "Improving Decision Making with Manpower Management Systems," *The Business Quarterly*, (1971, 35, 3), pp. 29-41.

Mahoney, T. and Milkovich, G., "Markov Chains and Manpower Forecasts", *(Office of Naval Research Technical Report #NR 151-323-7002, 1970)*.

Milkovich G. and Mahoney, T., "The Minnesota Manpower Management Simulation" in Simulation Games and Experiential Learning in Action. R. H. Buskirk, (ed), (1975).

Milkovich, G. and Krzystofiak, F., "Human Resource Planning Models and Affirmative Action Planning," Paper presented at Conference on Affirmative Action Planning, Cornell University, (1977).

Miller, J. R. and Haire, M., *Manplan: A Micro-Simulator for Manpower Planning*, (December 1967, MIT Working Paper No. 134).

Platz, A. L., "Linear Programming Applied to Manpower Management," *Industrial Management Review*, (1970), pp. 31-38.

Rudelius, W., "Lagged Manpower Relationships in Development Projects," *IEEE Transactions on Engineering Management* (1966, EM-13, r), pp. 188-195.

Sullivan, W. G. and Claycombe, W. W., *Fundamentals of Forecasting* (Reston, Virginia: Reston Publishing Co., 1977).

Sutermeister, *People and Productivity*, 3rd edition, (New York: McGraw-Hill, 1976).

A Model for Understanding
Management Manpower:
Forecasting and Planning
Noble S. Deckard and Kenneth W. Lessey

The key to a comprehensive view of management manpower planning is to look at the system from two perspectives. One is an independent or neutral view of what really happens to management manpower. This neutral view provides a tool, the forecasting model, to use in anticipating or forecasting what will happen. The other perspective is the organization's view of how to use management resources to achieve its objectives. This second view provides a tool, manpower planning, which is used to control the management manpower.

To develop an effective management manpower planning program, it is essential that models be developed to provide a framework to sort out all the pieces of information that are relevant. The model should be general enough to ensure that the variables included can be reviewed by each sub-unit to determine which are important and which have no impact, and be a guide for determining what happens in an organization concerning manpower. What the model can do is guide the investigation and help one get started, but it cannot be interpreted as an exact definition of what happens. Each organization must define what affects manpower requirements in its own situation.

FORECASTING

A central element in any manpower forecasting/planning system is predicting the need for and the availability of people to perform the management function for some future time period. This need to have the management function performed results from the organization's desire to accomplish its stated goals. The availability is concerned with the number of managers and the management skills of those managers.

The key to any forecasting procedure is to determine what causes things to happen the way they do. In this case, there is a need to know what determines the supply and demand for people which becomes the basis for predicting what will happen in the future. We can use this knowledge in two different ways. First, changes such as training and

"A Model for Understanding Management Manpower" by Noble S. Deckard and Kenneth W. Lessey. Reprinted with permission *Personnel Journal* copyright March 1975.

Noble S. Deckard is Special Studies Manager, Personnel Division, State of Oregon, Salem, and Kenneth W. Lessey is Manager of Maintenance and Engineering, Reichhold Chemical Company, Salem, Oregon.

Figure 1.

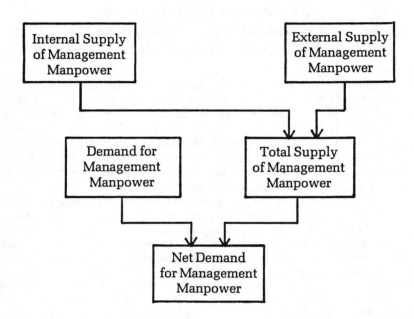

**Variables and Their Relationships to the
Net Demand for Management
Manpower**

transfers may be planned with anticipated effects of these activities projected into the suply and demand for people. But many factors are beyond the control of the organization and the organization cannot plan the changes in these factors. However, the forecast can still be used in this second setting by anticipating the possible changes in these uncontrolled factors and projecting their possible impact on the organization.

In many cases we need to make forecasts even though we do not know exactly what causes changes in the manpower system or the way these changes occur. This usually takes the form of management judgment or intuition. Partial information does not prevent us from forecasting but it does change the way we forecast. We can no longer forecast what will happen to the system if our assumptions are true. This may involve forecasting the implications of several plausible assumptions and preparing to live with the possible outcomes.

FORECASTING MODEL

The best way to communicate and work with a management manpower forecasting model is with graphic diagrams. Using a model enables one

Figure 2.

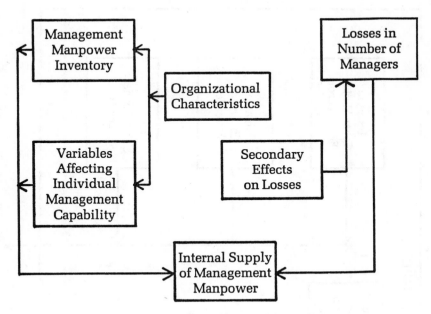

**Overview of Internal Supply
of Management Manpower**

to take all the bits and pieces of information about manpower and put them together in one package that is internally consistent and manageable.

There are many possible ways to group ideas on manpower forecasting. The one developed here is based on two concepts: the supply of management manpower and the demand for management manpower. Figure 1 shows these concepts and the way they are related. Each box shows a concept and the lines show the relationships. One box, "Demand for Management Manpower," is a result of the need of the organization to perform the functions defined as management. Another box, "Total Supply of Management Manpower," is the total supply of individuals that will be both capable and available to perform the management functions. The "Internal Supply" box represents those people who enter the organization through entry level positions. The "External Supply" box represents those people who enter the organization in positions above the normal entry level. The "Net Demand for Management Manpower" is the difference between the supply and demand for management capability. The remainder of the diagrams on forecasting (Figures 2 through 4) describe each of the Figure 1 boxes in detail.

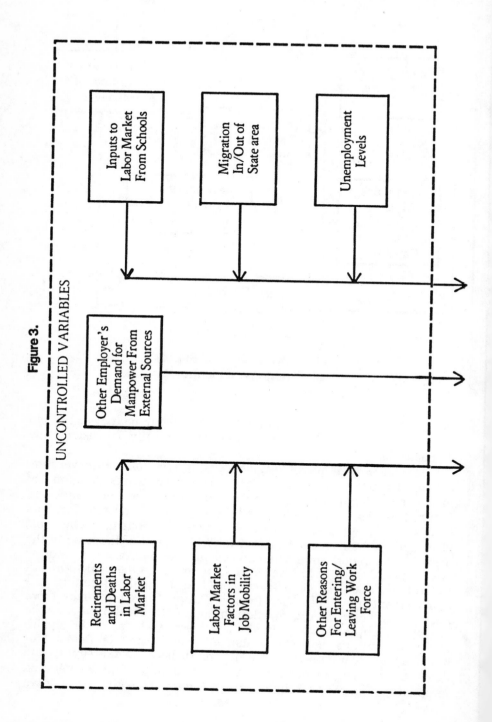

Figure 3.

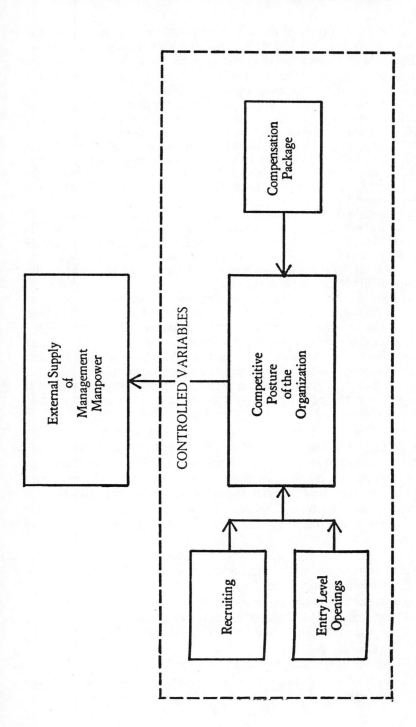

The internal supply of management people can be separated into three main sections (see Figure 2). One, the "Management Manpower Inventory," is an indication of capacity of the people currently in the organization to perform the management function. It is measured in terms of people and the management capabilities of each person. The second section includes the factors that can cause a change in an individual's ability to manage. These are labeled "Variables Affecting Individual Management Capability." The third section is the number of current managers that will leave the organization within some future time period. The other two sections, "Organizational Characteristics" and "Secondary Effects on Losses," do not directly influence the internal supply, but have an effect on the three main sections of the internal supply.

The variables in the two right-hand boxes are primarily measured in terms of numbers (Quantitative) and information about them is usually easy to obtain. The variables in the three left-hand boxes are usually measured in verbal terms (Qualitative) based on management judgment. Measuring tools for these factors are generally poor and the information is usually difficult and expensive to get.

The external supply of management manpower has been divided into two main segments (see Figure 3). The factors that have the biggest impact on the external supply of people are beyond the control of the organization. The variables and their impact on the supply are vague and very little information about these variables is available. There is more information on the second group of factors, controllable by the organization, but the impact of these factors on the external supply is vague. We have defined the competitive posture of the organization as the cumulative impact of these controllable variables.

The variables that affect the demand for management people are shown in Figure 4. Most of the variables are controlled by the organization, but are vague and difficult to measure. Most of them act through what can be called the need for management manpower. The primary sources of this need are the organization's objectives and the strategy for achieving those objectives. The need is the amount of manpower that would be required to carry out this strategy. The variables identified in Figure 4 are:

- Economic Plans of the Organization
  Budget increase
  Expansion of licensing or tax incomes
- Organizational Unit objective for the Program
  The specific goals and plans made by each unit in the organization.
- Objectives for Management Manpower for the Program
  The number of managers and the capability of each one of these managers.

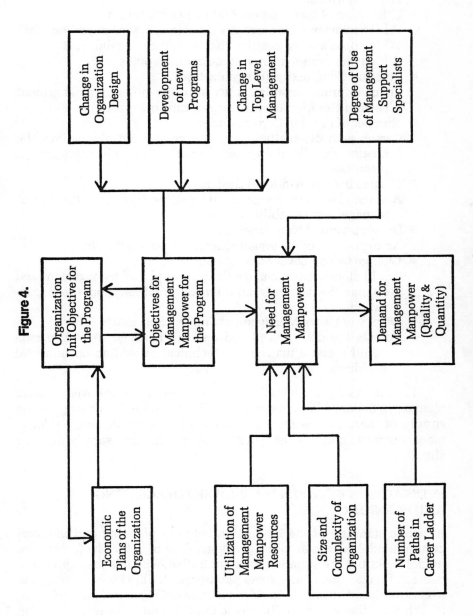

Figure 4.

Demand for Management Manpower

Formal training programs

Experience

Past performance

- Utilization of Management Manpower Resources

  Which managers are currently capable of more demanding jobs? Which ones are at a position that taxes their capabilities? Which one cannot meet the requirements of the job?

- Size and Complexity of Organization

  Small informal organizations can utilize different management capabilities from those of large formal organizations.

- Number of Paths in Career Ladder

  Career path alternatives; i.e., the greater the alternatives the greater the flexibility of selection from all management resources.

- Change in Organizational Design

  A major change in design could significantly change the type of management capability needed.

- Development of New Programs

  An expansion of the organization's services to its clients

- Change in Top Level Management

  Could significantly change the philosophy of management and change the demands put on managers throughout the organization.

- Degree of Use of Management Support Specialists

  Affects the demands placed on each manager. A staff person could assist a manager in technical or seldom encountered problems.

The forecasting model is the description of what is believed to cause changes in the need for managers as well as what causes a change in the supply of managers to meet that demand. The forecasting model is management's concept of what happens in the supply/demand situation.

INTERACTION BETWEEN MANPOWER FORECASTING AND PLANNING

An understanding of the interaction between planning and the forecasting model is crucial to the understanding of both. The forecasting model describes the situation to be controlled, which is the supply and demand for managers. Manpower planning describes how you are going to control the situation. It provides a framework to answer the questions: (1) What is it that we would like to accomplish; and (2) How are we going

Figure 5.

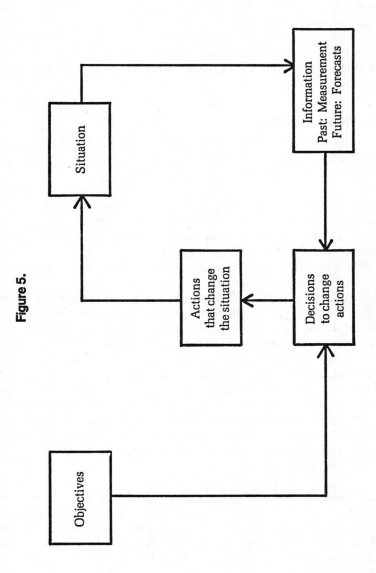

A Control System

to accomplish it? The interaction between the two is that it is necessary to know how the supply and demand situation works before it can be controlled.

There is another useful contrast between the forecasting model and planning. The forecasting model is a description of a natural system in the sense that these are the elements and relationships that exist. Manpower planning is a description of the design system in the sense that the organization can change the system if it has designed the system.

MANPOWER PLANNING

Planning includes three activities: (a) forecasting, (b) decision-making, and (c) actions. Figure 5 shows these activities and the way they are interrelated. The elements of any planning system are:

- The situation which we are concerned with as managers.
- Objectives or a desired condition for the situation.
- Actions that can be taken to change the situation. (If we cannot make changes that will modify the situation, then we cannot control the situation; if we cannot control the situation, there are no reasons to set objectives.)
- Information obtained about the situation under consideration. (This information can be divided into two classes, information about the past and the present. We have defined this collection of information as measurement, even if the measurements are made by casual observation and management judgment. The second class of information concerns the future. It is obvious that this information cannot be obtained through measurement. We can only anticipate or forecast what the situation will be. We use information about the past, anticipated future condition, and our objectives to make decisions about what actions we will take.) Decisions attempt to change the situation to a condition that matches our objectives.

Establishing manpower planning as the second step after manpower forecasting and the important emphasis placed on the designing of the program activities that are to occur, places management at the center of manpower planning. Policies and objectives for the manpower planning period must be established: this is a critical management function. The forecast gives a projected scenario of manpower supply and demand. Management must then decide and give direction to where and how the organization will achieve or modify that scenario.

Management must consider and concur with the assumptions used in the forecast. Next, top management designs the policies, objectives and programs that will guide the organization in utilizing its manpower resources.

The success of manpower forecasting/planning is greatly dependent upon management being a part of the program design. Generally, an organization should have a designated individual who will prepare the manpower forecast. The manpower planner then must consult with top management about the forecast and present a proposed manpower plan. Operating managers then provide their inputs to refine and improve the proposed manpower planning design.

A Human Resource Planning Model
Vincent R. Ceriello and Richard B. Frantzreb

INTRODUCTION

All organizations are comprised of masses of people at various skill and managerial levels. What most of these organizations have in common is that the employee population never remains constant. There is always growth, cutback, shifts, hiring, firing, and a great deal of lateral movement. Historically, most firms have hired on a replacement or demand basis. During periods of growth, they merely replaced at a greater rate than the rate of attrition; during periods of cutback or negative growth, replacement rate was lower than attrition rate. Manpower or human resource planning then was little more than developing time series (extrapolative) data and extending the trend line into the future a number of years.

To determine recruiting and training quotas for an organization today is a more complex task because optimal quotas depend heavily on uncertain future conditions. Additional considerations include expectations (with regard to that organization's growth), level of retirements

---

From *Human Factors*, Vol. 17, No. 1, 1975, pp. 35-41. Copyright 1975 by The Human Factors Society, Inc., and reproduced by permission.

Vincent R. Ceriello is with Hay Associates, Philadelphia, Pennsylvania, and Richard B. Frantzreb is with Bank of America, San Francisco, California.

and separations, promotions, transfers, and the proportion of trained personnel the firm will need to have in key positions at every level. Then there are external conditions such as macroeconomics, legal constraints, labor supply, social responsibility, *etc.*, which have impact upon the manpower planning problem.

An efficient solution to this rather complex problem is a computer-based simulation model. The simulation model, for these purposes, is a technique through which the computer attempts to represent the real-world and can react to "What if .... ?" questions. The model that has been developed by Manpower Planning at the Bank of America—called MPQ: Manpower Planning Quotas—uses historical and current data to translate staff totals into a series of equations and personnel inventories. MPQ gives the user an opportunity to specify all of the critical management policies regarding the selection and training of personnel. It then proceeds to stimulate the personnel experience of a single year—promotions, separations, retirements, and hires. The model then notes how many people will be required and from what sources they should be obtained; in other words, what the recruiting and training quotas should be. It repeats this simulation process for as many years as the user has specified, giving him the opportunity to change his inputs at the beginning of each year.

Many firms have grown in size and complexity to the point where manual forecasting is no longer possible. The Bank of America is no exception. With over 50,000 employees and some 1,000 domestic branches and 200 foreign offices, it is simply not possible to do this job without aid of a computer. Also, the number of variables that must be considered in any valid representation of human resources dictates the use of the computer. Because the computer performs tedious mathematical computations very rapidly, the model can generate training program quotas for one or more future years in about 15 min. of conversation with the computer at a remote terminal, during which time the computer is only "working" about 10 sec (CPU time). The conversational or interactive mode was designed primarily because this mode makes it easier to work with the MPQ model in altering the assumptions and data on a continuous basis. This rapid and relatively inexpensive process offers the user the possibility of experimenting with different promotional and hiring schemes to gauge the effect of each before the best one is selected.

BACKGROUND—FROM WHERE HAVE WE COME?

The Bank of America has maintained a sustained high interest in manpower planning for years, beginning with studies undertaken as early as 1955. These studies attempted to depict current manpower resources with exhaustive analyses of historical trends, retention and exit rates, and a rather complete profile of the staff. The summaries and recommendations contained therein indicated a critical need to do a better job of manpower planning but did not forecast a probable future posture for the bank.

Another major study was undertaken in 1962 in an attempt to again project staff needs, determine training quotas, and estimate the ratio of branch to administrative staffs. This study, entitled "Manpower Analysis and Training Quotas for 1962", brought to light major problems involving the readiness of qualified staff for promotions to fill vacancies, the need to establish realistic quotas of selection and training, and the effects of not meeting these quotas. It was a plea for action but not an action plan, except insofar as it caused management to create a manpower planning function.

In 1965, responsibility for manpower planning was assigned to the Organization Planning Department. Their studies formalized the projection of quotas and the inventory of manpower and had the title: "Manpower Study: Branch Males Grades 9—19 Inclusive, Conclusions and Recommendations".

This study was part of a major project involving branch staffing and developed many sound recommendations regarding promotional patterns, officer progression, training quotas, and manpower projections. The emphasis was on quantitative analysis. No attempt was made to address the qualitative aspects and the macroeconomics of California that would have an obvious bearing on any valid projection of staff.

By 1968, these studies were formalized and expanded and the presentation format was refined to include many charts, graphs, exhibits, and statistics. These studies were titled "Branch Manpower Analytic Projections" and "Training and Development Department Objectives".

The manpower planning unit of Organization Planning was reassigned to the Personnel Research section in mid-1969, where it remained until the creation of a formal Manpower Planning section in March, 1971. In this time period, various efforts were directed toward attempting to automate the manpower projection and quotas. Preliminary studies undertaken by the senior author in a consultant capacity proved the feasibility of such a project culminating in a proposal to top management in December, 1970. The project was assigned to Management Sciences Department, whose work ensued through February, 1971, when it was suspended pending the creation of a central responsibility for manpower planning. Concurrently, the consultant's development of a personnel information and reporting system containing many data elements pertinent to manpower planning in its data base was completed and installed in May, 1971.

Using all prior studies, approaches, and past history, the Manpower Planning section began an intensive investigation of the feasibility of developing a sophisticated manpower planning system. The previous attempts yielded valuable information on historical perspective but were most useful in outlining what was not being done—simulating the future in terms of both current data and most early future events and conditions. Since the future is so uncertain and subject to wide variations due to cause-and-effect relationships, a methodology was needed that could rapidly adapt to these changes in a way that did not require resident technical specialists. All attempts led to the assumption that manpower planning for the Bank of America could best be done on the computer using simulation and interactive computing (time-sharing). This meant that an external computer would be used to represent the present hiring, promotional, and exit policies of the bank, using the Personnel Data System, to produce recruiting and training quotas for 1, 2, or 10 years in the future.

The computer simulation model described herein was designed and developed in a space of four months, from June to September, 1971. It was written in the BASIC programming language referred to as *Call/ 360:Basic*. This language was used because of its simplicity, ease of modification, and short compile time (two CPU sec.).

The authors contemplated using ANSI COBOL or FORTRAN, since both of these languages are more powerful than BASIC. However, it was decided to trade power for ease of use and shorter compile and debug time. Future extensions of the simulation model will be developed modularly and should be written in a high-level language such as PL/1 or APL if the hardware configuration will support it.

DETERMINING RECRUITING AND TRAINING QUOTAS

The main objective of the MPQ model is to answer the question: at what level should we set next year's recruiting and training quotas?

To answer this question it must be recognized that optimal quotas depend on many factors.

Growth Rate of Staff
If the number of jobs for lending officers in grades 13-15 is expected to increase faster than that of other personnel over the next five years, recruiting and training program quotas must reflect this expectation.

Attrition Rates
If the bank expects to lose fewer employees through voluntary sepa-

rations next year than it has in past years, the quotas must account for this expectation.

Training Program Retention Rates

If the hiring criteria are revised so that the bank expects fewer people to drop out of a program before they are productively assigned, provisions must be made so that the quotas will be proportionally less.

Transfers and Promotions

If it has been the practice of the bank to place training program graduates in about 50% of the grade 14 lending positions, and it is decided that 80% is more acceptable, quotas must reflect this change even though the placement of training program graduates will not be affected by this change.

Targets for Training Program Graduates

At present, there are about 1,000 lending positions in grades 10—12. Of these, only about 30% are occupied by graduates of bank training programs. If this figure is considered unsatisfactory and placement of lending officers must be upgraded to the point that 60% are program graduates, the training program quotas would be substantially altered.

The optimal training program quotas can then be determined by the MPQ Model once these five projections have been determined. Needless to say, with the number of variables, criteria, and the mass of data involved, it would be difficult, if not impossible, to arrive at acceptable figures without the computer.

HOW MPQ WORKS

The MPQ model generates recruiting and training quotas by use of a forecasting and simulation technique. The model starts by considering the present personnel population of the bank. It then predicts how that population will change after one year of simulated promotions, separations, and other changes. These changes are then used to determine quotas for that year. In this way, the model is able to forecast several years into the future and predict the recruiting and training quotas for each year.

Since the simulation process occurs on a demand-pull basis, the effect of a year's personnel activity artificially creates vacancies at various points in the organization pyramid. These vacancies are eventually translated into quotas at several levels.

The MPQ model focuses on the bank's officers and support staff personnel. The model subdivides these personnel into four functional groups: Branch Manager, Lending Officer/Assistant Manager, Operations Officer/Assistant Manager, and Administration Officer. The model also subdivides the personnel into four grade groups: 6—9, 10—12, 13—15, and 16—19. This produces 16 categories of personnel (four functional groups times four grade groups) which are processed by the model.

Before the model can execute properly, it requests from the user the following inputs.

Planning Horizon.   MPQ can simulate 1 year or as many as 14 years at a time. A range of 2 to 5 years is considered optimal for these purposes.

Growth Rates.   The user initially selects two growth rates in the total number of personnel—one for branches, and one for administration. Before MPQ begins to execute, the user is given the opportunity to specify a different growth rate for any of the 16 categories of personnel described above.

Target Percentages.   If the user wishes to maintain a certain percentage of training program graduates in any of the categories, he must first set an overall target percentage. Before the model starts to execute, the user is given the opportunity to introduce differences in the target percentage. Before the model starts to execute, the user is given the opportunity to introduce differences in the target percentages or may bypass the option to set target percentages completely. If a target is set, MPQ will signal whenever promotions and separations produce a percentage of training program graduates lower than the target. Opportunity to change the assumptions built into the model until target percentages are met is another feature of MPQ.

Before the MPQ model begins execution, it gives the user the chances to change input data. For example, to test the effect of higher turnover in a particular grade or functional group, the user may alter the attrition rates by keying in the coordinates (row and column numbers) and the new data. If multiple runs of the model are being made, there is a feature to bypass the printing of training program graduate penetration and projected vacancies in each category of personnel.

When the MPQ Model starts executing, it does the following:

(1) determines the number of positions at the end of the year by increasing the present number of positions by the growth rate. This will initiate a demand for officers in each category;

(2) determines the numbers of employees who remain at the end of the year after voluntary and involuntary separations and retirements;

Table 1
Promotion and Transfer Percentages

Group Promoted From	Group Promoted To				
Row	BM/16—19*	LO/16—19	OP/16—19	AD/16—19	BM/13—15
(1) BM/C/16—19*	2%	0%	0%	0%	0%
(2) BM/O/16—19	0	0	0	0	0
(3) BM/M/16—19	3	4	1	0	0
(4) BM/N/16—19	0	3	0	1	0
(5) LO/C/16—19	2	.	.	.	.
•••					
(17) BM/C/13—15	7	4	0	2	2
•••					
(65) Credit Program (C)	0	0	0	0	0
(66) Operations Program (O)	0	0	0	0	0
(67) Management Program (M)	2	11	4	1	12
(68) No Program (NP)	0	0	0	0	0
(69) Direct Hire (NH)	0	0	0	1	0
Total	100%	100%	100%	100%	100%
Column	(1)	(2)	(3)	(4)	(5)

*Abbreviations:
BM — Branch Manager
LO — Lending Officer
OP — Operations Officer
AD — Administrations Officer
C — trained in Credit Program
O — trained in Operations Program
M — trained in Management Program
N — not trained

(3) determines the number of officers in grades 16—19 that will be promoted out of the system and reduces the number of officers in those grades in the four functional categories accordingly;

(4) compares the demand calculated in (1) with the supply calculated in (2) and (3). The difference is the number of officers that must be acquired by promotion to grades 16—19 from lower grades, from training programs, or from new hires;

(5) simulates the promotion of officers to grades 16—19 to fill the vacancies calculated in (4). A stored table detemines the sources of promoted personnel according to transfer percentages. This is illustrated in Table 1.

The model uses Table 1 by multiplying the total promotion requirements calculated in (4) by the percentages in the table to find expected number of personnel movements. For example, if 200 grade 16—19 lending officers (LO) were needed, eight (or 4%) would come from branch managers trained in the management program and currently in grades 16—19 (row 3). The numbers of officers in each grade and functional group are stored in the model, and the filling of vacancies is simulated by moving personnel from one group to another. In this example, the number of lending officers with management training in grades 16—19 would be increased by eight and the number of branch managers with the same program experience would be reduced by eight.

The MPQ model simulates all of the promotions and transfers in a given year by performing the calculations illustrated above for each cell of Table 1, starting at the upper left-hand corner and proceeding down each column. Since a promotion or transfer creates a vacancy, the net demand for personnel calculated in (4) is revised after completing column 1 and before proceeding to column 2.

The numbers calculated in rows 65 to 698 are cumulated throughout the simulation and saved as the training program quotas for the year being simulated.

(6) After the MPQ Model has simulated one year of promotions and calculated the training program quotas for that year, it may be directed to bring the year-end percentage of training program graduates in each grade and functional group. If not, it will proceed to the next year of the planning horizon and repeat the process until it has performed the simulation for all the years specified. It will then print the final percentage of training program graduates and list the quotas for each training program for each year of planning horizon. Table 2 shows a hypothetical output of training program quotas.

(7) At this point, the model will present the user with the option of repeating the simulation from the beginning with different inputs

Table 2

Sample Output of Quotas

	C*	O	M	NP	NH
Year 1	82	114	60	272	106
Year 2	77	121	64	278	97
Year 3	86	137	71	285	112

*C — Credit Program
O — Operations Program
M — Management Program
NP — no program (promotions from grades 1—5)
NH — new hires (direct placement)

by the command "GO" or will allow him to terminate the job by the command "STOP".

The promotional and transfer percentages (Table 1) are the heart of the simulations model and the results are very sensitive to the predictive accuracy of each percentage. In this version of the model, the percentages are based on actual promotions over the 18 months from January 1, 1971 to July 1, 1972, adjusted to depict normal patterns. It is not yet clear whether these percentages are valid and reliable predictors of promotional patterns for the next 10 years, but they are probably appropriate over a 1- to 3-year time horizon.

The percentages could possibly be made more reliable by going further into the past or if they were based on a more sophisticated study of promotions, such as linking the promotions to actual indices of promotability (performance, time in position, experience, age, mobility, etc.) The percentages could also be manipulated to test the effects of future management decisions such as promoting training graduates to higher-level jobs only, obtaining all operations officer in grades 10—12 from the Operations Program or entirely cutting-off the transfer of personnel from branches to administration, etc.

WHAT MPQ IS NOT DESIGNED TO DO

MPQ does not recognize individuals. It can manipulate only groups of people in summary format. Therefore, it cannot generate data on the future locations of specific people nor is it able to accommodate promotability readiness of individuals.

MPQ does not presently perform a financial analysis. The cost of each additional trainee is significant and would be readily quantifiable when such data are available. However, the benefit that each trainee provides now and in the future is very difficult to put in financial terms and the cost of hiring additional trainees at the prevailing rates is even more difficult to quantify.

MPQ does not presently generate probabilities of various situations occurring. It is deterministic and its quotas are a "most likely" case. Best and worst case examples can only be determined by altering the inputs.

WHAT MPQ IS DESIGNED TO DO

Assuming that MPQ is an accurate representation of the personnel policies of the bank for purposes of predicting the flow of manpower, it may be put to a variety of uses.

(1) MPQ can be used for calculating training program quotas in the absence of changes in promotion or placement policies and in the absence of changes in retention, separations, and retirement experience.
(2) The effects of changes in retirements, separations, and training program retention can be predicted so that the bank may properly account for any disequilibrium caused by the changes.
(3) The effects of different personnel policies involving promotions and transfers may be tested before actual implementation to determine their effects on promotion rates, levels of penetration of training program graduates, and training program quotas.
(4) Experimentation with various external factors, caused by economic or demographic conditions, can be performed so that appropriate tests of their potential effects can be taken into account.

Manpower Planning: A Markov Chain Application
Gordon L. Nielsen and Allan R. Young

INTRODUCTION

A trend in recent years has been to use computers in an increasing number of areas in business. Many articles have been written about the impact of EDP on the personnel function. Up until now, however, the main use of computers in personnel has been the automation of record-keeping. The resulting comprehensive, automated files have made available a wealth of manpower data. Attention is now being shifted from the establishment of these files to the use of the newly accessible information that they contain.

Concurrent with the growth of computer-based personnel information systems, emphasis on planning has been growing stronger. The generally accepted concept of management by objectives, originally formulated by Peter Drucker, has brought planning out into all areas of the firm. Given the newly available personnel information, along with the growing emphasis on planning, it is not surprising that personnel departments are now being called upon to perform in areas other than their traditional ones of selection and placement. Manpower planning is increasingly becoming an accepted personnel department function.

Being a relatively new function with not much of a built-up tradition, manpower planning in the personnel department is a task in need of tools. There is available a great body of statistical methods and techniques, presently being used in other, unrelated fields, many of which could probably be used by manpower planners.

One such concept in statistics that may be of immense value to manpower planners is that of the Markov chain. This research seeks to show the connection between manpower planning and Markov chains within the operational framework of management by objectives. Specifically, the attempt will be made to establish the Markov chain as a tool not to be overlooked by serious manpower planners.

Of the articles that have so far attempted to supply manpower planners with statistical techniques, two major criticisms have been voiced by experienced personnel managers:

"Manpower Planning: A Markov Chain Application" by Gordon L. Nielsen and Allan R. Young, *Public Personnel Management*, March-April, 1973. Reprinted by permission.

Gordon L. Nielsen is Associate Professor of Accounting in the College of Business Administration of Arizona State University. Allan R. Young is in statistical research in the Data Services Division of the Valley National Bank, Phoenix, Arizona.

1. The math that is presented in these articles is beyond the comprehension of those who need to apply it, and
2. Rather than creating more complex methods, what is needed is the simplification of existing tools so that they may be used by managers in practical situations.[1] The purpose of this article is to discuss the application of the Markov chain concept to the manpower planning situation in a non-mathematical language in the attempt to overcome the stated criticisms of existing literature in the area.

MANPOWER PLANNING: AN OVERVIEW

Manpower planning is a label that has been applied to a set of activities presently being practiced by many firms. The set of activities, furthermore, appears to be different in every firm engaging in them. That is, there is no fixed and simple formula which can be universally applied. Each organization must develop its own system in the light of its own situation.

With the variable nature of the process in mind, then, it is the purpose of this section to: (1) arrive at a general definition of manpower planning, (2) determine the common objectives of the process, and (3) present an overview of the typical steps involved in the manpower planning process. The motivation for presenting this overview is to establish an understanding of the need for the tools to be applied in a subsequent section of this article. A detailed enumeration of the tools and exact procedures used in the process is not presented because it would inhibit the clarity of presentation.

MANPOWER PLANNING DEFINED

Each author on the subject of manpower planning has his own definition of the process. Two excellent definitions sufficiently describe the process:

> The process by which management determines how the organization should move from its current manpower position to its desired manpower position. Through planning, management strives to have the right number and right kinds of people, at the right places, at the right time, doing things which result in both the organization and the individual receiving maximum long-run benefit.[2]

and;

> ... an appraisal of an organization's ability to perpetuate itself with respect to its management and a determination of the measures necessary to provide the essential executive talent.[3]

The two definitions, though quite different in wording, are similar in effect. Indicated in each is an evaluation of the present situation, an indication of future requirements that are known, and some sort of action plan to meet the future needs. Implied in the definitions is the purpose of manpower planning which is to make short and long-range plans for the continuous and proper staffing of the organization. The objective, then, is to have always at hand the necessary people to fill the open positions. The success of the process is, therefore, measured not by the sophistication of the procedures employed, but rather by whether the firm has the inventory of personnel that it requires when they are needed.

THE PLANNING PROCESS

In determining the nature of the manpower planning process, each firm has its own formula and each author has his own recommended set of activities. Most descriptions view manpower planning as a three-phase process. A macroview of the activities involved shows that there must be (1) a determination of future needs; (2) an evaluation and extrapolation of the present manpower inventory; and (3) an action plan for correcting any indicated imbalance between the projected manpower supply and demand. This three-part framework will be used to describe the individual components of the process.

Outside of this framework, but important in the process, is the planning period involved. Two major considerations are important in determining the planning period. They are:

1. The period must be long enough to allow time for adjustments to potential problems and needs revealed by the forecasts, and,
2. The period must relate to the other planning activities of the firm.[4] That is, the time period must be long enough to allow for recruitment and development, but it must not extend beyond the forecasting horizon of the firm. Also, since the firm's long-term capital investment plan may be a valuable aid in formulating the manpower forecasts, the two plans might well cover the same time period. Most authors suggest a five-year planning period. With the planning period defined, the process can begin.

CURRENT MANPOWER INVENTORY

The starting point for a description of the firm's existing stock of manpower is the personnel file. Generally there is available on each employee to be included in the inventory, information such as the employee's present job, training, education experience, age, sex, length of employment, and performance record. This information should be verified and updated if necessary. Any additional information can be obtained from personal interviews. The interview might also be the vehicle for determining an employee's interest in further advancement. All of this information should be collected and condensed into some workable format for later use. This could be in a catalog form for manual use, could be on punched cards for use in a unit-record data processing system, or could be entered into a computer memory in some form for future automated access. The result is a skills inventory for the manpower planning process.

The skills inventory, when completed, gives an indication of today's manpower situation. The next step involves extrapolating from this information to the potential manpower situation at the end of the planning period five years hence. The extrapolation process should begin with a thorough study of past attrition trends from retirement, disability, voluntary resignation, transfers, and involuntary terminations.

The determination of future losses due to these factors is not a uniformly simple task. The estimate of retirements can be quite easily obtained. A study of the present work force composition by age will reveal the needed information. Voluntary resignations, transfers, and other less regular losses can only be estimated from the firm's experience, and the judgment of the planners. If necessary, range estimates can be used.

In addition to determining estimated staff losses, the planners must estimate personnel gains. Here again, the planners must look both to the firm's past actions and to an expectation of future actions. At first glance the estimation of staff gains during the planning period seems somewhat redundant. This is so because part of the process is the development and implementation of action plans for recruitment and training of personnel. The estimate of gains in this phase of the project will identify the change in the manpower situation due to the continuance of present policies and programs. Later in the process a need may be identified to change these policies or augment the present policies with additional ones.

At the completion of this first phase of the planning process, the firm should know a great deal about its present stock of manpower. In addition the firm should have a good idea of what its manpower situation will be at the end of the planning period if present policies are continued. The next step then will be to determine what the manpower situation should be at the end of the planning period.

DETERMINATION OF FUTURE MANPOWER NEEDS

A firm's future manpower need is not an arbitrary figure. It is a variable that is determined and influenced by a number of factors, only some of which are controllable by the company. Whether or not the company has any control over these factors, their influence on the manpower situation must be estimated.

The first, and probably the most important factor that influences the firm's future manpower needs, is the company's own future sales and production plan. This plan is the basis for capital budgeting and long-range operating budgets, as well as the manpower plan. Preparation of a manpower plan without reference to the firm's other plans is irresponsible. The insight gained in the study of the present manpower situation should provide the means for transforming the production and sales plan into a manpower forecast. The influence of proposed new products or services will also be determined in this planning stage.

To further refine the manpower forecast, a study of the trend in manpower productivity is needed. Here again the planners must turn back to historical company information. New technological developments—such as the introduction of electronic data processing equipment or other new machinery—must also be accounted for. Since the capital investment plan for the period will be available, it should be possible to determine if abrupt changes in productivity will be expected.

Another factor partially controllable by the company is future growth. The staffing requirements of new ventures, or expansions of the company, should be predictable, based on past experience with expansion. The productivity factor and the effects of new processes or machinery should also be considered.

New policies or changed objectives of the company may also influence the future manpower requirements. The effects of these can be estimated and used to alter the basic forecast. Another related factor is the future organization structure. If the planners know, for instance, that the middle management structure is due to be radically changed, the future requirements will be somewhat different from the historical ones, and appropriate changes in the manpower plan can be made.

The last factors which are outside of the company's control, are changes in legislation that may affect the firm's business, actions by competitors, and changes in the general economic conditions like the business cycle. The effects of these factors are generally included in the sales and production plan but they should still be considered in this process.

It can be seen from these factors that the manpower planners must be in close communication with upper echelon corporate executives. A lack of a coordinated effort could well result in planned manpower requirements that ignore the impact of the proposed offering of a completely new service, a corporate merger, or the closing out of an unprofitable plant. A manpower planning group that continually provides a valuable service to management will not be excluded by that management.

ACTION PROGRAMMING

After the future manpower supply and requirements have been determined, the two forecasts must be studied to detect the presence of imbalances. All through the process the studies have been broken down qualitatively as well as quantitatively. That is, the forecasts must be developed on a disaggregative basis for general occupational groups, such as engineers, salesmen, and managers. Now, as a result of the two forecasts, the planners will determine which groups will pose potential problems. Objectives and policies for the planning period will now be established. These guidelines and goals provide operational meaning to the previous analytical work.

The major programs which may be changed a result of the forecasting phases of the process are recruitment, development, and internal transfer programs. If the forecasts indicate a potential shortage of a particular skill, the firm may want to step up its recruiting efforts in that area. In additional, if that particular skill is expected to be in short supply externally, the company may wish to establish, or amplify, existing development programs. Existing policies such as a strict promotion-from-within-policy may need to be changed. For example, if the major source of middle managers has been the company's pool of engineers, and if a shortage of engineers is indicated, the policy may need to be changed.

It should be clear by now that one of the greatest benefits of manpower planning is the integration and coordination of activities that affect manpower. With the whole picture available and with the consequences of actions identified, internal policies and programs are less likely to conflict with one another. Also, a basis for the establishment of meaningful and attainable objectives is produced by the process.

SUMMARY

The manpower planning process is a set of activities engaged in by a company which involves the determination of what manpower resources they have available, along with a determination of what manpower resources they will need, resulting in action plans to correct any imbalance between the two. Each phase in the process is designed to determine one of these three elements. The great benefits of manpower planning are a unification of the company's manpower strategies and programs and an awareness of the consequences of actions concerning manpower. The success of the process is measured by whether the firm has the right people that it needs at the right time and place.

The result of the analytical, forecasting phases of the process is the design of proper action plans to correct any indicated potential problems. Though it may appear fairly easy in light of the information gained from the forecasts to design these action plans and to set meaningful objectives, the dynamic nature of internal transfers, promotions, attrition, and development make this a very complex task. What effect, for example, would changing the manager-trainee training period from six months to one year, have on the availability of middle managers five years from now? Or, in a succession ladder, say through five levels of engineering skills, what would be the effect of shortening or lengthening the amount of time spent in each level? A statistical tool, not often used in the behavioral sciences, is available to help remove some of the confusion from handling dynamic situations such as those mentioned above. In the next section, then, is introduced the subject of Markov processes and their application to the manpower planning area.

MARKOV CHAINS IN MANPOWER PLANNING

To be truly successful in the prediction of workforce composition at the end of the planning period, the manpower planners must make some sense out of a complex system of internal employee mobility. As with many complex systems, the reduction of the system to a model for study may be very helpful. A useful model for the study of complex systems is the Markov process. The critical terms in the Markov process are *state* and *transitions*. A good definition of these two terms, and of the process itself is presented in an example by Ronald Howard in his book, *Dynamic Programming and Markov Processes*. His example concerns a frog in a lily pond and is as follows:

> As time goes by, the frog jumps from one lily pad to another according to his whim of the moment. The state of the system is the number of the pad currently occupied by the frog; the state of transition is of course his leap.[5]

The key idea in this little example is that the leap, or transition, is based solely on the frog's whim and not on any other prior conditions or plan. Just by proximity, however, the likelihood of his jump to each of the other pads in the pond may be estimated.

The key ideas of the Markov process have been applied to a variety of problems dealing with sequential decisions or events. In the previous section it was indicated that the first phase of manpower planning involved a current inventory of personnel skills, followed by an extrapolation to determine the availability of skills at the end of the planning period. The extrapolation is probably the most difficult part of the process. To accurately estimate the workforce composition at the end of the planning period requires a precise determination of expected staff losses and gains.

To simplify the whole procedure only a portion of the workforce usually needs to be included. That is, those skills which can be and typically are easily obtained from the external labor market need not receive the detailed study that those hard-to-obtain, internally developed skills will receive. Therefore, before the extrapolation begins, the skills to be included must be selected and sorted according to the difficulty of replacement. The total plan, then, may be arrived at through a variety of means, depending upon the resources available for the study and upon the value of the results.

The most detailed and critical extrapolation will be required for skills that are typically developed within the firm. For example, in a bank a loan officer or branch manager is generally developed over a period of years through exposure to a wide variety of training and operating experiences. The lead time, then, for the availability of one branch manager may be up to ten years. A skill that takes up to ten years to develop is indeed critical and must be planned for. When the forecast calls for five branch managers, each year, for the next five years, how do the planners know that the requirements will be met? In addition, because the branch manager position is probably the end of a fairly standard progression of positions, there are many more intermediate positions that must be filled. The obvious, and probably most often practiced, answer to the problem is to begin hiring at the entry level, and to continue hiring a few more each year than will be needed at the end, so that a constant stream of people will be moving through the progression, and, it is hoped, will be available to fill the branch manager and intermediate positions.

This simple solution to the problem present several problems. First, because there is a variety of exposures needed during the development period, some sort of schedule, or plan, will have to be developed which determines the amount of times to be spent at each level. Second, because the need which has been established is only an estimate, it is bound to vary. The progression, therefore, will have to be somewhat flexible. Third, the number of positions to be filled in each step through the progression is not the same. For example, there may be a need for fifteen in the second level, for thirteen in the third, for seventeen in the fourth, and only six in the last level. The movement through the progression, then, is not as simple and uniform as might be expected. To accurately predict the future workforce composition of a progression, therefore, is a very complex problem. Furthermore, the extrapolation is usually based on today's operating policies, so t'e opportunity to improve on past performance is lost. The situation is clearly too complex to be understood easily without special tools. It is in this analysis of complex needs in a progression that the Markov procedure can be of value.

In the manpower planning extrapolation problem, there is a workforce group at specified positions in the progression. A transition matrix will be used to specify the probability of moving from one position to any other position in the progression. The object is to determine the personnel composition at various times.

THE BASIC PROCEDURE

To illustrate the procedure, consider an assembly operation. In this illustrative operation, there are five specified worker classifications: Trainee, D, C, B, and A. Each classification is defined in terms of the worker's skill level and the various skill levels are attained through experience on the job. The work to be done varies in complexity, though each task is identified as requiring a worker with a specified minimum skill level. A task may require, for example, the C-level skill or better. For a given product mix, then, there is a specified requirement for workers in each of the skill levels. In this example, the workers in each of the skill levels, except for the entry level, are developed within the operation. The objective is not simply to have the correct number of workers in the final level at the end of the planning period, but it is also to have the correct number in each level on an ongoing basis. This objective is more difficult to achieve and therfore requires a more complex analysis. The Markov procedure allows the situation to be handled easily.

The first step in the procedure is the identification and quantification of present policies. Here, the planners should identify the current attrition and promotion rates for each worker classification. A study of the personnel records may show that during one year 60 percent of the workers in the D level are promoted to the C level and that 20 percent resign. Records may also reveal that no worker from the D level had been demoted to the trainee group, nor has any D-level worker been promoted directly to either the B or A level. This information exposes the likelihood, or probability, of a transition from one classification to another in the study period.

The promotion and attrition rates for the five illustrative levels on a quarterly basis are as follows: (expressed in percentages)

LEVEL	PROMOTION	ATTRITION
A	0	3.75
B	2.50	2.50
C	9.67	5.00
D	15.00	5.00
Trainee	80.00	20.00

The statistics are shown on a quarterly basis because the training program is assumed to take that long. Notice that at the end of the training period the successful trainees (80 percent of them) are promoted into the D level and the failures are terminated. Also, there is no promotion rate for the A level because it is the end of the line. At that point, the A-level worker may either leave the company or transfer to another position outside of the assembly operation-the effect on the assembly operation is the same in either case.

Having identified the appropriate attrition and termination rates, all that is needed to construct the model for operation is the workforce composition by level. The present composition is as follows:

LEVEL	NUMBER
A	50
B	60
C	80
D	90
Trainee	35

The system can now be presented in terms of a transition matrix. The purpose of this first phase is to determine what changes can be expected in the workforce composition if the present policies are continued. For simplicity, it will be assumed that all hiring will be done strictly for replacement. That is, a termination in any grade will effect a new hiring at the trainee level. The promotion and attrition data for a three-month period appear in the transition matrix.

		(To)				
		A	B	C	D	Terminate
	A	.9625	0	0	0	.0375
	B	.0250	.9500	0	0	.0250
(From)	C	0	.0967	.8533	0	.0500
	D	0	0	.1500	.8000	.0500
	T	0	0	0	.8000	.2000

   The transition matrix is even simpler than it looks. Data follow directly from the previous promotion-attrition schedule. Read the left-hand row designations as *from* and the column designations as *to*. Thus, going from Level A to A, i.e., remaining in level A, are 96.25 percent of the incumbents, or .9625. From A to terminate are .0375 of those in level A that quarter. From level B to A are 2.5 percent of level B incumbents, or .0250. Ninety-five percent of level B personnel stay in Level B, and .0250 of level B people terminate.

   Given both the present workforce composition, and the probabilities of transition for a three-month period, the next quarter's expected composition can be calculated as follows:[6]

$$
\begin{array}{c}
\text{(A) (B) (C) (D) (T)} \\[4pt]
\begin{bmatrix} 50, & 60, & 80, & 90, & 35 \end{bmatrix} \times \\[4pt]
\text{TIME 0}
\end{array}
\begin{bmatrix}
.9625 & 0 & 0 & 0 & .0375 \\
.025 & .95 & 0 & 0 & .025 \\
0 & .0967 & .8533 & 0 & .05 \\
0 & 0 & .15 & .8 & .05 \\
0 & 0 & 0 & .8 & .2
\end{bmatrix}
$$

A: $(50 \times .9625) + (60 \times .025) + (80 \times 0) + (90 \times 0) + (35 \times 0)$ = 49.6
B: $(50 \times 0) + (60 \times .95) + (80 \times .0967) + (90 \times 0) + (35 \times 0)$ = 64.7
C: $(50 \times 0) + (60 \times 0) + (80 \times .8533) + (90 \times .15) + (35 \times 0)$ = 81.8
D: $(50 \times 0) + (60 \times 0) + (80 \times 0) + (90 \times .8) + (35 \times .8)$ = 100.0
T: $(50 \times .0375) + (60 \times .025) + (80 \times .05) + (90 \times .05) + (35 \times .2)$ = 18.9

   That is, each element in the workforce-composition vector is multiplied by the corresponding transition probability in one column at a time, and the resulting products are summed from that column. The process is repeated for each column, and each column sum is the composition-vector element for the end of the quarter. The expected workforce at the end of the first quarter, then, is:

LEVEL	QUANTITY
A	49.6
B	64.7
C	81.8
D	100.0
Trainee	18.9

This new group composition is then multiplied by the transition probabilities to obtain the composition for the next quarter, and so on for as many quarters as desired. The transition matrix, it should be noted, remains constant because the operating policies do not change. At the

Table 1
Workforce to Composition by Quarters

Level	1	2	3	4	QUARTER 5	6	7	8	9	10
A	49.6	49.4	49.3	49.3	49.4	49.6	50.0	50.4	50.9	51.4
B	64.7	69.4	74.1	78.8	83.3	87.6	91.5	95.2	98.5	101.5
C	81.8	84.8	86.6	87.3	87.1	86.3	85.0	83.5	81.9	80.2
D	100.0	95.1	89.2	84.0	79.7	76.2	73.3	70.8	68.7	67.0
T	18.9	16.3	15.8	15.7	15.5	15.4	15.2	15.1	15.0	14.9

Level	11	12	13	14	QUARTER 15	16	17	18	19	20
A	52.0	52.7	53.4	54.1	54.8	55.6	56.3	57.1	57.8	58.6
B	104.2	106.5	108.6	110.5	112.1	113.4	114.6	115.6	116.4	117.1
C	78.5	76.8	75.2	73.6	72.2	70.8	69.5	68.3	67.3	66.3
D	65.5	64.3	63.2	62.3	61.5	60.8	60.2	59.6	59.2	58.8
T	14.8	14.7	14.6	14.6	14.5	14.4	14.4	14.3	14.3	14.3

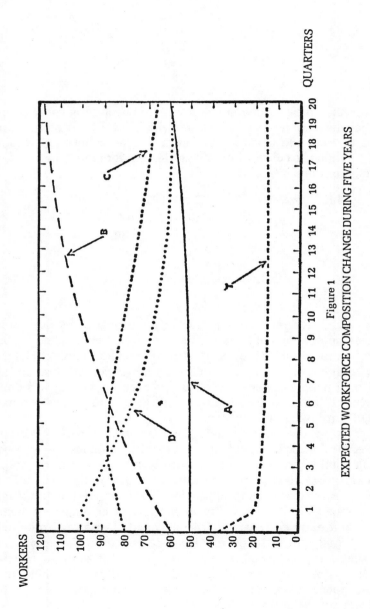

Figure 1

EXPECTED WORKFORCE COMPOSITION CHANGE DURING FIVE YEARS

end of four quarters, or one year, the employee-group composition will be:

LEVEL	QUANTITY
A	49.3
B	78.8
C	87.3
D	84.0
Trainee	15.7

Comparing the year-end composition with the beginning composition shows that the number of employees in the B level is rising (from an initial 60 to 78.8) and that the number of people in the entry level is dropping. When the calculations are carried out for twenty quarters, or five years, the composition is:

LEVEL	QUANTITY (After 20 Qtrs)	(Initial)
A	58.6	50
B	117.1	60
C	66.3	80
D	58.8	90
Trainees	14.3	35

Analysis of the five-year extrapolation, shown quarter by quarter in Table 1, as compared with the intitial situation, reveals that, if the current operating policies are continued, there will be a drastic change displayed graphically in Figure 1-in the workforce composition even if no additional people are employed. In this example, hiring was done only to replace losses in the system so that there were always approximately 315 employees in the system.

The example, then, demonstrates a very valuable use of the Markov procedure: the consequences of current operating policies are exposed. Using this relatively simple procedure illustrates that one of the major sources of future skills requirements is the present workforce itself. That is, the final workforce composition is a function of the transition probabilities, and each probability in the matrix is subject, to some degree, to control by management. Management, therefore, is provided with an extremely powerful tool in the transition matrix. By studying the policies that are represented by transition probabilities in the matrix, and by repeating the procedure with hypothesized, rather than historical, probabilities, planners have the opportunity to preview the consequences of various operating policies.

For instance, in the example, which the number of people in the A level (the end of the progression) remained fairly constant, the number of employees in the B level steadily grew. If the number of B employees was expected to remain the same during the period, some action would be needed to reduce the number of B-level employees, while retaining an adequate stock for promotion to replace expected A-level losses. The transition matrix indicates that only two and one-half percent of those in the B level will either be promoted or will terminate in a three-month period under current policies. This indicates that three solutions are available:

1. Increase the rate at which B's are promoted to the A level,
2. Increase losses in the B level through transfers out of the system, or,
3. Decrease the rate at which promotions from the C to the B level are made.

Each of these alternatives will have a predictable result on the future workforce composition. That result can be determined simply by changing the appropriate transition probability to some reasonable, estimated new value, and then repeating the procedure. The procedure can very easily be programmed on a computer to eliminate the manual calculations.

Each of the alternatives, besides having a predictable and quantifiable consequence on the system, will have a non-quantifiable human relations consequence. The human relations result should be much easier to evaluate after the other consequences have been identified. For example, in the case shown, if the third alternative is chosen, the planners must consider the effect on the C-level employees of having their training time (promotion rate) lengthened.

EXTENSIONS OF THE BASIC PROCEDURE

For simplicity the basic procedure example included two assumptions. The first, and probably the most unrealistic assumption, was that all hiring would be done for replacement only. This assumption resulted in a square matrix and a closed system. That is, at every stage of the process there was approximately the same total number of employees in the system. To account for growth in the number of employees, additions to staff can be added at the proper level in the progression and at the appropriate time. To illustrate this procedure, imagine that the planners anticipated (or hypothesized) that to meet growth needs, three people must be added to the trainee group every other quarter for the first two years. Now, Figure 1 shows the workforce composition that is multiplied by the transition matrix for each quarter of the projection. At the end of the first quarter there will be 18.9 trainees. If three people are to be hired at that point, all that must be done for the procedure is to add three to the 18.9 before beginning the second iteration. Similarly, this is done following the third, fifth, and seventh quarters. The hirees will move up through the progression in the fashion described by the transition probabilities and the consequences of this new hiring practices-such as timing or level of entry-can be simulated in the same way.

The other assumption that was made in constructing the example was that movement through the progression was uniform during the year: there was no seasonal variation in promotions or losses. For most applications, where the objective is a long-range projection, this assumption is valid. If, however, actual progress is to be compared with quarterly projections to check progress, the procedure can be further refined to reflect seasonal variations in the transition rates. To accomplish this refinement, the procedure requires several transition matrices, one for each season. If terminations are generally lower in the fourth quarter than in the other three quarters, the matrix describing fourth-quarter transitions would be modified to reflect the unusual movement. Any type of season variations, then, can be reflected in a unique matrix for that season. During the extrapolation process, the appropriate matrix is used for each quarter.

One additional use of the procedure, the mechanics of which are beyond the scope of this paper, is worth mention. In the discussion so far, the procedure has been used as a prediction tool beginning with today's workforce situation. A great many trials, using various transition probabilities and hiring practices, will probably be necessary to arrive at the desired results. An alternative to this situation is to begin with the desired workforce composition and, in effect, run the procedure backwards to determine what inputs are required with the specified transition matrix. To accomplish this, however, requires inverting the transition matrix which is a complicated procedure in itself. Planners with access to a computer may wish to try this powerful alternative. The basic procedure example, however, should provide an adequate tool for most cases.

SUMMARY

In this section following the discussion of the manpower planning process, a practical Markov application is demonstrated. By a thorough study of past actions, a simple quantification of policies is made and presented in the transition matrix. For the initial stage of the application, future consequences of continuing the past practices can be determined. The real importance of the whole procedure is, however, to explore alternative practices through a study of their related consequences. As a result of this alternative search, the planners can discover an optimum set of operating policies in light of the future manpower requirements.

When the optimum set of policies has been articulated, the basis for meaningful objectives has been established. Built into the procedure, as well as the basis, is an ongoing set of benchmarks by which the achievement of objectives can be measured. Use of the Markov procedure in manpower planning thus enlarges the scope of action programming by including the dynamics of day-to-day operations. The planners need not regard promotion and transfer rates as fixed—and therefore outside their influence—but rather may include them along with hiring in their list of available action tools.

NOTES

1. D. T. Bryant, "A Survey of the Development of Manpower Planning Policies," *British Journal of Industrial Relations* (November 1965), p. 290.
2. Eric W. Vetter, *Manpower Planning for High Talent Personnel* (Ann Arbor: Bureau of Industrial Relations, 1967), p. 15.
3. Edwin B. Flippo, *Principles of Personnel Management* (New York: McGraw Hill, 1966), p. 177.
4. Vetter, *Manpower Planning*, p. 41.
5. Ronald A. Howard, *Dynamic Programming and Markov Processes* (New York: John Wiley and Sons, 1960), p. 3.
6. The reader need not be versed in matrix algebra techniques. He can rely on the writers for technical accuracy.

CHAPTER 5
ESTABLISHING TASKING AND GROWTH PARAMETERS

A.   Analytical Foundations

Functional Job Analysis:
An Approach to a Technology
for Manpower Planning
Sidney A. Fine

Since shortly after the beginning of this century, scholars, educators and administrators have been seeking an effective technology to match men to jobs. The initial motivation for this search was clear; namely, increased productivity from increasingly costly production technology. Only after World War I did the idea gain momentum that a match that was suitable from the standpoint of the worker was good in itself, since the worker would be happier and better adjusted in a suitable job and, hence, more stable and possibly even more productive.

The initial approaches to this problem were those of Taylor, that is, time and motion study, in which the work situation was designed to reduce fatigue by way of simplification and repetition. This approach tended to view man as a machine. Another approach was by way of a psychograph, that is, matching a worker's traits such as aptitudes, interests, physical capacities, and the like to the requirements of jobs in those same traits. Here both job and worker were viewed as sort of jigsaw puzzles for which some hidden key needed to be found that would mesh them together. A third approach was to classify people according to certain predetermined categories like those in large bureaucracies, categories originally developed for pay purposes and budget control. Here the worker seems to be dealt with as a sort of package who belonged in the category if he had certain specified credentials.

"Functional Job Analysis: An Approach to a Technology for Manpower Planning" by Sidney A. Fine. Reprinted with permission *Personnel Journal* copyright November 1974.

Sidney A. Fine is a Senior Staff Member with The W. E. Upjohn Institute for Employment Research, Washington, D.C.

Needless to say, none of these approaches can be sustained in the value systems of today. Workers today are increasingly educated and sophisticated concerning their own worth as workers and their own self regard as persons. In this context, placement and counseling processes must be based on a technology of job and worker analysis that regards workers as whole persons, capable of growth and self-determination, not as cogs to be fitted into a hardware system.

This is what Functional Job Analysis (FJA) purports to do. Its fundamental concepts were developed about 25 years ago in the course of research that was carried on for the third edition of the *U.S. Dictionary of Occupational Titles*. This work was undertaken to improve job placement and counseling for workers registering for employment at local employment service offices. Since 1965, Functional Job Analysis has been applied to bring the disadvantaged and minorities, who had been excluded from the mainstream, into the labor force.

The question was: How do you bring these several millions of people into the labor force and provide them with career opportunities when workers already in the labor force do not have such career opportunities? Rather suddenly we became aware that our personnel systems, our manpower systems, were not geared to take such a problem in stride and were indeed quite shaky, often not reflecting our expressed values. Even in government merit systems, where we did have the semblance of a career system, they did not work very well because of assorted barriers mainly rooted in educational requirements such as diplomas, certifications, and licensing that frequently had little educational relevance for the work to be performed. The new entrants to the labor force simply did not have the credentials customarily required to achieve career status. So here we were promising something to people who had not been in the labor force, which many workers already in the labor force did not have. This situation prompted the realization that people had skills which were not being used and that much of the training being given was not relevant to the nature of the work in work organizations, not responsive to technological change.

Numerous government-sponsored programs were undertaken to train the disadvantaged in the skills they lacked for jobs experiencing shortages of applicants and to motivate employers to upgrade their current employees and hire the disadvantaged. There were numerous difficulties, and these programs have had only indifferent success. A primary difficulty was the extent to which knowledge and understanding about the work situation were misunderstood. Personnel systems, it was suddenly discovered, however unsystematic, nevertheless involved complex interrelationships that if tampered with could easily unlock a Pandora's box of problems. This is a basic consideration in FJA and the Systems Approach to Manpower Planning.

THE SYSTEMS APPROACH

Figure 1 represents the basic concept of the Systems Approach to Manpower Planning.

Figure 1
A Systems Approach to Manpower Planning

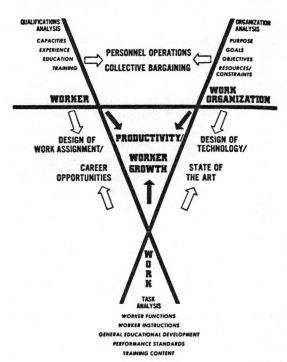

This concept is that work-doing systems which bring *workers, work organizations* and *work* together to produce something, inevitably have another output—namely, worker response to the work situation. This response is a complex of satisfacton/dissatisfaction depending upon the conditions that exist for worker growth. Worker growth refers to the worker's need (a) to feel he is dealt with as an individual, and (b) to find opportunities to realize what he defined as his potential. Although the word "growth" may seem to imply climbing a ladder and becoming president of the company, its use here is far more modest, intending merely to imply the concept of pursuing opportunity as the individual defines it, and this can mean remaining in a single assignment. Thus, to begin with, a human work-doing system must accept the fact that intrinsic to its existence is a dual purpose: productivity and worker growth. Increasingly, contemporary research seems to be confirming the fact that these two purposes are positively correlated.

It should be further noted that the three fundamental factors in our human work-doing system are inextricably tied together. To consider any of these alone in our attempts to achieve productivity, or to place undue emphasis on one or the other, tends to throw the system out of balance and to be counter-productive. Thus, undue emphasis on recruitment and selection of specific types of workers, too rigidly defined work assignments for pay and status purposes, and periodic reorganizations to reflect new approaches to management, by themselves upset the system and frequently have negative impacts on productivity over the long run, if not indeed, in the short run as well. The present approach asserts that since any change in one of the three factors is bound to have effects on the others, it is well to understand and consider the consequences of such changes beforehand.

Again, referring to Figure 1, let us examine in turn the structure of each of these components. In the Worker component, we are talking about those factors typically subsumed by qualifications analysis, namely the worker's capacities (physical, mental, etc.), experience, education and training. Our understanding of these factors and their relevance for work performance derives largely from the field of psychology applied to personnel analysis. In the Work Organization component we are referring to organization analysis, specifically, the organization's purpose, goals, resources, constraints and objectives and the way it structures itself to achieve them. In the Work component we are referring to task analysis—what actually is being done, performance standards, specific training, and the nature of the instructions to carry out particular tasks.

These structural elements or factors of our three fundamental components, interacting, is what generates the dynamic effects in the system. It is the dynamics that affects the designs, conformations and arrangements that result in positive or negative results in productivity and worker growth. The interaction between the workers and the work is the basis of the design of work assignments. The level of complexity of the assignment must relate realistically to the capacities of the worker. Similarly, in the design of career opportunities, you must again consider both the worker and the work itself, the relative complexity of the tasks, and the time necessary to acquire skill in relation to the training potential of the worker. In designing a technology—a work flow—the interaction between the work organization and the work itself must be considered. For example, the General Motors plant in Lordstown, Ohio, reputedly the most efficient of its kind, was designed to produce 100 small cars an hour, a goal deemed essential for profitability. There seemed to be little consideration given to the goal of worker growth. Hence, the work was designed to be extrememly simple, repetitive and fast-paced with practically all discretion on the part of the workers eliminated. As a result, grievances, slowdowns, and strikes multiplied. Contrariwise, a General Foods automated plant that produces pet food was organized with both productivity and worker growth as major goals, and although the tasks were also on the whole simple, the work assignments were designed to be varied. A totally different positive result was achieved in terms of productivity and satisfaction on the part of the workers.

The interaction between worker and work organization is manifested in personnel operations and collective bargaining. Collective bargaining, without full information about the nature of the work force, as well as the nature of the organization, limits the possibility of attaining lasting agreements.

Thus, the point of a Systems Approach to Manpower Planning is that by revealing the interdependence of the basic components of the manpower system—Work, Worker, and Work Organization—it makes clear why it is essential to consider the impact of any action on all three components in order to stay in control of everyday problems. It is only necessary to reflect how we have allowed ourselves to depend on "experts" in each of these areas of system dynamics to realize why many of our manpower problems do not seem to yield to solutions.

Who are the experts? In collective bargaining they are industrial relations and union people; in design of technology they are engineers; in design of work and career opportunities they tend to be psychologists and sociologists. These people are experts in their specialties, not in the system. In fact, they rarely communicate with each other. Clearly, we will have to turn more and more to the people who know the system if manpower problems are to be solved—namely, the managers and the workers.

THE TASK IN THE SYSTEM

Figure 2 attempts to show the impact and input of the Worker and the Work Organization upon the task, the fundamental unit of work, in the systems approach. This chart depicts the essentiality of a binocular view to understand and see the task.

If you look at the task being performed here only from the Work Organization point of view, you see a client being interviewed for some objective, let's say to establish his credit. This relates to the product or service concerns of the organization, and to its resources and constraints. On the other hand, if you look at the task only from the Worker point of view then you see primarily a behavior, a performance

Figure 2

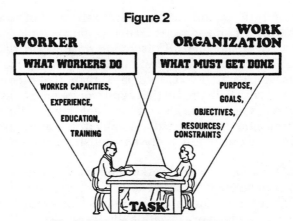

Task Analysis: The Whole Picture

influenced by the worker's general educational development, training, instructions, performance standards, and functional level to which he is assigned. In the first instance the language used to describe the activity is result or outcome oriented; in the second instance the language is behavior oriented. The language of job descriptions, of work analysis, has tended to favor the former, but Figure 2 should make clear that both points of view are essential to see the whole picture and to understand worker performance.

A CONTROLLED LANGUAGE
FOR TASK ANALYSIS

Figure 3, showing the three hierarchies of worker functions, represents the analysis of what workers do in their work assignments. It is a sort of taxonomy of how we expect them to function and the underlying base lines for our evaluation of their performance.

Figure 3
Worker Function Scales

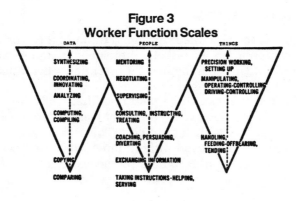

The twenty-eight functions shown were primarily generated by analyzing the language used to describe what workers did and what got done in 4,000 job definitions of the second edition of the *Dictionary of Occupational Titles.*

In this analysis, we found that the language of descriptions, particularly action verbs, predominantly related to what got done, that is, end results, and how the hardware involved was used. There were a couple of thousand such verbs. Very little of the language described worker behavior. In fact, the action verbs in Figure 3 were about all (and a few of these had to be conjured up) that could be found to describe what workers did.

Study of the use of these behavior-oriented verbs in job descriptions revealed that they tended to differentiate themselves as to whether the objects of the worker actions were things, data, or people. The verbs furthermore proved to have different levels of complexity implicit in their meaning more or less according to an ordinal scale, that is, where a particular level is more or less complex than another or can be considered as included in, or excluded from another. This finding was refined in the definitions of the functions and adopted as the scheme for the worker functions scales used to analyze all the jobs in the American economy. The last 3 digits of the 6 digit code of the approximately 23,000 jobs in the *Dictionary of Occupational Titles* reflects this analysis, indicating the relative levels of complexity of each defined job. This functional code proved useful in another fundamental way. It provided basis for understanding the involvement of the worker's physical, mental, and interpersonal resources and hence, the relevance of aptitude, interest, and personality measures.

The remarkable power of these scales cannot be over-stressed. By selecting three verbs, one from each of the scales, it is possible to describe any task, and in summary form, the job performed by any worker anywhere in the world. Take drill press or milling machine operators, for example, who happen to set up their machines. They could be classified as Operating-Controlling from the Things scale, which would mean that they do tending and feeding as well; Computing if they figure out the measurements of the work piece, and Exchanging Information to describe their relationship to their supervisor. When you describe their jobs in these terms, you tell the full range of their functioning. You have covered everything they do and everything they do not do. That is the nature of an ordinal scale. All of these terms are carefully defined and examples provided in *An Introduction to Functional Job Analysis.*[1]

It is possible to teach people with only moderate education (for example, secondary school) to use these scales in such a way that they achieve statistical agreement among themselves as to what actually is going on in a work situation. Many of the discussions, debates, and arguments over what people are doing will disappear because, even when they don't initially agree, by reference to these concepts they will be able to iron out their differences. The importance of such agreement about what is actually going on in a job for programs such as career analysis, wage negotiations, personnel selection, etc., hardly needs to be stressed.

THE STRUCTURE OF A TASK STATEMENT

Figures 4 and 5 shows the use of worker functions concepts in structuring and controlling a task statement, the fundamental unit of observation.

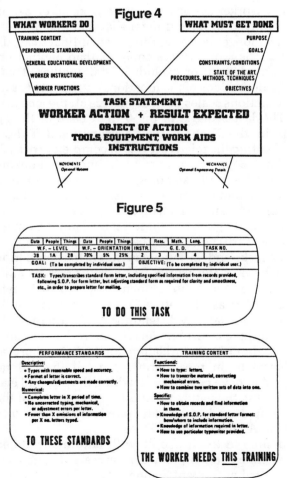

Figure 4

Figure 5

Figure 4 shows that a task statement consists of two parts, an explicit expression of a worker action and an immediate result expected of that action. To make the statement a meaningful self-sufficient sentence, the action verb is modified by the means (tools, methods, equipment) used, by the immediate object of the action if different from the result, and by some indication of the prescription/discretion in the worker instruction. A task statement at this level of detail and precision permits the inferences relevant to the categories of information indicated for What Workers Do and What Must Get Done. Should the statements get into the degree of detail represented by time and motion analysis and optional engineering details, they are then too fine for use in Functional Job Analysis.

Figure 5 is an example of what the master tool looks like with the applications paradigm (To Do This Task—To These Standards—The Worker Needs This Training, superimposed).

Consider first the section labeled TO DO THIS TASK. As already noted, this task is written according to a definite structure. When it is written in this way, it can be controlled for content and reliability and the controls are represented by the 10 figures shown at the top. Thus, for the task shown, the agreed-on ratings are that it is a Compiling, Taking Instructions, and Operating-Controlling task in which the Orientation (relative involvement with Data, People and Things) is 70%, 5%, 25% respectively. These percentages reflect the relative emphasis on the performance standards for the respective areas. Note that they add to 100% to reflect also the fact that in every task a whole person is functioning. The remainder of the ratings relate to 4 additional scales contained in the document mentioned earlier. These are scales of Instruction, Reasoning, Mathematics, and Language, the levels of which are also functional, that is to say, in terms of activities and behavior in work situations, not academically to reflect diplomas, certificates, and licenses.

When a task statement is controlled in this way, then it is possible to develop the performance standards and the training requirements. The standards indicated are the basis for management or the supervisor to achieve the productive work of the organization. They are also a guide to the worker as to what is expected of him. The training requirements indicated are standards which the organization must assure itself that the workers meet. In the case of the specific content, the organization must be prepared to assume the responsibility to supply it through its own training program.

Of course, it takes a while to learn the Functional Job Analysis technique, just as it takes time to learn any technology. But once acquired, something quite remarkable occurs. It becomes possible to develop a second vital tool, namely a bank of tasks for the organization.

In this manner, a 550 Task Bank for the social welfare industry in this country has been developed. There is also a Task Bank of about 60 basic tasks for 12,000 revenue agents in the U. S. In the process of development are Task Banks for clergymen, police, workers in personal care homes and in day care establishments. During the process of development, you discover that tasks typically repeat themselves in a functional pattern across occupations. The variations in similar tasks are always in some of the performance standards and some of the specific content training to achieve specific organizational objectives. Thus, the development of a Task Bank, although time-consuming initially, has permanence, the reason being that tasks have great stability, far greater than the jobs of which they are a part.

Reflect for a moment on what we have in this tool. We have units— task statements—which can be sorted and arranged in order to carry out many personnel operations. We can design jobs and career ladders and lattices. We can design work flow and rearrange organizational subsystems. We can organize pay systems. What has in the past taken weeks, months, sometimes even years to do, can now, with the aid of a task bank, be done in as little as one day by those familiar with the system. The more they work with it, the quicker and easier the various applications become. The information you need to approach a solution to various personnel problems is right at your fingertips. The solution itself still involves policy and experience, but the information for supervision, for training, for design, for pay purposes is there. It is reliable and stable information that is extremely flexible.

To summarize the main points, first, Functional Job Analysis is a technology of work analysis with which it is possible to achieve statistical reliability in the definition of basic units of information. It is not a perfect technology, but over the years it has evolved into an effective tool.

Second, it has helped us understand that requirements for the work system cannot and should not depend on educational credentials. Education has a more basic purpose than qualifying people for work, such as preparing people for life. Training, which does prepare people for work, should follow from specific needs of the work system. These needs become much more clear as a result of task analysis.

Third, worker growth, the development of the human resource, is as fundamental a purpose for the work organization as productivity. Although not yet a widely accepted idea by any means, it is more and more a significant part of the thinking of those concerned with manpower as exemplified in the discussions of the social responsibilities of industry.

Fourth, Functional Job Analysis is now increasingly being used to design jobs and organize career ladders to give workers opportunities within work-doing systems to achieve growth in their ability and in their incomes. It is also being used to determine the relative and optimal numbers of workers with the necessary kinds of skills needed to achieve a work organization's objectives.

A final use is the establishment of lines of mobility across related occupations such as those in engineering or secretarial work, and more recently in the Social Welfare occupations concerned with mental health, rehabilitation and education.

1. *An Introduction to Functional Job Analysis,* by Sidney A. Fine and Wretha W. Wiley, published September, 1971 by the W. E. Upjohn Institute for Employment Research.

Human Resources Development Through "Work Design"
Richard O. Peterson

The term *human resources development* is a relatively new one compared to terms like training, management development and personnel administration. Yet, the term has already become a kind of catch phrase, used as an "umbrella" for an assortment of traditional personnel functions as well as a symbol of the need to extend concerns and activities beyond the usual functions. The term is already being used uncritically and sometimes inappropriately, with little regard for its direct relavance to *organizational performance.*

The performance of any organization can be assessed in terms of at least four criteria:

- the quality and utility of the products and services it provides;
- the efficiency with which it provides those products and services;
- the organization's impact on society and the quality of life;
- the organization's impact on its employees and their lives.

Richard O. Peterson is Manager of Research in Work and Organization Design at AT&T, New York, New York.

To some organizational managers, human resources development concerns itself primarily with the fourth of these criteria . . . impact on employees. However, for human resources development to realize its potential in achieving organizational success, it must address itself to the full range of organizational criteria and must optimize the human resources contribution to each of them.

"WORK DESIGN" & ORGANIZATIONAL PERFORMANCE

One of the most powerful approaches in human resources development for enhancing organizational effectiveness is the emerging technology of work and organizational design. *Work design*, as it will be referred to in this article, is a set of principles and techniques for designing or redesigning the tasks and functions by which the work of the organization gets accomplished, for assigning them effectively among various jobs and job levels, and for supporting them with the necessary personnel-type systems of selection, training, supervision, evaluation, compensation, etc.

No matter what kind of organization is being discussed, the core of the organization must be considered the *work* to be carried out to achieve the organization's objectives. If that work is not effectively designed, arranged and allocated, no amount of elegant organization structure, sophisticated training or generous compensation system will bring about organization success. Stating this the other way, organizational effectiveness can often be increased by systematic analysis and, where appropriate, by improvement or redesign of its work and jobs. Figure 1 represents the successive layers through which human performance effectiveness must be built. These layers are:

- *Work:* The core of organizational performance; the sum total of activities and process that must be carried out to achieve specific goals and objectives.
- *Work Structuring Systems (Methods, Standards, Equipment, and Environment):* The direct facilitators or constrainers of performance; ideally, to be designed along with the basic work functions as part of fundamental work design.
- *Organization Structure:* The horizontal and vertical divisions of organizational functions to achieve various degrees of specialization, control, and responsibility; ideally, to be developed as an outgrowth of designing the inner elements of work and its structural factors.
- *Personnel Support Systems (Selection, Placement, Training, etc.):* The typical and traditional personnel functions and tasks needed to develop and sustain human performance in the

organization; ideally, to be designed on the basis of the more fundamental elements of work and its organization.

Figure 1. Human Resources Elements in Organizational Performance

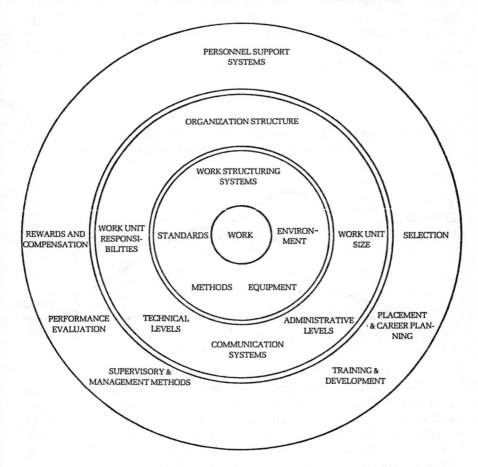

Attempts to improve organizational performance are often directed to one or more of the elements of the outer ring . . . the personnel support systems. Other popular approaches challenge the organizational structure, a somewhat more central issue. However, many problems of organizational effectiveness cannot be solved without going deeper into the design and structure of the work itself . . . seldom considered as a source of problems. To say it another way, human resource utilization may not be at its optimum without improving basic work design.

HUMAN RESOURCE UTILIZATION

A number of writers and practitioners point out that the distribution of jobs requiring individual talent, judgment and creativity does not appear to match the distribution of these capabilities among the employable population. The mismatch is in the direction of having more capability available than is required by existing jobs. Furthermore, the mismatch appears to be getting greater as the population gets more highly educated. Figure 2, adapted from Whitsitt,[1] is one theoretical representation of this mismatch.

Figure 2
Mismatch Between Task Difficulty of Existing Jobs
and the Talent Available Among Employable

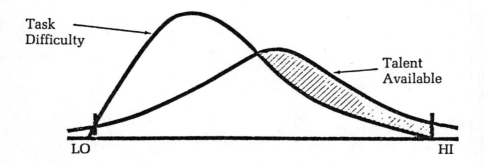

One researcher, Lawrence,[2] acknowledges that such a mismatch probably exists, but suggests that not everyone in the "underutilized" segment of the distribution wants work that utilizes his or her capabilities to the fullest. Even if we accept this caution, we must still recognize that there is a vast resource of underutilized talent among people wanting to use their capabilities more fully.

Some cases of underutilization can be reduced or eliminated through improved selection, placement, career planning or development. But eventually, the long-range solution must lie further into the core of the organization — the design of the work itself and the jobs among which the work is divided.

Thus from both a broad organizational point of view, the achievement of the full range of organization objectives, and from a narrower human resource utilization point of view, work design holds promise as a critical technology of the future.

WORK DESIGN STRATEGY

It is not enough to have techniques available to redesign work. The use of such techniques must be preceded by a diagnosis which determines whether or not work design *is* a problem, whether improving work design will contribute to organizational performance, and whether employees are likely to respond favorably to changes in the work design. Hackman[3] has cautioned against undisciplined use of work design techniques and, with his colleagues,[4] has provided a foundation for a systematic strategy which includes an intitial diagnosis. The strategy being discussed in the present article has evolved independently over the last 10 years of research at American Telephone & Telegraph (AT&T), but it is highly compatible with the Hackman concepts and approach. The AT&T strategy is currently being strengthened to take advantage of the research and experience represented by the strategy of Hackman *et al.*

The strategy has three fundamental phases:

I. Diagnosis of Work and Organization Design
II. Redesign of Work, Organization and Support Systems
III. Tryout, Evaluation, Implementation and Tracking

PHASE I
DIAGNOSING WORK AND ORGANIZATION DESIGN

Essential to any effort which might result in work design is an intitial specification of the problems it is hoped will be reduced or solved, and the criteria of organizational performance by which the overall effort will be evaluated. It is easy to be caught up in the enthusiasm for getting started and to be sure that results will be obvious when everything is carried out, but that is a complacency to be avoided.

When we agree with one of our "clients," an organization some-where in the Bell System, that we will help them look at work design, we prepare a written project plan intended ultimately as a "contract" for the application of the work-design strategy. The heart of that plan is a statement of the specific objectives of the project and how each will be measured. Some preliminary information and data have to be obtained from the client organization before such a document can be prepared. This information may include organization and job descriptions, current performance objectives and means of measurement and reporting, interviews with top management of the organization as well as with other employees, and interviews with people in organizations which interface with the target organization. The plan also includes a proposed diagnostic process to which the client must agree before actual data are collected.

We find it desirable to collect information and data of several types:

A. *Baseline data* which will be gathered before anything else is done, and again after any changes are made in work design: This baseline should include measures of the project objectives, the dimensions of work, employee attitudes about work and other job satisfaction facets, and any other measures which are likely to reflect on the ultimate success of the project.

B. *Work and organizational process data* which will provide the detail of how work gets accomplished, the detail on which actual work and organization design decisions can be based: This may include existing task analyses, work-flow diagrams, operating instructions, job descriptions, organization charts and descriptions, etc. It is usually necessary to supplement whatever is available with either individual or group interviews of job incumbents. Structured time logs have also been used as a source of information on activity, frequency, length, etc.

C. *Individual and demographic data* which help to define the employee population according to characteristics which may affect the design of the work: This may include data on past experience, training, need for job growth and challenge, etc.

Some measures exist for portions of the baseline data, such as the *Job Diagnostic Survey* developed by Hackman and Oldham.[5] Standard organizational measures of productivity, efficiency, quality, absence, etc., provide another source of available tools. The remainder of the data is collected with instruments and techniques either especially developed or adapted for the project.

Whenever possible, the data is analyzed by electronic data processing, with some statistical analyses if appropriate. Most of the process data cannot be so analyzed, but is systematically searched for potential work and organization design problems along the core-work dimensions, described below. The baseline data on work dimensons and the process data are compared and combined to produce a summary of the design problems.

The basic dimensions being used to evaluate the existing work design are:

- *Functional completeness:* a complete piece of work with an identifiable beginning and end.
- *User/turf continuity:* an ongoing relationship with one or more specific clients, users, customers, geographical areas, or types of equipment.
- *Variety of task and skill:* the degree to which there are varied tasks and varied skills used in the job.
- *Power to act:* the ability to make decisions concerning your own work functions.

- *Natural feedback:* individual, specific job-performance information that comes through the work itself or from users.
- *Opportunity for work-related growth:* the degree to which there are job functions which allow for expanded growth and development.

Although measures of some of these dimensions (under different names) are included in the *Job Diagnostic Survey* of Hackman and the *Job Dimensions Checklist* of Suzansky,[6] we felt it was necessary to develop and validate a more behavior-based instrument for measuring work dimensions. Therefore, we are developing and testing a "Work Dimensions Inventory" under contract to Applied Science Associates. It is currently undergoing validation to determine how each of the work dimensions relates to actual organizational performance.

PHASE II
REDESIGNING WORK, ORGANIZATION AND SUPPORT SYSTEMS

The results of the diagnosis may show that there is no need for work redesign. If that is the outcome, no work-design activities are undertaken. Problems in other performance support systems (e.g., training instruction manuals, compensation, selection, etc.) would be referred to the appropriate specialist group for their action, if necessary.

If work design is indicated by the kinds of problems identified, design task forces may be formed to begin work redesign. These task forces will probably include employees in the jobs under study. They are not only sources of important job and work information, but their potential contribution to the design of new work configurations is substantial, and their acceptance is critical. Work is redesigned along the six work dimensions defined earlier. Usually beginning with functional completeness, each dimension is examined with an eye to how that dimension can be improved without jeopardy to — and hopefully with improvement in — organization performance.

Alternative configurations and redesign ideas are reviewed with the client. Recommendations are also made regarding changes in other aspects of the personnel support systems needed to effect or sustain the proposed work-design changes. Additional details on the work-design process and its background are presented in the *ASTD Training and Development Handbook*.[7]

PHASE III
TRYING OUT, EVALUATING, IMPLEMENTING, TRACKING

Depending on the scope of the recommended changes, decisions must be made regarding how the redesigned jobs will be "tested." This can range from small-scale tryout in one protected part of the organization, all the way to complete conversion of present jobs to new ones.The judicious approach is usually between these two — in as typical a setting as possible, where usual job pressures and situations will be encountered, where organizational performance can be observed and measured.

The newly designed jobs can be further adjusted on the basis of the tryout and its subsequent evaluation. Only then can plans be developed for implementation on a wider basis, to be accompanied by ongoing evaluation wherein the established objectives and measures are tracked through periods of typical operation and variation.

CONCLUSIONS

Human resources development must be oriented toward the achievement of all objectives of organizational performance: quality, efficiency, societal impact, employee impact. Human resources activities are often focused on personnel support systems such as training, selection, compensation and performance appraisal. While it is imperative that these systems be effective to optimize human resource utilization, the more basic core of human performance — the work itself — may be at fault. Techniques and strategies are becoming available for examining and redesigning work and its structuring systems. Current research and experience with this technology of work indicates high payoff when it is judiciously and expertly applied.

REFERENCES

1. Whitsett, David A., "Job Enrichment, Human Resources and Profitability," in J. R. Maher (ed.), *New Perspectives in Job Enrichment*, Van Nostrand Reinhold, New York, 1971.
2. Lawrence, Paul, "Individual Differences in the World of Work," in E. L. Cass and F. G. Zimmer (Eds.), *Man and Work in Society*, Van Nostrand Reinhold, New York, 1975, Chapter 2.
3. Hackman, J. Richard, "Is Job Enrichment Just a Fad?" *Harvard Business Review*, September-October 1975, 129-138.
4. Hackman, J. Richard, Greg Oldham, Robert Janson, & Kenneth Purdy, "A New Strategy for Job Enrichment," *California Management Review*, Summer 1975, 57-71.

5. Hackman, J. Richard, & Greg Oldham, "The Job Diagnostic Survey: An Instrument for the Diagnosis of Jobs and the Evaluation of Job Redesign Projects." Technical Report No. 4, Department of Administrative Sciences, Yale University, May 1974.
6. Susansky, James W., " The Effects of Individual Characteristics as Moderating Variables of the Relation Between Job Design Quality and Job Satisfaction," Stevens Institute of Technology, 1974.
7. Peterson, Richard O., & Bruce H. Duffany, "Job Design and Redesign," in Robert L. Craig (Ed.), *The Training and Development Handbook* (Revised Edition), New York, McGraw-Hill (in press).

B. OPPORTUNITIES FOR GROWTH

A Model for Human Resources Development
David G. Muller

Numerous texts and articles are available which deal with the development of human resources. Many of the sources are excellent, offering an appreciation of the importance and complexity of human resources development to those who have the time and interest to research the subject. But too often the enormity of the field frustrates the researcher's attempt to harness his or her understanding of the subject into a form which is readily understood by others.

What seems to be needed is a concise, coherent presentation of what is meant by human resources development and what it consists of. The person responsible for the function would find support much easier to come by if the total concept of human resources development could be depicted in a manner which clearly shows the relationships of its components and how they constitute the whole—and to do it on one page. This article offers such an illustration—"A Model for Human Resources Development."

It's important to note the model is titled "A Model" and not "The Model." The author has found this version particularly useful as a vehicle to display the strengths and weaknesses of his own company's developmental efforts. The reader may well find it desirable to modify the model or some of its terminology to serve his or her own purposes.

The model to be built in the following pages is an attempt to answer two questions—"Why should a company invest in the development of human resources?" and "How is it accomplished?" The first question can be answered quickly and simply. The second question is not as easy. Its answer leads us into an array of company-sponsored activities but even then the question is not completely answered. All the model can do is to show what a company might offer. It does not and cannot show what the employee will accept. Recognizing that motivation is an internal phenomenon, we can only hope that the model and all it represents helps to establish an environment which fans the flames of self-development.

"A Model for Human Resources Development" by David G. Muller. Reprinted with permission *Personnel Journal* copyright May 1976,

David G. Muller is Vice President and Personnel Director, Ohio National Life Insurance Co., Cincinnati, Ohio.

BASIC PURPOSE

The development of human resources is a costly and time-consuming function. Line management has every right to ask why it should invest in the process. Texts abound with impressively complex answers which are not likely to be remembered. Many of them include reference to the psychologically self-fulfilling advantages of development activities which are valid and are not debated here. The aim here is to abbreviate the basic purpose of human resources development into a form which is readily acceptable to the line management reader. Maximum Utilization Of Human Resources is such a purpose statement (Figure 1) and is the goal toward which the entire model is directed.

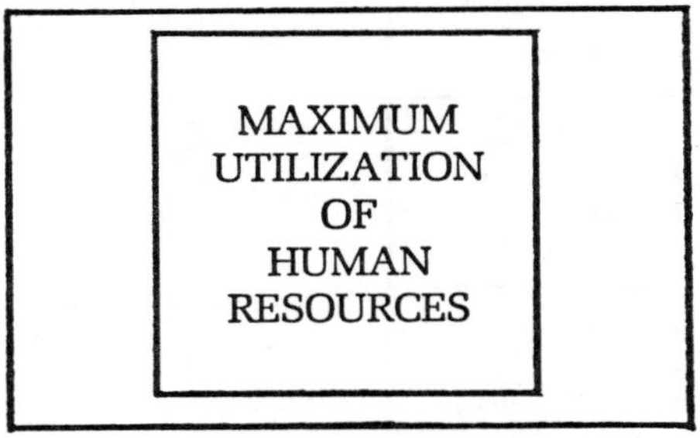

```
+-----------------------------+
|  +-----------------------+  |
|  |                       |  |
|  |      MAXIMUM          |  |
|  |     UTILIZATION       |  |
|  |         OF            |  |
|  |       HUMAN           |  |
|  |     RESOURCES         |  |
|  |                       |  |
|  +-----------------------+  |
+-----------------------------+
```

Fig. 1

PRIMARY ELEMENTS

Assuming the reader accepts the basic purpose statement as a valid response to the question "Why human resources development?" the model proceeds to answer the "How?" by breaking the process down into six primary elements (Figure 2).

The first of the primary elements, Assure Organizational Climate Conducive To Development, is an essential one but must be considered as tangential to the purpose of the model which is to display the development process per se and not the environment surrounding it. The means by which the organizational climate may be made conducive to development could well be the subject of a separate model. It might include the insertion of development responsibilities in management job descriptions, a reward system for development efforts, appropriate allocations of money and time to the process, and most important—the active involvement of top management. The well-publicized implementation of a "Model for Human Resources Development" is, in itself, an effective means of assuring a conducive climate.

The sixth primary element, Assure Fair Tangible and Intangible Reward Systems, is also an essential but tangential one. It is shown on

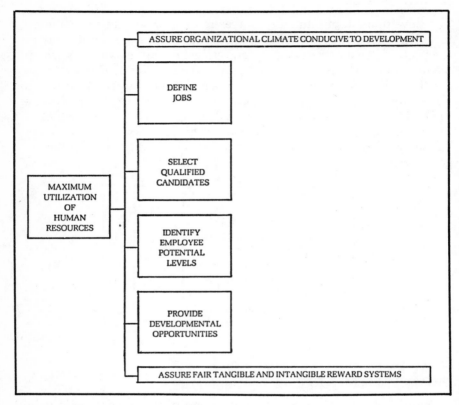

Fig. 2

the model being constructed to preclude its being ignored or forgotten. But to expand on it here would lead the reader away from the thrust of developmental activity and into such areas as job evaluation, salary surveys, pre-requisites and employee benefits.

The second through fifth elements are more germane to the process of human resources development and are therefore explored further in the model and in the following paragraphs.

DEFINE JOBS

The definition of jobs goes beyond the documentation of job content in job descriptions when viewed with an eye toward maximum utilization of human resources. As shown in Figure 3, Current Needs of the organization can be better met by applying Job Design, a process

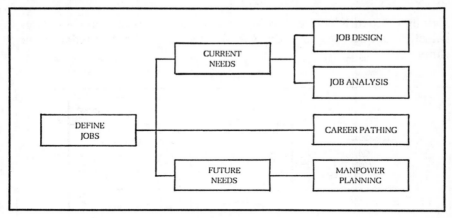

Fig. 3

designed to increase productivity by assigning to an incumbent, to the extent possible, those tasks which take fullest advantage of one's capacities, interests, and ambitions.

Job Analysis—the observation and study of a job to determine its component parts—furthers maximum utilization as it enables the establishment of performance standards and paves the way for work simplification. Its results are of value to a number of processes including job evaluation, employee appraisal and recruitment.

Career Pathing is shown in this segment of the model because it is a different form of job definition which facilitates the employee development process and helps the manager prepare to staff for Future Needs. Career Pathing is an impersonal process. It is the establishment of a logical progression of jobs to be occupied by an employee as technical and/or managerial expertise is acquired. Career paths are roadways pre-built by the organization to be followed by interested and capable employees. These paths, or roadways, may lead to traditionally required positions in the organization or to positions which are planned for the future as part of the Manpower Planning process.

Job definition for future needs is but part of the manpower planning process. Marketing, financial, and consumer-related skills are a few of the other talents called for in forecasting future staffing requirements and taking timely action to assure the organization's readiness to meet those requirements. Manpower planning is included in the model because human resources development has an important role in the process. It is not the initiating force.

SELECT QUALIFIED CANDIDATES

Having defined jobs in a developmental sense as discussed above, the selection of qualified candidates for jobs is viewed by the model in the same light (Figure 4).

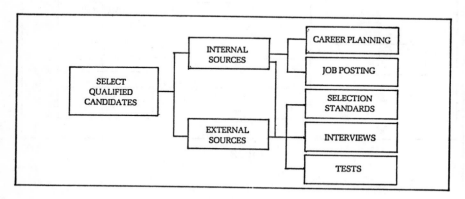

Fig. 4

Selection is made from either Internal or External Sources. The techniques applied in either case are similar except that two of them—Career Planning and Job Posting—are applicable only to in-house selection. And they both contribute to the developmental process.

Career Planning personalizes the Career Pathing concept. It is the decision-making process of an individual, often in consultation with others, as to which pre-built roadway or career path he or she is best equipped to undertake—or whether the decision is to not travel at all. There is reason for Career Planning to be shown here as well as in the appraisal-assessment segment of the model. It is part of the internal selection process when the employee's aspirations extend beyond his or her current organizational unit and he or she is hesitant to discuss with the immediate boss the prospect of leaving the unit. When it is part of the internal selection process, career planning consultation often takes place in the personnel or development staff offices.

The in-house posting of available jobs, with the qualifications required, is a common internal selection tool. From a developmental view, perhaps its greatest value is that it provides employees with a legitimate channel through which they can communicate their qualifications and aspirations outside their own areas, and through which they can receive some indication of how others assess their future potential.

The application of Selection Standards, effective Interviews, and job-related tests are included in the model not only because they are indicators of developmental needs, but because a new look must be taken at these traditional activities in view of today's regulatory compliance requirements.

IDENTIFY EMPLOYEE POTENTIAL LEVELS

This primary element—the identification of employee potential levels—is often mistakenly considered to be the starting point for determining developmental needs. The model shows that a number of training and development needs are already identified in the job definition and candidate selection stages. It is true, however, that at this point the need identification becomes highly individualized as we enter into Appraisal of Performance and Assessment of Potential (Figure 5).

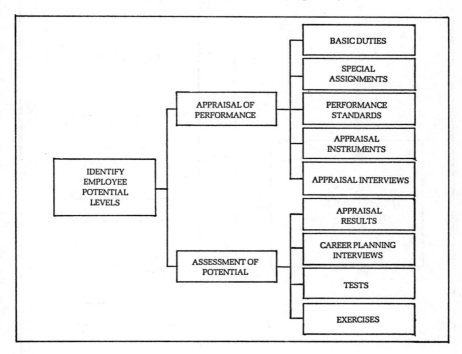

Fig. 5

The incumbent's performance of his of her Basic Duties and Special Assignments is measured against any existing Performance Standards and commented upon in writing; Appraisal Instruments are usually used for this purpose as well as to provide a discussion outline for an Appraisal Interview with the employee.

Appraisal Results are one of the primary inputs to the potential assessment process. The Career Planning Interview is repeated here in the model because it is conducted in this instance by the appropriate line manager. It is a natural follow-up to the appraisal interview and another major input to assessing potential.

In the larger or more sophisticated organizations, Tests and Exercises are also utilized to assess potential. Ideally, these activities are carried out within the framework of an assessment center. The assessment center concept is not shown on the model, however, since its in-house usage is usually feasible only in the largest organizations.

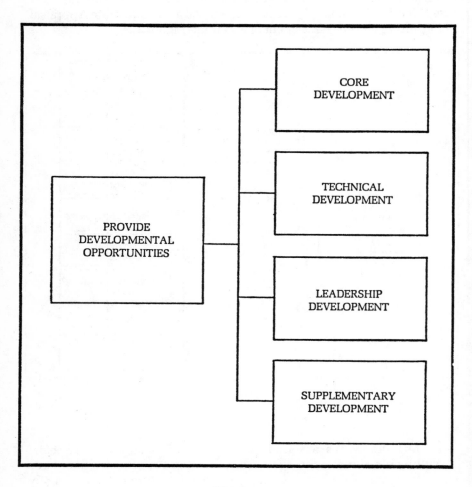

Fig. 6

PROVIDE DEVELOPMENTAL OPPORTUNITIES

The training and developmental needs of the organization are discovered as a result of the activities associated with each of the three preceding segments. Having identified them, the model's fifth primary element is to Provide Developmental Opportunities. Because this involves a wide variety of possible programs, it is convenient to divide them into four categories (Figure 6), in order to readily recognize a form of development in need of attention.

CORE DEVELOPMENT

Core development refers to those developmental programs which contribute to an employee's basic knowledge of the organization, the industry, and the procedures pertinent to the job (Figure 7).

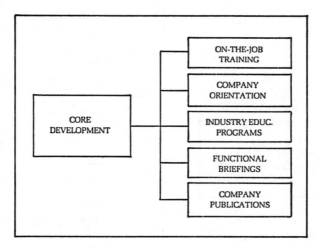

Fig. 7

Much of core development occurs through On-The-Job Training. Company Orientation programs contribute to the process as do Industry Educational Programs, such as those offered by the American Institute of Banking or the Life Office Management Association. Functional Briefings are any form of brief introduction to a particular technical function within the organization. Company Publications including written procedures, or organization and personnel policy manuals are also important contributions to core development.

TECHNICAL DEVELOPMENT

Programs in this category are aimed at increasing the incumbent's technical proficiency (Figure 8). On-The-Job Training must be included as the most common activity for this purpose. Manual Skills training programs are common in industrial settings, often in the form of vestibule training. Certification Examination Programs such as the CPA, Bar, and Actuarial programs are technically oriented, as are a wealth of On-Campus Programs, Industry Meetings, and Professional Association Meetings, attendance at which is frequently company-sponsored.

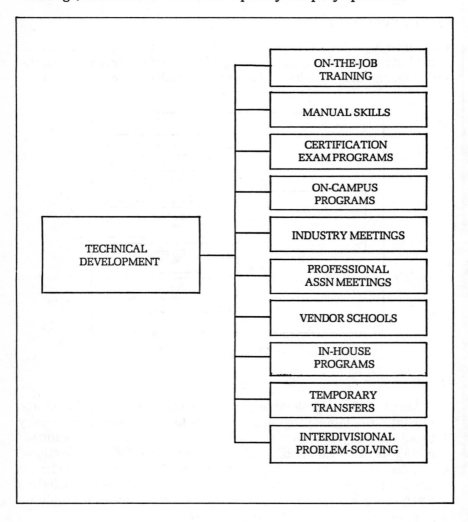

Fig. 8

Vendor Schools such as those offered by IBM and the 3M Corporation are valuable supplements to technical development. So, too, are a wide range of In-House Programs developed within the organization or purchased for in-house use.

Temporary Transfers to another area within the company to increase one's technical knowledge is a frequently used technique. Also frequent is the assignment of an individual to a temporary task force or committee to participate in Interdivisional problem solving.

LEADERSHIP DEVELOPMENT

Programs designed to improve one's leadership skills form the third category of developmental programs (Figure 9).

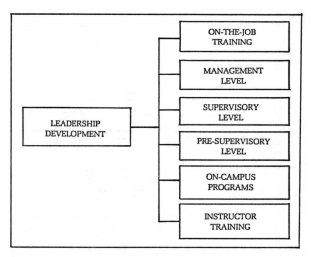

Fig. 9

It should not be surprising that On-The-Job Training again leads the list of activities in this area. The array of corporate programs devoted to core, technical, or leadership development will always be secondary to the information gained and attitudes developed on the job. The model deliberately lists on-the-job training in these segments to emphasize that point.

Leadership development is a vital ingredient at the Management, Supervisory, and Pre-Supervisory Levels of the organization and the program content varies at each level. On-Campus Programs are often used as an expansion of in-house facilities for leadership development. Instructor Training is highlighted in the model as an indication that a good leader must be a good trainer.

SUPPLEMENTARY DEVELOPMENT

Supplementary Development is the term chosen to identify those developmental activities which, while not directly related to a technical specialty or leadership level, offer helpful or enhancing experiences to any employee (Figure 10). Training to improve one's Oral or Written Communications skills are excellent examples of supplementary development. Learning to strengthen one's Personal Counselling, Time Management, or Interpersonal Relations are additional examples. Community Activities is shown in the model as an often overlooked training ground for leadership. The development-minded organization will encourage its employees to become involved in suitable community activities and to assume leadership roles in them if possible.

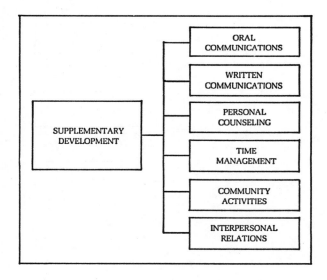

Fig. 10

THE COMPLETE MODEL

Having read about the segments of a Model For Human Resources Development sequentially up to this point, the reader may well have experienced some of the same frustration in trying to harness the complexity of the subject which was mentioned in the critical comment about other texts and articles made at the outset. Indeed, that is the whole purpose of this article—to illustrate how easy it is for the reader to follow each point as it is being made about human resources development but how difficult it is to tie it all together in a manner which is easily followed by and acceptable to line management. The complete model depicted in Figure 11 on the following page brings the segments together clearly and concisely—on one page.

One entry is shown in the complete model which was not illustrated earlier. It's the Training and Development Needs entry in the center of the model and it's the entry that ties all the other pieces together. Every one of the activities connected with Define jobs, Select Qualified Candidates, and Identify Employee Potential Levels yields evidence of the organization's training and development needs. And based on those needs, the development programs to the right of that key entry are offered.

SUMMARY

The model described here was originated in response to a perceived need to give shape and form to the myriad developmental activities that exist in many companies, and which often appear to be unrelated. It was conceived to give a wholeness, an identity, a cohesiveness to what it is we mean when we speak of the development of human resources.

Top management is understandably hesitant to support recommendations which appear to be piecemeal or unrelated to a larger purpose. The importance and relevance of a recommendation may be understood by the development staff—we read the books—but it is quite another matter to convince senior line management of the need for a particular developmental activity in a total program. The model provides a vehicle to facilitate discussions of human resources development issues with line management. Having accepted the validity of the model and having helped identify in-house weak spots on it, line management is inclined to be far more receptive to strengthening recommendations from the human resources development staff.

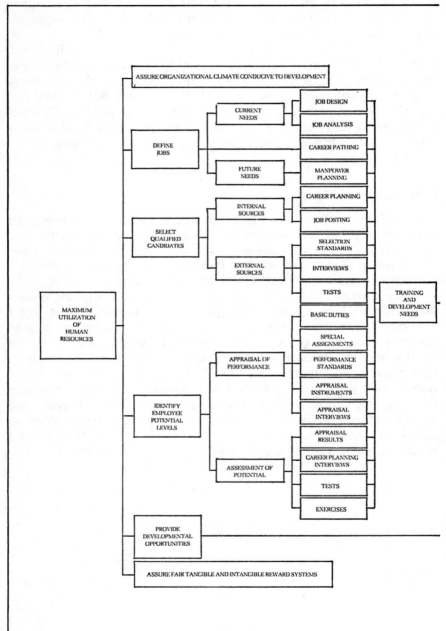

Fig. 11

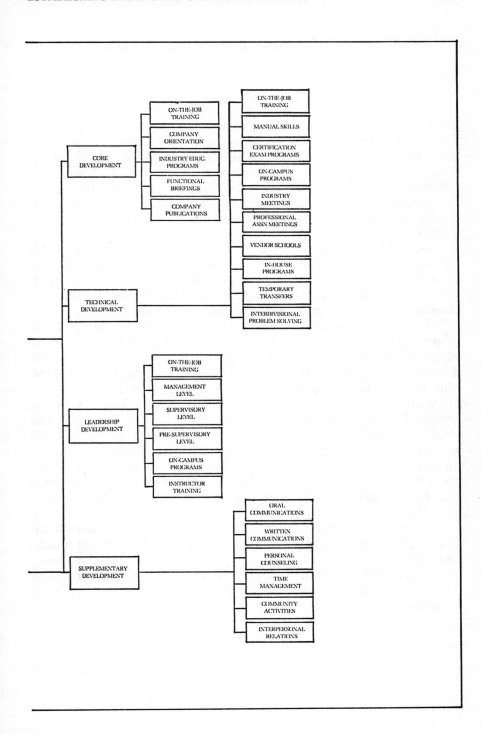

Career Planning in the Organization
Sam Gould

An increasing emphasis is being placed upon career planning systems within organizations. This growing concern for career planning has three root causes. First, employees at all levels within organizations are demanding to have more of a say in the direction which their career takes. Secondly, career planning is the only sensible approach to rapidly moving women and minorities into higher level managerial positions to fulfill the organization's Affirmative Action Plan. Thirdly, a rapidly changing environment necessitates careful grooming of men and women to fill executive positions ten and fifteen years in the future. This grooming can only occur efficiently through careful planning and programming of the individual's job related experiences and training. These three forces appear to be propelling career planning into the forefront of concerns for human resources practitioners.

Career planning comes in many shapes and sizes. Frequently, career planning will incorporate various training programs, designation of career paths and methods for identifying and tracking employees with high potential. A shortcoming of many career planning programs is that they have not been viewed from a systems perspective. As a result, they have not been integrated into the personnel system. Career planning approaches have suffered from three reoccurring problems. The first deals with participation. Who should participate in a career planning program? If all employees are forced to participate the program is bound to be plagued with individuals who have little interest in developing their own careers. The results of this lack of interest will be reflected in the overall quality of the program. Hence, participation should be selective.

A second problem is the lack of participation of employees in the career planning process. The author is reminded of a young middle manager who was assured by his superiors that his career was being planned and closely monitored. The only problem was that the manager had no input into the process. As a result the manager resigned in frustration. This approach to career planning is not atypical.

Reprinted from *Human Resource Management*, Spring 1978, pp. 8-11, Graduate School of Business Administration, University of Michigan, Ann Arbor, MI 48109.

Sam Gould is Assistant Professor of Management at the University of Texas, San Antonio.

Third, career planning is often done independently of organizational requirements. If the organization does not know what positions will be open and when, career planning cannot be realistically maintained. The employee must not only participate in the career planning process, but must also have some time frame of reference. Too often employee expectations are raised through some element of the career planning process—only to be dashed when the desired opening does not occur. A similar sequence of events may result if the employee is not fully and accurately informed of his or her performance and state of development in relation to achieving career goals. The result may be feelings of disappointment, frustration and betrayal when the career system does not consider these factors.

THE CAREER PLANNING SYSTEM

The career planning system has three key components: (1) Personnel Assessment, (2) Personal Assessment and Goal Setting and (3) Organization Assessment. Personnel assessment involves selecting participants to participate in the program as well as assessing their current and potential performance.

The most likely persons to successfully participate in a career planning system are those who are highly involved in their careers, have a high need for achievement and an internal locus of control. The extent a person is involved in a career varies among individuals. High involvement generally signifies that work is a central life interest from which the individual derives a great deal of satisfaction and which may define a large part of the person's identity. A high achievement need indicates that the person has a tendency to set moderately difficult goals which he or she strives to achieve. Such a person requires feedback from superiors and peers to maintain that drive for goal achievement. An internal locus of control signifies that the individual believes that success or failure is to a large extent due to his or her own actions rather than to some outside force.

PERSONNEL ASSESSMENT

Assessing current performance and the employee's potential is a second function of the Personnel Assessment component of a Career Planning System. Performance feedback is essential for the development of achievement oriented individuals—the type most likely to benefit from a career planning system. Yet superiors are often unable to give meaningful feedback either because they lack the proper interviewing skills to effectively communicate performance data or because the performance appraisal system does not provide meaningful standards upon which performance can be evaluated. Often performance appraisal stresses evaluation of personality characterisitics rather than productive behavioral characterisitics.

Management by Objective (MBO) is one method by which performance appraisal is made more objective. Another promising approach is the Behavioral Anchored Rating System (BARS). The BARS differs from either MBO or traditional performance appraisal in that specific behaviors are identified for a particular class of jobs. Several statements are then constructed which are indicative of a range from ineffective to very effective for each identified behavior. Using BARS, the manager chooses for each relevant behavior the statement which most closely resembles the subordinate's behavior on the job. By dealing with specific job related behaviors, defensiveness on the part of the subordinate is minimized and specific developmental recommendations can be made.

Most good appraisal techniques including MBO and BARS are subject to the criticism that while they may measure performance adequately in one job, they do not necessarily predict how good a person will perform at the next higher level. The assessment center is a technique which appears to have high validity in predicting employee potential. The assessment uses multiple assessors or judges to assess the performance of several individuals engaged in a simulated managerial task. The center normally consists of a series of structured and unstructured exercises which the candidates perform under the watchful eye of the assessors. The assessors themselves may be managers from the organization who are trained to perform the assessment task. This technique may be used to supplement performance appraisal. The center may last two or three days. Specific recommendations are made to participants regarding their developmental needs. Assessment centers are currently used by several large and medium size organizations for identifying the potential and development needs of selected employees.

PERSONAL ASSESSMENT

A second key component of a career system is personal assessment and goal setting. Commitment to reaching career goals is strengthened by direct employee participation in the determination of career goals. In order to set meaningful career goals, an individual must have a clear self-concept, the type of person he or she would like to become. This requires the individual to clearly define values, interests and skills. Several sources exist for aiding employees in investigating these personal factors and some are listed among the references for this paper. Several organizations have put together personal assessment exercises for their employees.

To effectively plan a career the individual must understand the nature of those jobs to which he or she aspires. Therefore, skills, training and job experiences required for each job must be known. In addition, the skills and training required at each step along the path to the ultimate goal should be defined so that proficiency can be evaluated at each step in time. This leads to the third key component in a career planning system—organization assessment.

ORGANIZATIONAL ASSESSMENT

Organization assessment involves the analysis of the sequence of jobs of the path by which a particular career goal may be reached and a forecast of positions which may become vacant. Assessment of career paths should be done for all key positions in an organization. This involves defining the particular jobs, training and skills which are required to perform this job and those which will be required of future job incumbents. Career path assessment begins with the key position and works backwards through a sequence of jobs which will ultimately prepare an individual for that key position. There may be multiple paths for any one job.

An important variable to most employees planning a career is the time it will take to reach certain of their goals. This time is a function of (1) the speed with which an employee can develop the required skills, (2) the frequency with which the desired positions become available and (3) the number of employees who will be competing for the position. Adequate personal assessment will provide the employee with an estimate of how fast he or she can develop the requisite skills. However, the speed with which positions become vacant and the competition for each job can only be accurately assessed through a manpower forecasting system. Manpower planning within the organization should not only provide insight into the frequency with which positions open, but also provide the lead time necessary to adequately develop candidates to fill these positions. Thus, manpower forecasting is essential to the maintenance of a smoothly operating career planning system.

ADMINISTERING THE CAREER PLANNING SYSTEM

Adminstration of the career planning system involves two activities: (1) developing a plan and (2) joint goal setting. The components of a career planning system provide a basis upon which a career plan can be established. The career plan will be unique to each individual. This uniqueness is a reflection of the uniqueness of each individual's values, skills, interests and aspirations. The career plan must contain a statement of the individual's ultimate career objective. This is the top position which the person would like to achieve at some point in the future. This is often a difficult objective to establish. It requires a firm knowledge of self as well as a knowledge of the higher level positions in the organization. An adequate personal assessment is mandatory for success at this stage. Choosing this end goal is a tentative decision which requires frequent reanalysis. A change in the end goal will require a change in the path by which the new end goal will be achieved. Sometimes the change may require only a slight mid course correction while other more drastic changes may require a return to some beginning point from which a new direction can be plotted.

Once an end objective is determined, intermediate positions and developmental skills can be outlined. It is at this point that career paths established by an organization become helpful. These provide a guide for plotting one's course to the end objective. The career paths also help the individual identify an immediate promotional objective. This objective is the next step up the organizational hierarchy. Specific developmental steps now need to be outlined for achieving this immediate promotional objective. This leads to the second primary activity in administering a career planning system—joint goal setting.

Goal setting in the career planning system involves identifying developmental steps required for achieving the immediate promotional objective and then attaching a time frame to these goals. This goal setting process must be a joint venture with both the individual and his superior participating. Identifying the developmental steps will involve a projection of the job related experiences, skills, training and education which the person must receive and master prior to becoming a candidate for the position. These steps may involve lateral transfers to other jobs at the same level to broaden the person's job related experiences and knowledge. It may require further training or experience in the person's current position. Or it may require that the person complete formal educational requirements.

A key factor in setting developmental goals is an understanding of the person's current performance and stage of development. This is where the personnel assessment component of the career planning system becomes essential. Accurate appraisal in this area will strengthen the goal setting activity. Also important is the setting of a time frame for accomplishing these goals. This is a difficult but necessary part of the goal setting process. Timing must be viewed as a forecast not as an absolute. It will depend on several factors as discussed earlier and will therefore always be a variable. Manpower forecasting will be the only guide available for this part of the goal setting process and hence it is a very important basis for introducing realism into the career planning process.

Administration of a career planning system requires that frank discussion and joint goal setting occur between the supervisor and subordinate on a periodic basis. Career goals must be established realistically with consideration for (1) the individual's self assessment of needs, interests, values and aspirations, (2) the likely opening and position vacancies which are likely to occur and (3) an objective assessment of the person's capabilities and stage of development. These factors may require supervisors to cultivate counseling and coaching skills to a greater extent than now exists.

A final issue that needs to be dealt with is motivation. Not the motivation of the employee but rather motivation of the manager to invest time and energy in developing subordinates—i.e. in taking his or her role as a career coach seriously. Typically, developmental efforts of managers are penalized. Time spent in developmental efforts takes away from more pressing issues. Further, once the employee is developed he or she is often transferred out of the manager's department and the coaching process begins over with a new employee. Effective administration of the career development system requires that managers be rewarded for their development of subordinates. This may require that performance evaluation of managers and supervisors be partially based upon how effectively they develop their subordinates to assume positions of greater responsibility.

SUMMARY AND CONCLUSIONS

Organizations must have two goals to maintain their position. That is to make a profit (or operate within budget) and develop people. Developing people is the process whereby the organization can continue to operate efficiently in the future. Effective career planning requires that human resources practitioners take a systems perspective when they design career planning programs. Too frequently career planning is approached in a disjoined fashion. New training programs are established or career ladders are defined and included in the personnel manual without proper consideration for other system components which are required for the system to work effectively.

Figure 1. Elements of the Career System

REFERENCES

1. Bolles, Richard N., *What Color Is Your Parachute?* Berkeley: Ten Speed Press, 1972.
2. Crystal, John and Richard N. Bolles, *Where Do I Go From Here With My Life? The Crystal Life Planning Manual*. McLean Va: Crystal Mgt. Services, 1974.
3. Hall, Douglas T., *Careers In Organizations*. Pacific-Palisades: Goodyear, 1976.
4. Jennings, Eugene E., *Routes to the Executive Suite*, New York: McGraw-Hill, 1971.
5. Van Maanen, John, *Organizationl Careers: Some New Perspectives*. New York: Wiley, 1977.

CHAPTER 6
HUMAN RESOURCE INFORMATION SYSTEMS

Establishing the Human Resource System Data Base
Lyman H. Seamans, Jr.

Human Resource Information Systems are "coming of age" in personnel. For most companies, personnel is no longer low on the priority list for a computerized application. Rather than being relegated to the tail end of a previously designed payroll system, the personnel department is getting its own computerized system, sometimes even as a front end to the payroll system.

The increasingly complex and growing demands of governmental agencies, as well as a need for company management to know facts with which to make decisions, are just two situations which have pushed the personnel system's priority to the top. In this environment, it is extremely important that a Human Resource Information System be designed as a management tool, not just as a producer of reports. This article examines some of the do's and don't's relative to development of the data base of personnel information which forms the heart of any well-designed Human Resource Information System.

One of the most important points to recognize is that the system we are discussing will be for the use of and operation by the "people oriented" functions of the organization. Thus, the requirements of the data base are for "information" rather than accounting or other functionally-oriented data. Many of the reporting requirements will not be known at the time of design and those that are known will need to be flexible with respect to pressures in the future. The HRIS must be geared to the day-to-day operation of the personnel function, must be capable of

---

"Establishing the Human Resource System Data Base" by Lyman H. Seamans, Jr., *The Personnel Administrator*, November 1977. Reprinted by permission.

Lyman H. Seamans, Jr., is Vice President and Consulting Manager for the Human Resource Management Systems Division of Benefacts, Inc., Baltimore, Maryland.

being operated by the personnel department and must be responsive to these needs.

When a decision has been made to modify an existing system or design an entirely new one, the first decisions required relate to the system's scope. Since one cannot be all things to all people in this determination, a decision must be made relative to the areas of applications and the specific needs of the functions of personnel to develop the proper data base of information. These functions may include: wage and salary, benefits, attendance, applicant information, skills inventory, education and training data, etc.

The next step is to assign a project team of key individuals from various personnel functions and representatives from data processing. It is extremely important that the design tasks be a joint determination. A project manager should be assigned, preferably from the user function.

The establishment of the data base of "need to know" information is the single most important and critical job involved in the design of a Human Resource Information System. Reports in an HRIS should always be viewed as a secondary concern. Although the previous comment may sound like heresy to any well trained and experienced systems analyst, in personnel defining the data elements of needed information must be the first task. Most systems in any other area would certainly begin with a definition of output and report requirements. However, the personnel department is rarely able to determine all of the precise reporting requirements that will be needed for the future. Furthermore, so much time could be spent in determining the precise format and sorting characteristics of fixed reports that the design of the system may well take several years, which can not be afforded in light of today's needs. Therefore, it is essential that the reader understand that a Human Resource Information System is one system that demands definition of the data base prior to dealing with outputs and report requirements.

The data base must conform to current corporate policies and procedures regarding waiting periods, eligibility considerations, vacation and sick leave eligiblity, attendance regulations and other corporate policy concerns. If current policies are vague or conflicting, change the policies before attempting to design the system.

The next area to be examined is the existence of current coding structures within the personnel function. Have job titles been standardized and a coding scheme assigned? Has an organization code been established to enable the personnel department to define "establishments" for Equal Employment Opportunity and affirmative action reporting? Have salary and wage ranges been established and do they consider regional and/or geographical variations? Have major groups of employee classifications been defined within the organization? These are all questions that need to be answered much before beginning development of this system and the data base. Once the proper coding structures have been developed, the job of designing the system is ready to begin.

The very next job is to examine all existing forms, records and reports used in the administration of personnel. This examination should include not only those documents and forms which are "official" but indeed those "little black books" which often reside in the file drawers of interested managers. All too often a great idea for record-keeping and display can be elicited by reviewing the storehouse of information that many managers keep.

All available documents and plans must be examined in this preliminary process. In the employee benefit and insurance area, the actual plan documents and policies should be reviewed. Employee handbooks and booklets are useful to communicate generalities of plans to the employee population but are virtually useless in defining the data base. Examine the area of salary administration regarding plans, ranges, salary survey needs, eligibility criteria for company benefits, salary grading plans, etc. In the labor relations area, bargaining agreements, automatic wage progression schemes and data needs for regular negotiations should be reviewed. In the human resource planning area, such things as promotability, potential, performance review and developmental activities should be examined. The training area needs to determine what types of courses might be maintained within a data base and what types of plans can be formulated for developing training and career objectives. The area of safety information can be a real payoff for an HRIS. Having available information relative to the type of accident, duration of absence, costs, location of injury, time of day, etc., will provide an opportunity for examination of trends in safety with an eye towards alleviation of hazardous areas and conditions.

In the areas currently being legislated by the federal government, the capability for an HRIS to record and maintain Equal Employment Opportunity information along with affirmative action program goals and plans amounts to one of the bigger payoff areas. Increasingly the government is almost expecting that companies will have computerized information available for analytical purposes in this critical area. Another area of great concern involves benefit and welfare plans which have been impacted more recently by the signing of the Employee Retirement Income Security Act (ERISA). This Act is guaranteeing each employee's right to retirement and pension benefits, legislates that employers communicate with individual employees relative to their earned benefit and with appropriate federal agencies relative to these benefits.

The next task will be to organize the pieces of information

developed from the review into certain general categories. The first and probably most important category will be information utilized for control and operation. Examples of these types of data are employee status codes, organization and location codes, job and position codes and salary grading codes.

The next category of information to be considered relates to those items of personal information that the corporation requires about individuals. Such things as sex, marital status, date of birth, race, home address, telephone and other facts are involved. It is in this most critical area that current proposed legislation relating to privacy must be considered. The report of the Privacy Protection Study Commission recommends that public and private organizations inhibit the collection, maintenance and access to data which can be used to violate the privacy of individuals. Therefore, it is essential that the organization define the "need to know" as well as the "right to know" this information.

Job data is another major category which needs to be defined. Such things as job codes, titles, salary grades, job classifications and the regional variations involved should be addressed. Information relating to the benefit plans of the organization should be reviewed. Each plan should be defined for such things as status in the plan, options elected, effective date, amount of coverage, beneficiary designation, etc. Pension plan administration is becoming increasingly important and requires maintenance of data relative to service and earnings history for long periods of time. Depending on the retirement plan, it could be required that the system maintain consecutive years of earnings running 10 years or longer. Service history relating to breaks-in-service and bridging situations will require suitable logic. Additionally, calculation routines to provide plan administrators with the basis for making interim and final benefit calculations can be a major benefit of an automated HRIS.

Another category of Human Resource Information relates to applicant data. Governmental legislation has impacted virtually every organization in the private sector concerning maintenance of "applicant flow" statistics. While the government only requires basic "head count" data, organizations are finding that the maintenance of education, skills and other information related to applicants can be extremely beneficial in enabling the organization to retrieve data for previous applicants who have applied for positions that are currently available.

No Human Resource Information System would be complete without various degrees of historical information. Mere examination of current "cardex" and similar records points out the daily dependency on historical information used in the process of personnel administration. Thus, it is essential that the personnel data base consider maintaining sufficient historical data to satisfy the everyday needs of personnel administration as well as the compliance needs legislated by the government in areas such as EEO and ERISA.

The foregoing areas of information are by no means exhaustive but they will point out the need for a thorough examination of all information needs involved in the process of Human Resource Mangement.

Now it is time to draft the actual elements of information that will comprise the Human Resource Information System Master File for each employee of the organization. The very first thing to do is to develop a preliminary list of elements of information to be used as a starting point for the project team. It would be extremely difficult to start this process using only a blank piece of paper. The initial list should be as inclusive as possible and should be organized with a logical grouping respecting the functional orientation of the various elements.

A useful device in this process is some type of data element definition form which enables the team to progressively define each element and its relationship to other elements and to the system. This data element description form should contain columns relating to: element name and description, type of field (alphabetic, numeric, or alphanumeric), source of input (initial and subsequent), on which predesigned forms or profile documents the element may print, editing characteristics to be applied, indication as to whether the element is utilized in interfacing to another file such as payroll and space for any comments or descriptive information relating to each element. A form containing these items of information will be extremely useful in considering all aspects of each element to be designed into the HRIS.

As the project team reviews the list of data elements, they should keep in mind that many elements will not have to be directly input into the system, but can be derived or calculated on the basis of other input elements. One example is the capability of producing a normal retirement date from the date of birth of the employee as input. Additionally, certain groups of elements will be maintained for a period of occurrences for historical reference.

The procedure for maintaining these elements could be called bumping or rolling. In this instance, when a new element or group of elements is input, the information resident at that location would be moved one step in history, causing the former historical information to be moved back a prior step and so forth. An example would be maintaining current salary information along with the two or three prior salary occurrences.

One more consideration which needs to be understood by the project team is the use of tables of data which relate to things such as jobs, salary ranges, organization codes, etc. Tables are extremely useful in Human Resource Information Systems since they are records within the system capable of being updated and changed as elements relating to certain control fields are modified. An example of a table might be one which is controlled on a job code and contains such things as job title, EEO job category, salary grade, FLSA status, salary survey indicators, etc. Using these tables requires only that the control element such as job code be directly input to the system. The system would then edit the validity of the code against the table and of the employee information. Also, as certain elements such as job title are changed, it would only be required that a change be made to the table, which would then transfer the changed data to all of the master file records using that key field. Another useful table would be in the benefits area. Certain contributions, coverage amounts and formulae can be contained on the table, available as future situations dictate change to these elements. In this way the system remains flexible and is capable of substantial change without re-programming the entire system.

It is also necessary that the date base of information allow for expansion areas. The necessity for this obviously depends on the nature of the file and whether or not expansion is provided within the company's software conventions. If not, utilizing a fixed length record concept, the designers will want to leave expansion areas throughout the master file record for later addition of elements as they are defined in the future.

As the project team reviews the sample elements they need to answer certain important questions:

1. *Accuracy*—determine the source of the element and the means which can be applied to establish validity of each element. If a high degree of accuracy cannot be insured, then it might be wise not to include the element on the system.
2. *Timeliness*—determine the method of input to be utilized as well as the means which can be provided to speed input to and output from the system.
3. *Completeness*—be certain that all factors relating to each element and its relationship to other elements has been determined. Such things as effective dates and other concerns should be reviewed and discussed.
4. *"Need-to-know"*—each element needs to be critically examined with respect to the necessity for the organization to keep, maintain and have knowledge of that piece of information. It is essential that extraneous and superfluous information be omitted from the system. If the color of a person's eyes or their height and weight have no definite relationship to the business, they should not be included. Also, concerns regarding each persons privacy must be addressed in this critical area.

5. *Utility value*—decide how often and for what purposes each element of data will be required in the conduct of the firm's business. It may be that the cost of collection and maintenance far exceeds the value to be derived from the element. Examples of elements which may have marginal value are name of school, business telephone extension number, etc.

6. *Interfacing considerations*—many data may be duplicated in or available from other computerized files of information. A determination must be made as to whether the item should be duplicated on the HRIS or left resident on the other file for access. If it is included on both files then consideration must be made for a method of interfacing to insure that the information on both files is consistent.

It is quite likely that the project team will review and redraft the elements of data five or six times before deciding that they are complete. Once the project team feels that they are reasonably complete, they should turn their attention to report requirements and outputs of the system to insure that all elements of data are available or that information can be calculated or derived from the elements to be included. It is important that report concerns not extend to actual formats at this point since these decisions can be made after solidification of the data base.

The final draft of the elements of data should then be distributed for review by all persons on the project team and for other personnel functionaries respecting their areas of responsibility. The elements should also be reviewed by others in the data processing area to determine file sequencing and considerations for tables and the like.

The data base and its careful construction is a must in insuring the success of the Human Resource Information System. Of equal importance is the need for people in the personnel function and individuals in the data processing area to work closely together. A successful HRIS is probably never finally complete and will always need to be flexible and expandable to meet the needs of the times. The system should also be monitored and continually appraised to make certain that it is meeting changing needs.

Each organization's Human Resource Information System must be designed to meet the needs of that company only. The personnel department, as the prime user, should be held responsible for defining what information and data elements should go into the system and which information will be required from the system. Data processing specialists should be held responsible for how the information is to be processed within the system. It is only with the proper attitudes and working relationships between these two groups and with a common goal, to develop an efficient and effective Human Resource Information System, that all corporate and system objectives can be achieved.

Time-Sharing & Information Systems
Frank Pfeilmeier

Scores of organizations, large and small, are utilizing computer time-sharing for their personnel information management needs. The responsiveness and power of this tool are impressive and at times almost unbelievable; however, it is not a panacea. The trick, as with computers in general, is to review the potential of time-sharing in light of an organization's unique requirements and make a prudent judgment of its value.

Now, more than ever, the information needs of personnel management are intense. Personnel receives a steady flow of requests for reports, analyses, forecasts, projections and opinions from management, corporate counsel, various public and private agencies, etc. The reality of this, to the practicing personnel professional, is quite obvious, but for organizations managing large work forces, efficient and practical means of generating these answers are rarely self-evident.

At this point, there is no reason to elaborate on the nature and source of the problem facing personnel professionals today—the information squeeze. The real necessity is to provide professionals with a frame of reference from which to evaluate the potential of computer time-sharing within their organizations. There is little doubt that time-sharing, in the proper situation, is a significant resource, and it will continue to be so as management information needs in the personnel function intensify. Scores of organizations, including smaller local companies with several hundred employees and huge multinationals with many thousands of people, are presently using these services for a broad spectrum of personnel applications.

WHAT IS TIME-SHARING?

Typically, time-sharing has been defined purely in technical terms. For example:

> Computer time-sharing provides many users simultaneous access to a common central computer which each user can use as his/her own for a variety of individual purposes. Connection to the computer is normally

"Time-Sharing & Information Systems" by Frank Pfeilmeier. Reprinted with permission *Personnel Journal* copyright February 1978.

Frank Pfeilmeier is Personnel Systems Consultant for Tymshare, Inc., Cupertino, California.

made through a typewriter-like device called a terminal, using common telephone lines. With these terminals, users can literally talk to the computer and receive answers and reports directly over their terminal in seconds. Since many users share the central computer, each pays only for those computer resources actually used.

Many of us are exposed to time-sharing on a frequent basis. For example, automated bank teller processing and airline counter reservation/ticketing systems often use time-sharing for these specialized tasks. Significantly, although the previous definition refers to the time-sharing tool in purely technical terms, these two examples highlight an essential fact, that raw computer power, regardless of the level of sophistication, is an undeveloped tool. Time-shared personnel systems must also refer to programs, techniques and support resources committed (as with the two previous examples) to the specialized requirements of personnel information. In the absence of this, time-sharing represents only raw potential. With these specialized features, it becomes a truly viable, cost-effective tool.

SEVERAL ESSENTIAL SYSTEM REQUIREMENTS

Any personnel information system—manual, in-house computer, out-of-house computer, or a combination of these—should meet several performance criteria in order to effectively respond to the changing requirements of personnel information. Seven system parameters, and the logic behind them, provide a valuable reference in evaluating alternative approaches.

These basic system requirements are:

- Accuracy
- Flexibility
- Dynamic
- Modularity
- Comprehensive
- Cost performance
- Control.

Accuracy:

Naturally, any automated personnel system must maintain a high degree of accuracy. However, since computers are inherently accurate, severe problems in this area are likely a result of system design and/or programming errors. In fact, most data errors are caused by operator error or misunderstanding, as well as information "falling through the cracks" due to problems in paper flow. Since the potential for human error is everpresent, the system must be extremely easy to use and should include reliable data validations (e.g., valid job code) and reasonableness checks (e.g., new salary less than $10,000 per month) which are built into the computer programs.

Flexibility:

Since each organization's structure and information needs are unique, the automated personnel system must be adaptable to these features whenever compromise will affect performance. Also, since the information squeeze on personnel often demands one-time, unpredictable analysis and reporting "due yesterday," tools must be provided for *ad hoc* inquiry to the personnel database, varied information retrieval and analytical routines for calculations, summations, etc. The most comprehensive and accurate personnel database is worthless without effective means of using the data on a day-to-day, on-demand basis.

Dynamic:

Automating the personnel system in many organizations represents a data processing enigma since the system requirements are rarely well defined and never permanent. Ideal data processing problems are structured, organized and stable (e.g., order inventory, accounts receivable, etc.), and personnel is, at best, a moving target. Changing business conditions, compliance regulations and management policy present an environment to which the system must adapt with minimal disruption. Without proper consideration for change, today's automated personnel system may soon become less productive and in time obsolete.

Modularity:

As previously stated, the personnel system must be flexible in adapting to each organization's unique situation. Additionally, system priorities may also vary from company to company. Personnel responsibilities are primarily functional (EEO, compensation, welfare benefits, retirement benefits, etc.) and the information needs of each function, although interrelated, are somewhat unique and independent. Given this fact, with proper design foresight the automated system may best be installed step-by-step, addressing immediate problems first and deferring less critical functions. Simultaneously implementing an overall automated personnel system can be a disruptive, lengthy process. Using a phased modular approach, the entire process can be relatively painless, and a solution to imminent needs can be delivered in short order.

Comprehensive:

Although the system need not be all-inclusive from a functional standpoint, those modules which are implemented should each be comprehensive, including the tracking of all key data items (salary, job code, increase reason, etc.) with potential relevance. It is a simple matter to build in elaborate system features initially, but only too often changes or additions after the fact may create an inefficient patchwork quilt effect.

Frequently deficiencies of this kind occur with the tracking of employee work history. Although from a management information standpoint it is certainly essential to have an accurate picture of each individual's current status, critical issues often involve an analysis of progression over a variable time period. For example, EEO employment progression, manpower planning and compensation planning and analysis all require comprehensive data over a span of years. Systems should avoid unreasonable restrictions on the number of employment history transactions which are stored by the computer, and system design should track changes in all key employee data elements. These include job data, salary data, organizational location, performance and review data, corporate status (i.e., exempt/nonexempt, full time, part time, etc.), as well as relevant dates and reasons (merit, promotion, transfer, etc.).

Cost Performance:

Cost performance breaks into three basic areas:

- Initial Cost: Costs to implement an automated personnel system can range from thousands of dollars to hundreds of thousands, and a discussion of them is well beyond the scope of this article. Costs can only be evaluated in light of the system's response to information needs, while being careful to also evaluate less tangible initial costs such as disruption of personnel department activity and lost productivity due to extensive implementation periods, false starts, etc.
- Operating Costs: Ongoing operating costs are minimal compared to the potential benefits from a responsive system. However, as with most purchases, you get what you pay for, and careful attention must be paid to performance. Systems not meeting the five performance criteria previously discussed are too expensive at any price.
- Maintenance Cost: The potentially most expensive element of an automated personnel system may be costs necessary to maintain the level of performance required by personnel. Lost productivity

and out-of-pocket costs can reach astronomical proportions if, due to errors in judgment, the system implemented cannot respond to the changing needs of personnel and requires constant work to maintain acceptable performance. Again, attention to basic performance criteria will pay significant dividends in overall system results.

Control:

As a matter of personal opinion (argued by many), overall control of the automated personnel system should reside within personnel. Rather than abrogating responsibility for the design and performance of a system, personnel must assume a posture of leadership in providing computer systems staff with definitive guidelines and requirements throughout the system selection and implementation process. Furthermore, constant attention must be given by personnel to monitoring system performance, ensuring continued responsiveness as management information requirements change over time.

WHERE DOES COMPUTER TIME-SHARING FIT IN?

Commercial computer time-sharing companies grew up during the mid-60s, capitalizing on the needs of mathematicians and engineers for more convenient, responsive computational resources. During the past decade, raw computer power has become much less expensive, and commercial time-sharing services have consequently tried to provide more specialized capabilities with a value added beyond pure computer power. Also during this period, in dealing with thousands of users for every conceivable type of computer application, many vendors have developed flexible, generally applicable tools for data management, data analysis and information retrieval.

In this context, during the mid-70s the need for effective personnel information increased, creating a tremendous opportunity for time-sharing suppliers to apply their general purpose management information tools to this highly specialized field. In response to this need, several vendors have developed effective personnel information systems. (It is important to note that any further reference to time-sharing personnel systems alludes less to technology than to the application of available tools as a specialized product.)

With the appearance of time-sharing on the personnel systems scene, there are now several very distinct alternatives to be evaluated:

- Inventing your own system to be processed on in-house equipment through large-scale batch processing, in-house time-sharing machines, minicomputers, etc.
- Purchasing software packages to be processed on in-house equipment.
- Utilizing an already developed personnel information system on an out-of-house commercial time-sharing or batch service bureau.

In fact, a fourth alternative exists which involves a *multimode approach* utilizing a combination of alternatives, exploiting specific advantages of each. Unfortunately, there is no clear-cut way to predict an organization's optimal approach. The correct alternative can depend on a number of variables, including organization size and growth, available data processing resources, industry needs and abstract elements such as management personality. Variables such as these determine the basic elements of system need and environment. Once these needs are determined, a logical systems approach can be selected using one or all of the basic alternatives.

THREE BASIC APPROACHES

There are three basic approaches to time-sharing, and these are a function of the in-house data processing environment:

- Fully *self-contained*, stand-alone systems using an out-of-house time-sharing package;
- Specialized functional modules *complementary* to an in-house personnel system; and
- Specialized capabilities and techniques *supplementing* an automated in-house system.

Having established a basic definition of the time-sharing approach and the overall requirements of automated personnel systems in general, each of the three basic approaches to time-sharing should be presented in detail.

SELF-CONTAINED SYSTEMS

Building a comprehensive automated personnel system is a lot like piecing together a puzzle. Personnel consists of many interrelated functions, and the information needs of each function are unique. However, the heart of a personnel system consists of data capture and records maintenance. Reporting and analysis are only relevant if the required personnel data is accurate and comprehensive and can be updated in a timely manner with minimal clerical effort.

Figure 1 suggests the interrelationship of many unique functional modules and stresses the fact that efficient data capture and records keeping are the core of any integrated system.

Figure 1. Comprehensive Personnel Systems

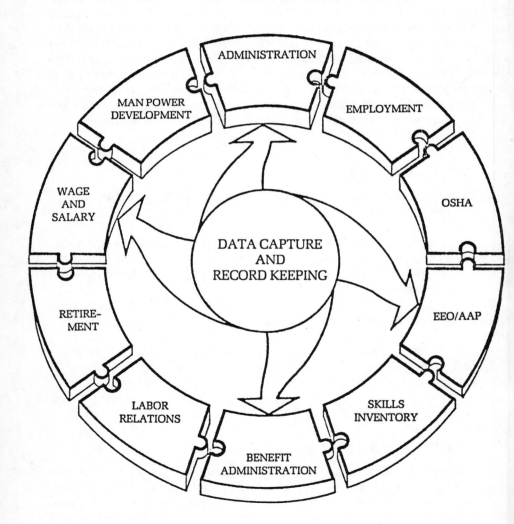

In smaller companies, with little or no inclination or resources to process peronnel information on in-house computers, a time-sharing system is a viable alternative and often becomes an integral part of the personnel department. At USLIFE Savings and Loan Association in Los Angeles, several time-sharing modules have been linked together to support their total personnel administration system. Beginning with data entry/maintenance and ending with extensive reporting and data inquiry (via a computer terminal in their office), USLIFE uses time-sharing for a variety of personnel work, including salary and promotion planning, affirmative action and welfare benefits administration.

USLIFE's personnel coordinator chose the time-sharing system to replace a number of nonautomated methods because none of them could provide information that was completely reliable or up-to-date. In this example, time-sharing has become an integral part of USLIFE Savings and Loan's day-to-day operations and has been very responsive in providing necessary personnel information. For example, during a recent transit strike, the time-sharing terminal was used to arrange an impromptu carpool program for the associaton's stranded employees.

At Allstate Savings & Loan, a similar system has been implemented for much the same reason. Faced with future growth which would substantially increase Allstate Saving's size, their personnel division needed a system which would support high levels of service to the employees and management with minimal increase in clerical staff. Using time-sharing with support from the vendor's personnel system specialists, the system was implemented within several months at minimal costs.

How do the time-sharing systems at USLIFE and Allstate rate in light of the seven requirements previously outlined?

Accuracy: Both organizations were able to achieve high levels of accuracy and data integrity using the computer terminal for input. At USLIFE (350 employees), data entry and validation require less than one clerical day per week, the ease of use avoids confusion, and the program automatically checks input data for errors and returns an error list to the operator for immediate correction and reentry.

Flexibility: The time-sharing terminal is repeatedly used to inquire into the database, using conversational statements. For example, the command necessary to count employees by department presenting their total and average salaries is:

```
sum cnt. employee and payrate
and ave. payrate
by department
end
```

DEPARTMENT	EMPLOYEE COUNT	PAYRATE	AVE PAYRATE
PHILADELPHIA	10	7860.00	786.00
DENVER	7	6160.00	880.00
EL SEGUNDO, CA	3	2395.00	798.33
SALT LAKE	6	4840.00	806.67
MANHATTAN	13	10319.00	793.77
TAMPA	4	4125.00	1031.25
LOS ANGELES	13	11205.00	861.92

Dynamic: A major consideration of the Allstate Savings decision was the system's ability to respond to changes caused by projected growth. Recently, a merger doubled Allstate Saving's work force. Proposed system changes should require no more than one programmer week.

Modularity: In both cases, the immediate system requirements were limited to several functional modules which were integrated without complications.

Comprehensiveness: At Allstate Savings, the system is tracking employee status and work history in such detail that, although it was not an initial goal of the system, clerical efforts in posting of historical data on the employee folder are minimal, with attendant cost savings.

Cost Performance: Although actual system cost figures are not available, the staff productivity within USLIFE's personnel department has been enhanced.

Control: With a computer terminal located within USLIFE's department, essential information is available to personnel upon demand with total self-sufficiency.

Using these two examples, time-sharing appears to pass the performance tests, as well it must. As a stand-alone system, there is no backup other than manual resources. The next two approaches—services complementary and supplementary to an in-house system—assume the presence of resident in-house capabilities, and the role of a time-sharing system is to fill a gap or weakness not suitably addressed with a stand-alone in-house system.

COMPLEMENTARY FUNCTIONAL MODULES

Comprehensive personnel information systems consist of numerous interrelated functional modules, each of which represents a specialized, potentially complex body of knowledge. Since software alternatives are essentially make, buy or rent (time-sharing) it is logical that reinventing the wheel by writing customized programs for all complex areas such as EEO, retirement benefits and ERISA, skills inventory, etc, may not be efficient or cost-justified. With the complementary approach, the user makes or buys less complex functional modules and complements the overall system with functional modules processed on a commercial time-sharing system. Time-sharing is used in this environment for a number of reasons:

Specialized software is available which satisfies the organization's needs.

The module must be *implemented quickly,* and with the flexibility of time-sharing, time frames of 30 to 60 days are not unreasonable.

Unique technical requirements lend themselves particularly well to time-sharing (e.g., on-line terminal inquiry at any time, or the need to access a central database from mutliple locations via the time-sharing phone network).

The time-sharing vendor provides *consulting expertise* from personnel system specialists, valuable in qualifying functional specifications that are vague or poorly defined.

Organizations using this approach to time-sharing have access to in-house computer power and are satisfactorily processing major elements of an automated personnel system. For whatever reason, a functional gap in the overall system exists, and time-sharing can successfully fill this need.

Security Pacific National Bank in California has developed an efficient and comprehensive computerized personnel system internally, but even with this resident computer power, they have found time-sharing to be a valuable complement.

Security Pacific's personnel department was developing an inventory of employee skills to support its aggressive staff development activities and to aid in finding qualified candidates for open positions from among its own employees. However, the department found that the bank's in-house data processing facility could not easily accommodate all aspects of this specialized module due to two factors:

Internal data processing priorities and commitments were such that in-house resources were unavailable to create candidate search and retrieval routines in a short time frame. To maintain personnel's objectives, they turned to a commercial time-sharing vendor, and the skills system was running within two months.

Utilizing experienced support resources available from the time-sharing vendor, the bank was able to minimize the internal staff required to support their skills system.

Using time-sharing, the Security Pacific National Bank employee skills system is performing well, their own management group can use it with little computer training, and the flexibility of the system ensures that the personnel department can identify participating employee candidates with appropriate requisite skills.

In this case, the specialized module is effective due to an ideal fit of time-sharing technology with unique performance requirements. Under different circumstances, the sheer complexity in certain aspects of personnel requires that individuals or organizations possessing in-depth technical experience of these problems develop a "packaged" approach.

The West Coast firm of Olanie, Hurst & Hemrich, compensation and benefits consultants, has applied its experience in the retirement benefits field and developed sophisticated time-sharing systems presently being used by many of their clients. They serve medium to large companies in the administration of their retirement plans and have used time-sharing computing to handle complex systems requirements, such as the computing and updating of accrued pension benefits, profit sharing and savings plan accounting, and individual employee benefit statements.

One particularly interesting application is a pension benefit system built for a major airline. It calculates accrued pension amounts, optional forms of pension, early retirement adjustments, Social Security and forecasted pension benefits. It's a great employee relations tool, because the airline can give its employees almost instantaneously the numbers they need to make plans for their retirement. By using time-sharing, the airline gained the on-line capabilities they need for processing terminees and retirees at a fraction of the cost it could have taken to put the whole pension record-keeping system on-line internally.

Organizations using time-sharing as a complement to in-house personnel systems can find functional solutions which would be difficult, if not impossible, to develop entirely in-house—at a fraction of the developmental expense. In addition, the time-sharing vendor working with the benefits consultants can provide the client with responsive, on-going local service and support.

As with the previous method, supplementary time-in-house computer resources and a comprehensive automated personnel information system exist and satisfactory systems solutions have been developed, responding to basic needs in all essential functional areas of personnel information. However, even though "package" requirements for functional modules do not exist, time-sharing products applied to personnel systems still have value. For the most part, in-house systems are implemented in a "batch" environment: fixed, structured programs and capabilities are established with scheduled processing for data revisions and reporting. It is normally assumed that once established, the system should undergo little change and that retrieval or analysis of data not generated on fixed reports will be minimal. Certainly the fixed in-house system, if well designed, can meet the majority of personnel's information needs, but as we are all too well aware, the periodic need for "off the wall" data analysis, retrieval and one-time reporting is a problem for personnel today.

Time-sharing tools specially applied to personnel can provide needed flexibility without the need for additional capital expenditures or very costly reprogramming. For example:.

> *Special techniques* exist to quickly (in as little as 24 hours) and easily transfer current in-house data to a compatible time-sharing computer for further analysis.
>
> Structured, yet flexible, in-house *reporting languages* can generate one-time or variable reports without costly, time-consuming programming.
>
> *Mathematical models* have been designed to perform projections and forecasts which are relevant to compensation, human resources planning and affirmative action.
>
> Easy-to-use *statistical models* exist for analysis of variance and correlation, trend analysis, forecasting, etc. These tools have been applied very effectively to affirmative action problems, particularly those involving "utilization analysis."
>
> *National time-sharing communications networks* can provide convenient access to the central in-house database from personnel units throughout the country.
>
> Sophisticated *graphical techniques* (plotting histograms and cross-tabulations) can present visual displays of data otherwise presented in voluminous tabular report format. For example, this sample graph (Figure 2) shows a detail plot representing the total compensation structure of a typical company, including the respective position of each employee. Also, by plotting only select data, comparative analysis is provided visually.

Figure 3 depicts a comprehensive system utilizing supplementary time-sharing tools to provide responsive management information capabilities.

With these powerful analytical tools supplementing large-scale in-house efficiency, many larger companies have upgraded the flexibility

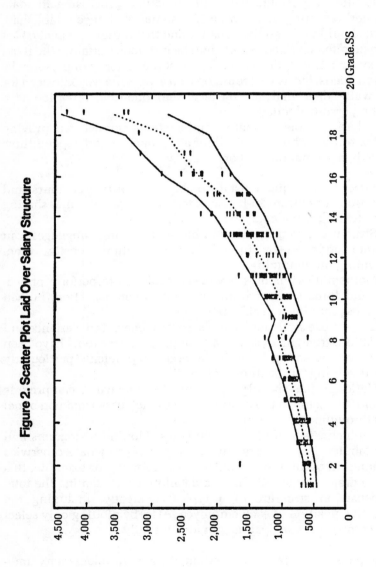

Figure 2. Scatter Plot Laid Over Salary Structure

Figure 3. Supplementary Services

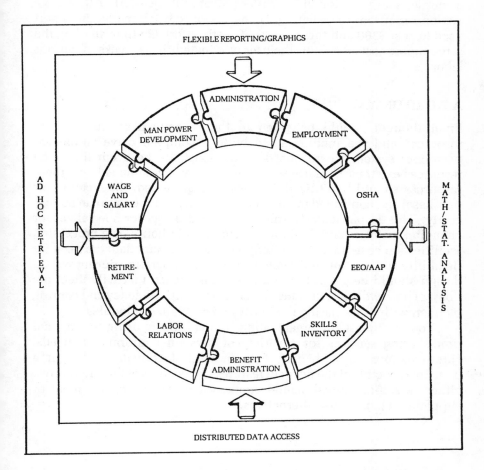

of their system, increasing the usability of data with minimal expense. For example, several *Fortune* 1000 companies with very powerful in-house payroll and personnel systems have "hired" time-sharing to enhance the management information capability of their batch processing systems. These companies decided to use time-sharing because it allows immediate examination of data, interactive question-and-answer sessions with the computer, quick report preparation and graphical presentations—all at an office time-sharing terminal.

The ability to easily move personnel data between existing internal data processing and out-of-house time-sharing systems has proven simple and efficient, enabling the merger of in-house computer data with flexible reporting and analysis using time-sharing. This development provides great potential cost savings. Recently, for example, a large nationwide retailer prepared its quarterly Affirmative Action report on time-sharing. Using in-house batch mode, the report used to cost $300 and three weeks of costly effort. On time-sharing, the same report costs $35, and the user eliminated those weeks of tedious labor.

A WORD OF WARNING

Final thought should be given to those companies with internal resources and the inclination to build a comprehensive automated personnel system where one does not exist. In the event that such resources exist, particularly when the employee volume is large, these resources should be utilized. However, as discussed, the creation (or purchase) and continued maintenance of personnel software can be very costly. This is particularly true if the need exists for specialized or changing modules and flexibility. Structured in-house data processing facilities are cost-effective, but often do not accommodate the need for flexibility and continued coverage. Careful consideration during system design should be given to a multimedia approach that will effect the "best of both worlds": in-house batch processing efficiency and control, blended with time-sharing flexibility and specialized modules.

Today, at least 200 organizations in the U.S. are using commercial time-sharing services for a variety of personnel information needs. Hundreds more might benefit if personnel professionals would gain a better perspective of the relevant features and benefits of this alternative, either as self-contained stand—alone system or as a complement or supplement to in-house alternatives.

Evaluating Computer-Based Human Resource Information Systems: Costs vs. Benefits
Frank F. Tetz

As management struggles to increase profitability (or reduce costs) it is especially appropriate to look at the impact of a computerized human resource information system. How much does it cost? How much is it worth? These questions must be answered, not just at the time management is considering installation of a human resource information system, but through a constant evaluation process after it is operational. This evaluation requires assessment of the system with regard to:

- effectiveness in meeting both immediate and projected needs of decision-making managers
- costs and offsetting savings in time and money compared with former methods of meeting information requirements.

INFORMATION SYSTEMS IN HUMAN RESOURCE MANAGEMENT

Before discussing specifically how to evaluate a human resource system for a particular situation, it is worthwhile to consider the over-all place that management information systems have in Human Resource Management.

The human resource manager is uniquely fortunate to be dealing with the most vital, complex and expensive resource of the industrial equation—the human being—and there is a growing acceptance of the idea that a systematic approach to the management of people is one of the biggest, single challenges facing top management today.

Computerized management information systems are valuable and essential tools for meeting these challenges. They are not devices nor objectives which must be served in their own right. The system necessarily takes second place to the job to be done, although some degree of accommodation to an information system may be required to make it effective.

"Evaluating Computer-Based Human Resource Information Systems: Cost vs. Benefits" by Frank F. Tetz. Reprinted with permission *Personnel Journal* copyright June 1973.

Frank F. Tetz is Consultant with Towers, Perrin, Forster & Crosby, Philadelphia, Pennsylvania.

FACTORS INFLUENCING SYSTEMS

In performing the job of managing our human resources, we cannot avoid having information systems of some type, whether or not they are computerized. These systems will grow "like Topsy" unless we plan them carefully. Overcoming the proliferation of special purpose systems—each operating independently of the others with little or no interchange—is one of the key factors influencing installation of a comprehensive human resource information system. Why have these special purpose systems been spawned with such frequency? Correspondingly, why are human resource information systems so necessary? Some reasons are:

- *the increasing difficulty including all useful information in decision making.* Without a comprehensive human resource information system, decision making is often necessarily based on limited information. The inclusion of all useful information which would contribute to a decision process is becoming more and more arduous. The natural result is to ignore some information and rationalize that we are being selective in what we consider.
- *a need to make more and quicker decisions.* Our increasingly complex society requires that decisions with far-ranging consequences be made in a shorter time frame. The gestation period for change is shortening in business generally. More action is taken in a given period of time than was the case two, five, or ten years ago.
- *organizational growth.* Organizational growth has the obvious effect of requiring additional information and results in even greater impact of our decision-making.
- *increasing costs for information maintenance and reporting.* Clerical costs have increased as additional records and reports to support changing requirements are developed.

THE EVALUATION PROCESS

Assessment of the effectiveness of a system should be made in the context of its objectives. These goals can be divided into "immediate" and "long-range" to achieve reasonable pay-back within an acceptable time frame/cost.

Typical goals provide immediate value through replacement of routine approaches for gathering, storing, and reporting information. Far more than just meeting today's requirements, however, a human resource information system provides a new capability for record maintenance and reports. Furthermore, it allows extension of human resource applications into new areas requiring complex analyses with numerous variables. The speed and depth of information availability in a sophisticated system will contribute substantially toward the quality of decision-making.

Typically, a human resource information system "signs up" an employee and initiates records for both personnel and payroll; triggers actions such as benefit plan membership, salary review, service awards; and satisfies special reporting requirements such as:

- meeting the growing requirements related to equal opportunity "Affirmative Action" programs
- providing essential data for bargaining unit contract administration and negotiations
- gathering human resource information for shareholders' meetings/annual reports
- compensation studies/surveys
- benefits planning.

SYSTEM BENEFITS

Although few studies of tangible benefits from installation of a human resource information system have been undertaken, some personally documented findings of system impact include:

- Improved accuracy resulted. Even facts as straightforward as population counts were found to be off by as much as 15% prior to system installation.
- Clerical effort was reduced. There was no longer any need for manually posted employee record cards.
- Labor negotiations, EEO, BLS, Pay Board reports, and other peak information requirements did not interrupt the regular work load.
- Consistency was provided. It became possible for the first time to relate data between functional groups such as payroll, wage and salary, insurance, etc.
- Savings came about, for example:
  - processing new employees—as much as ⅓ less time.
  - providing routine information—reported saving of 55%-90%
  - meeting increased EEO information needs—averaged 80% less effort
  - routine monthly reporting—60% less effort
  - handling seniority record keeping—up to 90% less effort
  - furnishing data to payroll—50% less
  - special reports (One plant reported $27,000 in savings per year

using a computerized personnel system instead of EAM for *special reports alone.* In addition, there were documented clerical savings of over 600 hours per year in providing data to payroll, over 800 hours per year in weekly reporting, and almost 500 hours in preparing monthly, quarterly, and annual reports.)

In many situations, however, users report that they have not yet achieved all possible savings, even after several years of system operation. Why? There are many reasons, including neglect of these positive actions most often required for obtaining greater value from a human resource information system:

- overcoming resistance to change
- increasing awareness of the system's capabilities
- organizing in a way more suited to the system, such as utilization of a Human Resource Information Center concept (this does not mean that a system should dictate the Human Resource organization)
- demonstrating adequate support from both Human Resource and technical functions so that the system will perform as scheduled/ required.

To achieve the foregoing benefits/savings through an operational computerized human resource information system, "one-time" costs will be incurred in the development of the system and in conversion to it. *Continuing* costs will result from operation and maintenance of the system. These costs must be compared with current costs which will be reduced or replaced to determine a true measure of the investment in the system.

DEVELOPMENT COSTS

"One-time" developmental costs include those for system design planning, detail design, software development, operation planning, documentation, management orientation, training, conversion, and parallel operation.

In an AMA study by R. T. Bueschel several years ago*, six firms reported the average cost for in-house development of a personnel system, programming and conversion costs included, was about $15 per employee. In other instances, costs have been quoted as low as $6 per employee for systems installed with outside assistance, and as high as over $30 per employee for development and installaton, because the scope of the systems, operating environments, and population sizes differ widely. However, experience can be a significant factor in reducing costs. For example, conversion costs alone were reduced more than threefold over a period of several years as a human resource information system was phased into the diverse operations of a major multi-location manufacturer. Development costs can likewise be reduced through application of experienced talent.

The wide range of costs serves only to reinforce the belief that it is useless to compare such figures.

OPERATION COSTS

Consideration of operational costs is extremely important because of their recurring nature. These include costs related to human involvement, forms, data preparation, data control, system maintenance/documentation, and system reporting.

The AMA study showed nine firms reporting an average operating cost for a "system of comprehensive personnel records," including machine time and data preparation, of $5.50 per year for each employee. These costs are so dependent on variable factors that again, there is no general yardstick which can be applied with consistency and accuracy. Some of these factors are size of population, application of system options/capabilities, frequency of processing, volume of data, interfaces with other systems, organization and system administration/utilization, communications with remote locations, and internal billing practices.

Some original pre-installation estimates of $4-$5 per employee annually eventually ranged in actual practice from $2-$7. Why such a range? In some cases, higher costs reflected a correspondingly higher usage of the system. On the other hand, in too many situations the system cost resulted from inadequate controls, improper scheduling, and alarmingly high system operation set-up time in the computer room. The approach to the system operation can make a significant difference in its operational costs.

OFFSETTING COSTS

The estimated costs of a human resource information system should be tempered by the realization that there are current information costs which will be reduced or replaced. These offsetting costs include those for salaries, both for manual development of information and for its utilization by personnel, other staff activities, and operating management. They also include costs of mechanized systems with their associated data preparation, processing, and control.

JUSTIFICATION BASED
ON GREATER CAPABILITY

Computerized human resource information systems are not usually justified on the basis of savings and staffing reduction, even though they should result in directly attributable savings. What is more significant is that the Human Resource Management effort can be directed toward more meaningful and productive tasks in the time now spent on information development, maintenance, and reporting. More important, the additional capability for obtaining and manipulating information will allow the Human Resource function to provide substantially greater service to operating management than ever before. This service is all the more significant with the human resource becoming an increasingly critical—and expensive—factor in management.

CONTINUING EVALUATION NECESSARY

The evaluation process should not end with the installation of the system. The effectiveness of operational systems can be measured on the basis of factors other than costs. When faced with an assignment to do just that in a short period of time with a system operating at two dozen locations with over 60,000 active employees, the approach used was a carefully structured "self-review" questionnaire with detailed assessments by Human Resource Management, Management Information Systems, and Auditing. With respect to each element in the system, in addition to costs, the evaluation considered:

- extent of use
- does it meet the location's needs completely?
- problems in meeting the organization's need—system, people, equipment
- most important benefits.

Selected in-depth follow-up was undertaken after the survey was completed. This included structured interviews with all levels of personnel and operating management. Results were then analyzed and used as the basis for determining system improvements, the direction of further development efforts, and cost re-allocation.

Evaluation of a computerized human resource information system is an important process whether an organization is considering its installation or already has an operational system. Definite approaches have been developed for such evaluation to assure that essential factors are brought to the attention of management.

The writer's experience has indicated the following conclusions from such an evaluation:

1. The most *immediate* benefit is the greater accuracy of data with savings in clerical effort. The most *significant* value is the availability of the data resource with quick access by the Human Resource staff through a retrieval system designed for their use.
2. A computer-based system is essential today for most personnel operations, although size/complexity are major factors in the type of system applied to a particular situation.
3. Human Resource or Personnel operations with computer-based systems have made them a "way of life," and, therefore, have become *dependent* upon them. It would be costly and impractical to operate with former methods in these situations.
4. *Savings* over prior methods for collecting, maintaining, and reporting information have been substantial—and usually more than anticipated—even though such systems have not normally been "sold" on the basis of savings. Savings have been in terms of increased capability and cost avoidance, rather than staffing reduction—although there have been instances of such an effect on staff. Most important, computerization assists the company in using the talents of its people more fully.
5. *Resistance to change* continues as a factor which limits the system in making its maximum contribution toward most effective and economical operations.
6. A requirement for system success is a high level of Top Management, Human Resource Management, and Technical Systems interest and support. The Human Resource activity should provide the leadership in system design, installation, and operation, with the Systems activity assuring adequate computer scheduling, controls, and reliability.

* AMA Management Bulletin #86—"EDP and Personnel."

New Directions in Manpower Planning and Control

Peter P. Pekar, Jr., and Elmer H. Burack

This paper deals with manpower problems and prospects which are already with us or anticipated in the near future. The overall intention of any manpower system is to develop a comprehensive framework for the understanding and the effective use of manpower resources in any organization, as well as a practical apparatus for the analysis and resolution of specific manpower problems at the operating level. The breadth and practicality of any approach should permit several different types of problems to benefit from what is offered.

Previous manpower planning techniques have concentrated on recruitment and placement, manpower audits, appraisals, education and development, and aspects of motivation and compensation. In other words, manpower planning has been for the most part used to manage growth and forecasting future manpower needs. This paper not only addresses growth through a manpower systems design model, but considers the more serious and perplexing problem of manpower reductions because of economic stagnation or decline.

Needless to say, in manning of new facilities, and the closing of old ones, the availability of information on the credentials of potential candidates will greatly enhance planning flexibility. Any system which can provide management with the greatest array of candidates and job functions to choose from will contribute importantly to the lessening of expensive phase-in, phase-out or de-bugging of new facilities. Also, any system should build on present data and not start from scratch. The following management information system design meets or exceeds all of the above criteria and permits a more effective utilization of personnel. The design is divided into the following sections:

- Employee Data Base
- Performance Ranking Criteria
- Identification of Job Functions
- System Design Model
- Role of Computer
- Conclusions

"New Directions in Manpower Planning and Control" by Peter P. Pekar, Jr., and Elmer H. Burack, *Managerial Planning*, July/August, 1977. Reprinted with permission.

Peter P. Pekar, Jr., is Director of Business Analysis of Quaker Oats Company, Chicago, Illinois. Elmer H. Burack is Professor of Management at Illinois Institute of Technology with the Stuart School of Management and Finance.

EMPLOYEE DATA BASE

Two matters of concern in the design and development of a manpower information system are the breadth and depth of data to be collected. Clearly, information is the foundation upon which a manpower system feeds, however, the extent of information must be limited to only what is meaningful and necessary. It is the author's opinion that the following bodies of data are necessary to have an effective manpower information system. A discussion of each category follows:

General Employment Data

The general employment data file is designed to profile each employee by age, sex, marital status, work station, ethnic background, health, citizenship and exempt or non-exempt status. The following information is foundation to a manpower data base.

Data Needed

- Employee name
- Social Security number
- Area identification number (IDU)
- Business unit identification number (IDU)
- Job identification number (IDU)
- Date of birth or 5 year average, e.g., (31-35 years)
- Date of hire
- Sex code
- Marital status code
- Number of dependents (Per current W-4 Form)
- Occupational category code (Equal Employment Opportunity)
- Employment status code, exempt or non-exempt
- Medical status code
- Physical limitation code
- Citizenship status code
- Union representation code, if any

Education and Training

Since managerial, professional and technical personnel differ widely in complexity, education information helps determine interests and worth. It must be recognized that what is being discussed here are descriptions of educational experiences and complex combinations of academic skills and without specification of job experiences, motivations and drive are somewhat misleading. However, classifications, such as these, help to determine skill transferability within and across occupational lines, determine who holds particular skills and facilitate the expansion of employee alternatives for job movement. The following educational information should be considered for a manpower system.

Data Needed

- Highest educational code
- College or trade or technical school fields of study
  First Field code
  Second Field code
  Most recent attendance code
- Degree or certification code
- Year of degree or certification (or last year attended)
- Patents, awards and publications
- Other occupational skills

Prior Employment History
A prior employment file would help assess previous experience. Such information would provide a measure of employee worth. This file should have the following information.

Data Needed

- Military Service
  - Military service branch code and dates
  - Highest rank
  - Primary duty
  - Type of discharge code
- Armed Services School fields of study
  first field code
  Second field code
- Prior Employment - External
  - Employer's name (last five)
  - Industry code
  - Position titles
  - Job descriptions
  - Training programs
  - Prison record code
  - Disadvantaged program code

Any manpower information system should reflect an employee's job assignments. It must be understood that this file only profiles an employee's history and position and does not indicate whether he is critical to a function or not. This will be discussed later. It is important to note, however, that this section does highlight an employee's progress within the organization.

- Internal Employee History
  - Original grade level
  - List past five positions held
  - Date started
  - Current grade level
  - Years with company
  - Description of current duties

Salaried Hourly Employees Information
This file features base salary, grade and bonus status.

Data Needed

- Current base salary
- Grade level
- Bonus status
- Quartile range

Termination Data
This file would contain such information as termination date, reasons for, rehire recommendation, severance pay and pension eligibility.

Data Needed

- Severance pay
- Pension eligibility
- Rehire recommendation
- Termination date
- Reasons for termination

A sample of personnel data information is illustrated in Figure 1.

PERFORMANCE RANKING CRITERIA

Since an employer deals with his supervisor on a continuous basis, his supervisor should then be the best judge of the employee's performance. Therefore, each supervisor should be asked to rank his people according to the following performance criteria.

Figure 1. Sample Employee Personnel Data Information

EVALUATION DATA

COMPANY IDU_____SUBHOLD IDU_____AREA IDU_____JOB TITLE _____
JOB IDU_____PERFORMANCE RANKING_____APPRAISER'S NAME_____DATE _____

GENERAL EMPLOYMENT DATA

NAME_____SOCIAL SECURITY NO._____EEO CODE _____
PLACE OF BIRTH_____DATE OF HIRE_____SEX _____
MARITAL STATUS_____NO. OF DEPENDENTS____EXEMPT_____NON-EXEMPT_____
MEDICAL STATUS_____PHYSICAL LIMITATION_____
CITIZENSHIP_____UNION REPRESENTATION _____

EDUCATION AND TRAINING

HIGHEST EDUCATIONAL CODE: COLLEGE, TRADE OR TECHNICAL SCHOOL (NAME)_____
FIELDS OF STUDY (1)_____, (2)_____, (3)_____ DATE OF RECENT ATTENDANCE _____
DEGREES AND/OR CERTIFICATIONS_____YEAR OF DEGREES OR CERTIFICATIONS _____
PATENTS, AWARDS AND PUBLICATIONS _____

OTHER SPECIALTY OR OCCUPATIONAL SKILLS _____

PRIOR EMPLOYMENT HISTORY

MILITARY
MILITARY SERVICE_____DATES_____HIGHEST RANK_____
PRIMARY DUTY_____TYPE OF DISCHARGE _____
ARMED SERVICES SCHOOL FIELDS OF STUDY: FIELD (1)_____ FIELD (2) _____

EXTERNAL
EMPLOYER'S NAME (LATEST FIRST) (1)_____ (2)_____ (3)_____ (4)_____
INDUSTRY TYPE (E.G., MANUF.)   (1)_____ (2)_____ (3)_____ (4)_____
POSITION TITLES   (1)_____ (2)_____ (3)_____ (4)_____
JOB DESCRIPTION
    (1) _____
    (2) _____
    (3) _____
    (4) _____
PRISON RECORD CODE_____DISADVANTAGED PROGRAM CODE_____

INTERNAL
DATE STARTED WITH COMPANY_____ORIGINAL GRADE LEVEL _____
LIST ALL POSITIONS HELD (CURRENT FIRST) (1)_____ (2)_____ (3)_____ (4) _____
DATE STARTED WITH CURRENT POSITION_____CURRENT GRADE LEVEL_____YEARS WITH COMPANY ____
DESCRIPTION OF CURRENT POSITION_____

SALARY INFORMATION

CURRENT BASE SALARY_____ GRADE LEVEL_____ BONUS STATUS_____ QUARTILE RANGE _____

TERMINATION DATA

SEVERANCE PAY_____ PENSION ELIGIBILITY_____ REHIRE RECOMMENDATION_____ TERMINATION DATE_____
REASONS FOR TERMINATION _____

- U - UNSATISFACTORY
- Performance does not meet the requirements of present position.
- M - MARGINAL
- Developing at slower rate than majority of contemporaries. Needs development for greater responsibility.
- EF - EFFECTIVE
- Performance meets job description standard.
- EX - EXCELLENT
- Performance exceeds standard and is above the level of majority of contemporaries.

For example: The president of a corporation would be responsible for appraising all people shown on Figure 2. In turn, each of the executives would appraise the next level. This process would continue

Figure 2. Example of Evaluation Level I

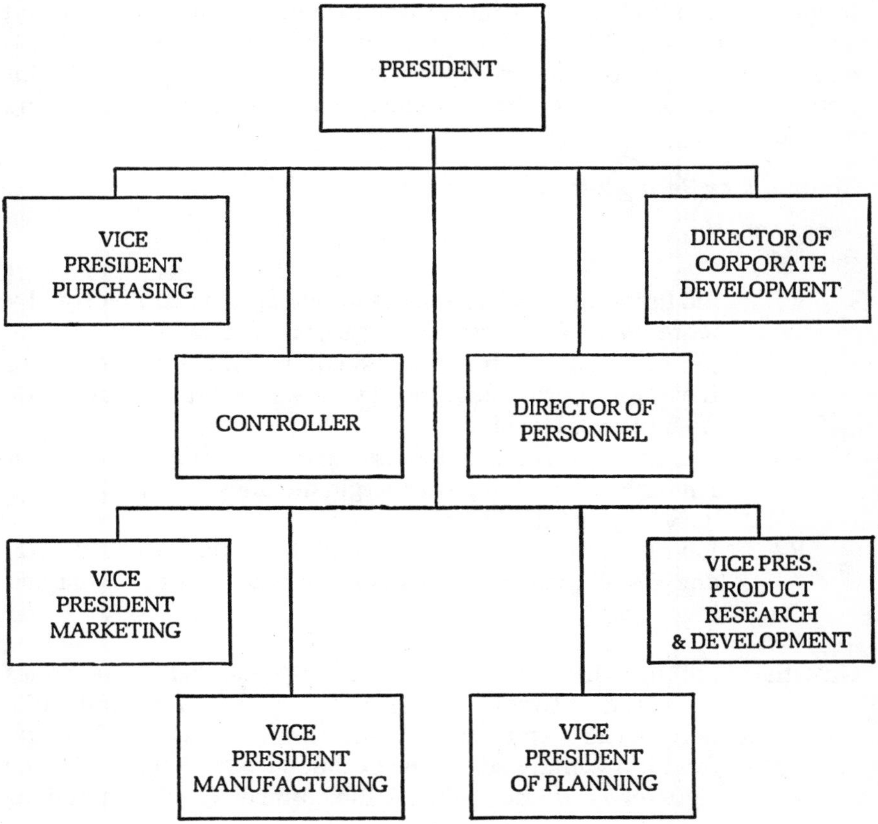

until all levels are screened. In order to minimize bias that occurs in such a scenario, it should be noted that any appraisal will always be reviewed by the appraiser's superior who is also acquainted, although not intimately, with the individual being appraised.

IDENTIFICATION OF JOB FUNCTIONS

There are two main objectives of any manpower system. The first, in periods of growth or expansion, is being able to identify which new jobs should be created in order to support planned expansion. Second, in times of decline or recession, is the ability to recognize which jobs should be eliminated in order to maintain the organization at a reduced level. Also, management should try to retain excellent employees in periods of crisis.

Since an employee's data file contains his performance ranking, it becomes essential to recognize which job function needs to be eliminated or expanded vis-a-vis corporate performance goals and objectives. Hence, it is a requirement that each job be distinguished by identification numbers (IDU), according to company business unit and area. Contingency ratings covering expansion and decline should also accompany each job function. These ratings would be determined for both growth and recession by area managers. The following job rating structure is suggested.

Contingency Rating System

Recession
Rating

R1	Job function which is non-essential, if gross margin drops by more than 5% but less than 10% from planned level.
R2	Job function which is non-essential, omitting personnel in Level R1, if gross margin gravitates between 11% and 20% from planned level.
R3	Job function which is non-essential, excluding personnel in Levels R1 and R2, if gross margin declines between 20% and 30% from planned level.
R4	Job function which is non-essential omitting Levels R1, R2, and R3, if gross margin falls more than 30% from planned levels.
Growth	Job function which needs to be expanded, if revenues increased between 5% and 10%; between 11% and 20%; between 21% and 30%; or greater than 30%. G signifies a job function which needs to be expanded. The first space to the right of G would indicate the number of new functions

needed to support growth between 5% and 10%. The next
space represents the number needed for growth between
11% and 20%. This process then continues for each growth
rate respectively.

The identification framework is systematically shown in Figure 3.
For example, suppose a severe decline in revenue is experienced in the
southern region, (i.e., gross margins are projected to decline by 25% in
the next fiscal year.) Since management would have previously
indicated which jobs could be eliminated in such an event, it then
becomes a simple task to retrieve all southern related job functions
through the data bank. A sample termination list is shown below:

Job Number	Title
13330001 R1/G 0, 2, 3, 4[1]	Salesman
13330002 R2/G 0, 0, 0, 0	Financial Analyst

SYSTEM DESIGN MODEL

Figure 4 shows schematically the manpower system design model and
the interfacing of all data. The boxes on the far left involve the basic
inputted data, i.e., job titles, IDU's, contingency ratings and personnel
files. The jobs, titles and contingency ratings are stored in one file with
personnel data with performance rankings being kept in another. The
remainder of the model deals with manipulating the data base in times of
growth or recession.

If recession for a particular unit was forecasted, the data bank would
supply a list of all job functions which could be eliminated. The data
bank would also supply personnel files for all of these occupants. In
addition, a sorting out of Ex-rated personnel for possible retention
would also be done. After these people have been distinguished, the data
bank would identify all corporate personnel with U, M, and EF
performance ratings. A matching exercise could then take place in hopes
of replacing some of these marginal people by the Ex-personnel. It is
important to note that not all Ex-personnel would be retained. However,
this system would optimize management's ability in retaining the best
possible people. After all decisions have been made, the total cost of
termination would be summarized.

If on the other hand expansion was forecasted, the data bank would
provide a list of new job functions needed. Employees with similar job
functions could be identified and reviewed for possible promotion to fill

Figure 3. Classifying Job Functions

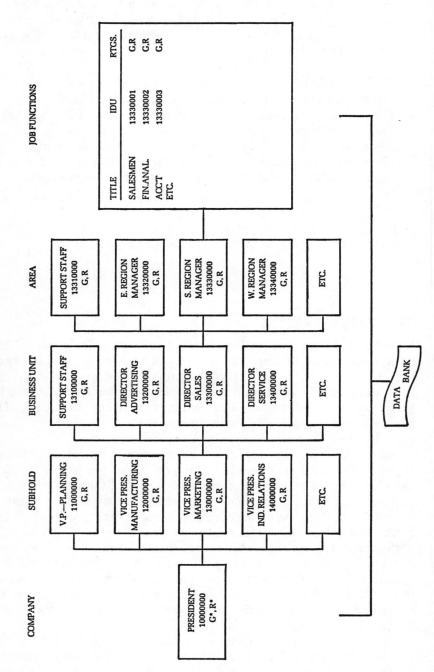

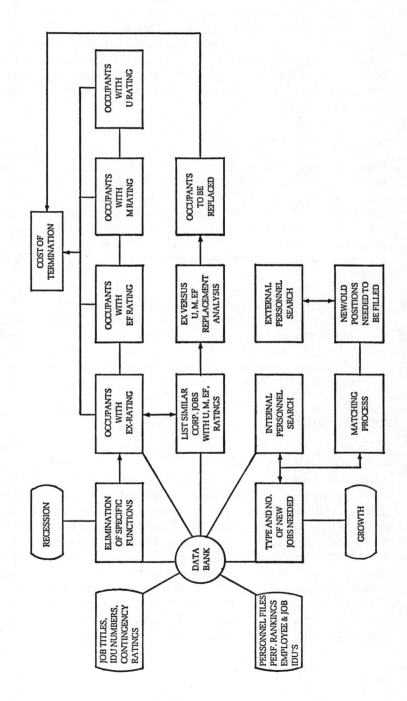

Figure 4. Manpower System Design

these positions. In any event, new needed positions would be recognized and a-search for occupants started.

The manpower system here offers flexibility and rapid access, but is no better than the information supplied it. Therefore, careful consideration must be given to all forms and data needed. This is a time-consuming undertaking but is indispensable in order for the model to operate effectively.

ROLE OF COMPUTER

Reaction management, which is simply reacting to the consequences of change, takes time and is generally tedious. However, developing a more objective, orderly base of information and data, as stated previously, helps ease the tightness of such situations. Clearly, the indicated system is complex and requires rapid retrieval. A computer data base information system would service both current required reports, as well as information pertinent to future issues. Such a system would:

a) Significantly decrease the time in analysis

b) Identify qualified candidates and provide accurate summaries in sufficient detail to significantly increase or decrease positions.

c) Provide basic reports for employment salary control, and comparative analyses between business units in their use of manpower and staffing.

CONCLUSIONS

In the proposed system, data could be updated annually, systematized and made more comprehensive, thus more accurate, for manpower planning and programming purposes. The system will permit more effective monitoring of manpower levels and costs which will permit a more effective utilization of personnel. The computer-based information system will provide detailed intelligence about skill deficiencies and need. Finally, it should mention that the proposed design is an overall system. Therefore data could be gathered in stages in order to permit immediate analysis of pressing problems. It should be noticed that a full organization structure diagram has to be constructed so that the previous mentioned levels of visibility can be defined, and identification numbers assigned. The data then has to be collected and filed. Only after this, can data be assembled and needed reports created.

CHAPTER 7
EVALUATING THE EFFECTIVENESS OF HUMAN RESOURCE PLANNING STRATAGEMS

Evaluating the Practical Effectiveness of Human Resource Planning Applications
James W. Walker

In the past several decades, large organizations have put into use a wide range of programs and practices aimed at the improved utilization of their human talent. The thousand largest business and industrial organizations in the world together spend in excess of $10 billion each year in human resource management activities, excluding the value of time spent by individuals and managers away from work for purposes of training, development, interviewing, performance planning and review, and other activities.

A discipline of human resource planning (manpower planning) has developed and is now widely used to guide management in planning and conducting these activities, and allocating these financial resources. Nearly all of the organizations in a recent survey of major U.S. and Canadian firms indicated that they practiced manpower planning (Walker, 1973). These organizations also indicated, however, that these practices are extremely traditional and rudimentary. The tools being used in manpower planning do not appear to be adequate to meet the needs of management for proper evaluation and planning of investments in the human resource area.

If the major financial investments being made are to yield the returns that they should, more rigorous tools need to be added to the discipline of manpower planning. This paper proposes a four-stage model of human resource planning.

Reprinted from *Human Resource Management*, Spring 1974, pp. 19-27, Graduate School of Business Administration, University of Michigan, Ann Arbor, MI 48109

James W. Walker is a Principal of Towers, Perrin, Forster & Crosby, Inc., Boston, Massachusetts.

Through human resource planning, management prepares to have the right people at the right places at the right times to fulfill both organizational and individual objectives. With the proper planning and evaluation, management is able to attract, retain, develop, and utilize talent to meet organizational challenges of the future. At the same time, the organization is able to provide employees with realistic and satisfying career opportunities. The human resource planning process may be viewed as having three elements:

1. Through *forecasting*, management anticipates talent requirements by examining both individual and organizational plans.
2. Through *programming*, management plans actions that will meet these needs and at the same time support key individual career decisions, as follows:

   organizational and occupational choice by attracting, recruiting, and orienting new talent to the organization.
   job assignment by matching individual interests and talents with opportunities.
   performance and development planning and review by helping individuals perform effectively and develop their capabilities.
   retirement by helping individuals prepare for satisfying retirement.

3. Through *evaluation*, management assesses the effectiveness of this forecasting and programming in terms of both organizational and individual impact.

In each of these elements of the human resource planning process, organizations display a variety of practices. The types of practices vary with the circumstance of the organizations, including the number of employees; the geographic dispersion; the stage of development of the organization; the technologies involved; the economic, social, political environment; and the personalities and experiences of key executives.

We find that practices in each element of planning may be viewed in terms of a four-stage evolution, linked to circumstances such as those noted above. Simply put the organization uses a combination of tools and management practices suited to its needs. This evolutionary view of human resource planning, outlined below, must be considered tentative and subject to validation through further research. At this point, nevertheless, it serves as a useful framework for auditing human resource planning practices and for evaluating their effectiveness.

The four "stages of human resource planning" represent successive levels of complexity and scope in the systems, procedure, and activities that make up an organization's human resource management. Stage I represents a rudimentary, basic approach to an organization's needs as might be applied in a small organization or an entrepreneurial organization in its early stages of growth. For such an organization this approach is quite proper and appropriate.

Stage II represents a short-range planning cycle, and a sensitive but largely paternalistic approach to human resource management. It represents an effort by an organization to supplement its informal, personal management style with more formal, objective tools. Today, many organizations, particularly those in the range of 3,000 to 10,000 employees, are in this stage.

Stage III represents "state-of-the-art" practices in human resource planning involving use of computer capabilities and coordinated activities aimed at satisfying both short-range and long-range needs. Major business organizations are operating in this stage, where the focus is improved career management.

Finally, Stage IV represents the ultimate in human resource planning practices, requiring in many aspects tools that may be on the drawing boards. Practices here are innovative and experimental. As a management process, Stage IV may be viewed as futuristic at this time, even though the techniques are widely discussed in the popular and professional literature and are the focus of attention by manpower researchers.

While organizations appear to develop more advanced systems as they mature and grow, there should be presumed no normative progression from Stage I to II and so on. All organizations should not necessarily operate in the Stage II, III, or IV. Rather, each organization should operate in the stage—the human resource planning system—best suited to its present needs, its past successful experience, and its projected immediate future requirements. Above all, it appears that practices are well-planned when they are consistently applied within one of the stages. These points will become more clear as the elements of the four stages are examined more closely.

THE FOUR SYSTEM STAGES

As shown in Exhibit I, the ways organizations may forecast future talent requirements and human resource management needs range from the very informal and subjective to the very quantitative, formal, and analytic. Similarly, as shown in Exhibit II, the ways organizations plan actions to meet needs range from the very simple, personal, and informal, to the very systematic, open, and comprehensive. In the Exhibit, practices are identified as they relate to each of the primary aspects of career management.

Each of these approaches to human resource planning requires a

Exhibit I.

FORECASTING: The way we anticipate future talent requirements and
Human Resource Management needs

I	II	III	IV
—Managers discuss goals, plans and thus types and numbers of people needed in the short-term.	—Annual planning and budgeting process includes manpower needs.	—Using computer-generated analyses, examine causes of problems and future trends regarding supply and demand (the flow of talent).	—On-line modeling and simulation of talent needs, flows and costs to aid in a continuing process of updating projecting needs, staffing plans, career opportunities and thus program plans.
—Highly informal and subjective.	—Specify quantity and quality of talent needs as far out in time as possible.	—Use computer to relieve managers of routine forecasting tasks (such as vacancies or turnover)	—Provide best possible current information for managerial decisions.
	—Identify problems requiring action: individual or general.	—Analyze career paths and career progress using computer data files.	—Exchange data with other companies and with government (such as economic, employment and social data).
	—Analyze management succession and readiness of successors.		

Exhibit II.

PROGRAMMING: The way we plan actions to satisfy talent
requirements

I	II	III	IV
—Individuals recruited and assigned to jobs as needs arise.	—Recruitment based on projected short-range needs and on analysis of past recruitment and selection experience.	—Recruitment coordinated among organizational units and linked to plans for the future flow of talent in the organization.	—Fluid exchange of talent on reciprocal basis among organizations and with government.
—Necessary on-the-job orientation provided.	—On-the-job orientation supplemented by formal orientation programs.	—Long-term indicators of individual career interests, capabilities and performance are considered in recruitment and selection.	—College recruitment begun during training so as to guide individual preparation.
			—Recruitment is corporate-wide for managerial, professional, and technical talent and the market is multinational.

Exhibit II. (Continued)

The way we match individual talents and interests with opportunities

I	II	III	IV
—Informal knowledge of individual capabilities and readiness is relied upon for new assignment results in matching. Managerial judgment and personal contact are of prime importance.	—Career information is communicated to employees.	—Internal search precedes outside recruitment; the information system is used to search for individuals interested in and qualified for vacancies.	—Individuals plan their desired career program in an open "internal labor market" in the organization.
	—Internal search is conducted for all assignments, including review of available appraisal data and personal biographical data.	—The chain effect of assignment is fully considered and planned. A comprehensive job posting or career tracking system is used.	—Individuals may initiate reviews of their qualifications for vacancies as they arise (position or job). Assignments may cross departmental and functional lines on the basis of career paths.
	—A limited job posting system may be used.	—Individuals provide data on skills, preferences, and development needs in advance of vacancies for consideration in matching process.	—Managers review individual plans and provide developmental opportunities needed to prepare individuals for planned future responsibilities; level with individuals when plans are unrealistic and provide out-placement assistance when suitable opportunities are not available.
—Managerial replacement planning is informal, based on personal knowledge and on "heir apparent approach."	—Systematic backup planning includes use of charts, appraisals, and/or management-level development committees.	—Management succession candidates are prepared for career to fill projected needs on a pooled basis.	—Management succession results from effective normal career development and progression covering employees. An annual management review of human resource planning ensures effectiveness of action.

The way we help individuals perform effectively and develop their capabilities

I	II	III	IV
—Job descriptions provide guides for managers in directing the work of others.	—Managers interpret position responsibilities with individuals and coach individuals to assure understanding and commitment to them	—A goal setting and review process draws together individual plans with task/role aspects of a job.	—Individual plans work (roles/tasks) and development actions in the context of career planning.
—Individual development results through work experience and some formal training.	—Managers appraise results and individual capabilities and potential.	—Managers coach individuals, provide career guidance, and mutually review progress with individuals.	—Full information is shared with individual so that plans may be realistic and attuned to company needs.

Exhibit II (Continued)

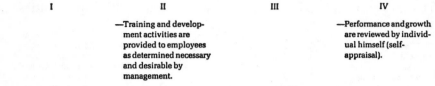

I	II	III	IV
	—Training and development activities are provided to employees as determined necessary and desirable by management.		—Performance and growth are reviewed by individual himself (self-appraisal).

The way we help individual prepare for a satisfying retirement

I	II	III	IV
—Pension benefits and pertinent information on them and company retirement policy are provided.	—Pre-retirement counseling is provided to encourage individual preparation both financially and psychologically.	—Retirement is viewed as a career step and is prepared for as such by individuals.	—Individuals move in and out of "retirement" through mobility (with vested pension benefits).
—Service is recognized with awards program and retirement honors.	—Early retirement is possible with reduced pension benefits.	—Retirement timing is flexible through gradual retirement and other options.	—Sabbaticals, special leave programs, and project assignments are available.
			—Individual differences are recognized and honored by company actions—without reliance on age and seniority as overriding factors in career progress, development or compensation.

different base of information—both in terms of the type and extent of data and the nature of the system by which those data are gathered, stored, and made available for management use. In Exhibit III, the pertinent data required for or provided by each stage of human resource planning are displayed. While providing personnel data is not an integral part of the planning process, it is critical to it. Information provides the foundation for human resource planning and especially for the third major element: evaluation—the way we ensure that human resource planning is effective. This last element of human resource planning is the focus of this paper.

EVALUATION

Techniques used to evaluate the effectiveness of human resource planning and human resource management generally are simple, subjective, and traditional. Analysis of current practices indicates that in most business organizations the various human resource activities are subject only to a personal review by key managers. The philosophy prevailing seems to reflect such assumptions as:

Exhibit III.

INFORMATION: The way we keep track of information on talent in the oganization

I	II	III	IV
—Basic employment data: • Personal education, experience • Biographical data	—Appraisal data added: • Performance • Potential • Qualifications • Limited data on skills and interests	—Qualitative data added: • Individual interests • Self-appraisal data • Job preferences • Specified individual skills and knowledge areas • Psychological assessments	—Behavioral attitude data added: • Role/task elements • Behavioral characteristics of individuals and jobs • Investment and benefit measures
—Manual files contain basic personnel data.	—A semi-automated data storage and retrieval system is used.	—Comprehensive human resource information system with turnaround documents for personnel decisions and updating and a generalized retrieval program.	—Information system is • Corporate-wide • Multinational
	—It may be an expanded payroll file or a stand-alone file.	—Essential calculative capacities (e.g., correlation, modeling).	—System is on-line providing access to data for retrieval analysis and updating.
	—Provides basic reports, general listings and summaries for managerial use.	—May be for division, group or location (e.g., U.S. only).	—The data system initiates personnel actions, analyses of special problems.

"If it works, don't fix it."

"If we wanted things different, we'd make things different."

"We look at results—and we're making profits, aren't we?"

This traditional approach to evaluation becomes more critical only where major problems emerge, such as:

- a union organizing drive among employees
- a period of cost-control emphasis
- a period of low or declining profitability
- a sharp upturn in employee turnover
- a tight labor market, with inability to recruit needed talent.

Then a series of special studies, attitude surveys, and other analyses are often conducted to help management determine the best course of remedial action. Many companies look to their competitors for a guide to their own human resource planning effectiveness. Such insightful questions are addressed as:

"Where do we stand with other companies?"

"What are other companies doing differently?"

"What are the trends?"

When a need for reconsideration of existing practices is recognized, the common procedure is to conduct a special study of the issue. For example, if there is some concern about management development not being adequate, a task force or committee may be formed. If manpower planning itself appears inadequate to meet company needs, a specialist may be commissioned to survey practices of other leading companies and recommend remedial actions. The result is usually a specific set of recommendations aimed at revising or replacing current practices with a new approach based on the information gathered. This new process remains in place until a need for further change is strongly felt.

This traditional evaluation approach is not necessarily inadequate. It is simple, personal, direct, and responsive to important business needs. It may be slow, but it is inexpensive and avoids frivolous changes and actions. It is subjective, but relies on business judgment—a key to business success. In small organizations and in organizations with human resource planning in Stage I, this approach may be perfectly appropriate and sufficient. As the needs for more rigorous evaluation in human resource planning develops, new tools and different procedures may be introduced.

Such additional, more rigorous, tools and procedures for evaluation might include the following:

- in-depth review of specific policies, systems, programs, and activities—with regard to the manner in which each is actually applied, and its merits (Gordon, 1973).
- interpretation of quantitative data—including rates and levels of participation in programs, movement of talent, turnover, and absenteeism.
- interpretation of employee attitudes—based on periodic employee attitude surveys or other forms of organizational climate audit.
- review and interpretation of activities by an external party, such as a consultant—permitting a possibly more objective view and evaluation and further inputs regarding comparisons with practices of other organizations.
- measurement of direct expenditures of such programs as recruitment, training and development, or training of disadvantaged employees (Rohan, 1972).
- analysis of turnover costs and the causes of turnover (Bassett, 1972).

- analysis of the breakeven point/payback period of new hires.
- analysis of productivity changes, the impact of incentive compensation on productivity, and other factors affecting productivity.
- analysis of recruitment results—optimal sources of recruits, recruitment practices, costs of recruiting versus developing talent available internally.
- analysis of staffing mix to optimize personnel costs.
- analysis of the economics of layoff and retention of good talent during periods of staff reductions
- analysis of talent requirements associated with possible mergers and acquisitions.

These types of evaluation procedures may be found in industrial practice today, but they are not widely used. They are concerned primarily with: a) examination of current practices in light of costs, employee or management perceptions, and results; and b) measurement and analysis of cost and variations in costs under decision alternatives.

These evaluations may be conducted readily in most major business organizations. The data are available; the tools are available. They provide substantive, factually-based information for management's consideration in making decisions. They are, however, merely supplemental to basic, rudimentary managerial judgment. They do not provide estimation of the benefits related to costs, nor do they constitute an ongoing evaluation process to guide management planning and budgeting. The techniques that provide for this type of evaluation include cost-beneift analysis, human capital budgeting, reporting of human resource data, and estimation of human resource values. These techniques are not fully developed for application in the human resource planning area. They are used, however, in other functional areas of management and thus may be applied effectively where they are appropriate and where individuals understand how to apply and interpret them. We will review each of these techniques briefly.

1. Analysis of cost in relation to estimated benefits is a direct application of a well-accepted tool of financial analysis. This tool is particularly applicable to evaluation of specific training and development programs, evaluation of fringe benefit and compensation changes, and evaluation of new systems and organization structures (Thomas, 1969). Cost-benefit analysis can be a useful element in the evaluation of alternative programs that may be implemented in an organization. For example, a division of Xerox Corporation evaluated various proposed personnel expenditures in terms of cost-effectiveness and technical and operational feasibility.

The various proposals were then ranked and the best were adopted (Cheek, 1973).

2. Cost-effectiveness evaluations are essential for human capital budgeting—a process whereby management allocates available resources for human resource programs through a budgeting process, normally a part of the management budgeting and planning process. At a minimum, a company attempting human capital budgeting establishes common budget lines in all divisions covering training and development outlays, recruitment expenses, relocation expenses, and other major types of expenditures. This tool permits an ongoing review of these expenditures as investments.

3. The very process of reporting basic human resource data to management can prompt consideration of human resource planning issues in the context of regular business planning and management. Some companies, for example, provide human resource data and plans as part of the five-year business planning process. This information provides a basis for increases and shifts in capital allocation for human resource development and utilization to meet the organization's anticipated needs. Of course, payroll costs, staffing levels and projections, and results of special studies would supplement basic budget-line data.

4. Some companies have attempted to estimate the value of their human resources—as information useful in planning layoffs, further developmental actions, compensation changes, and other types of decisions where asset values are helpful information. Granted, this is not common practice, and the rationale for developing measures or estimates of the worth of employees and executives is not always clear. The insurance industry has encouraged such an effort, with limited success, for purposes of establishing key man insurance in business organizations. The effort has also been of considerable interest and attention in academic research and publications (Flamholtz, 1971; Lee, 1972; Likert, 1967, 1973; Waters 1972). As a matter of information, there are primary approaches for estimating human resource value:

Accrued costs: an accounting approach based on historical asset-costs/predicted-values, i.e., an organizational systems approach that examines human facts in relation to organizational performance.

Replacement value: a "market value" approach pioneered by the insurance industry in the 1950's and 1960's.

Economic value: a discounted present-value approach based on projecting earnings of the individuals and/or other pertinent variables.

There are numerous variations on each of these themes, but these are the primary ones recognized today. Others include a goodwill approach (either based on total stock value or net worth), a discounted total earnings approach (part of the present value of future earnings is attributable to the human element, and a value-structure approach (in which skills groups are ranked ordinally and then priced as a structure according to the market value).

To date, the value of such surrogate measures of human resource value has been largely one of drawing attention of managers to the sizable investment in people. With extremely few exceptions, this information has not been used in human resource accounting systems, it remains primarily an academic exercise.

Beyond human resource evaluation and the various evaluation techniques outlined there is a great deal of interest in a broad-scope process of human resource accounting. Under this umbrella name, researchers have developed processes for continuous monitoring and reporting of investments and values, computerized simulation of alternative human resource investment decisions, and ongoing accounting and financial reporting for human resources. At this point you may take these to mean pretty much what you wish, as they are still largely undefined and subject to much further development. The thrust is in the same direction as that of the techniques now being used—toward more rigorous evaluation of human resource expenditures. These broad processes, however, are such major departures from current business management practice that they can best be described as futuristic (Alexander, 1971).

The pioneering steps taken by William Pyle, Director of the University of Michigan's Human Resource Accounting Program, and the R. G. Barry Corporation, an Ohio-based manufacturer, have been widely publicized. The company, with the assistance of the University of Michigan, has reported human asset information in its annual financial statements since 1969. The accounting system uses a replacement cost, and company-developed standard costs are added. The initial steps taken at Barry were to place "people on the balance sheet" in terms of accrued costs. Steps to supplement and refine this data and to make it useful as management information have followed (Pyle, 1970).

STEPS FOR EVALUATION

So what should an organization do to evaluate properly its human resource planning effectiveness? Which of these varied tools and techniques should be applied? Is human resource accounting the ideal process to be implemented, or is subject evaluation best suited for some organizations?

In the context of human resource planning as an evolutionary process, there is no one best evaluation technique. Different evaluation techniques and measures apply to each stage of human resource planning practice, as displayed in Exhibit IV. Management should use the evaluation practices that are consistent with the forecasting and programming practices used and the personnel information available.

Exhibit IV.

EVALUATION: The way we assure that human resource planning is
effective

I	II	III	IV
—Policies, systems, programs, and activities are subjectively reviewed.	—Policies, systems, programs, and activities are reviewed and evaluated. Available quantitative data, attitudes of participating individuals, and practices in similar organizations are examined. This may be conducted by a third party for improved objectivity.	—Cost-benefit analyses of systems, programs and activities are conducted; expenditures are budgeted according to priorities resulting from these analyses.	—Computerized simulation of alternative human resource investment decisions and the long-term impact of of human resource investment and amortization practices.
—Problems, strengths and value received from expenditures are evaluated intuitively.	—Direct expenditures— outlays for acquisition and development of human resources—are measured and reported.	—Indirect costs are estimated, accounts on all costs and measured benefits, and the estimated net organizational impact are reported for management consideration.	—Direct and indirect investments and related values accruing to the organization are monitored.
	—Analyses of turnover, productivity shifts, recruitment results, and other manpower patterns are conducted so as to identify problems.	—Surrogate measures (such as replacement cost, accrued cost, or economic value) of human resource value are developed and applied suited to the organization's circumstances, technology and market.	—This information is included in accounting, financial analysis and reporting processes for management and investor information.

As discussed in this paper, an organization should operate in the stage—the system—best suited to its present needs, its past successful experience, and its projected future requirements. Above all, it should strive to be consistent in its practice so that time and resources will not be wasted.

This suggests that pitfalls endanger many well-intended managers who seek to apply human resource accounting techniques, human capital budgeting, computerized simulations, or other advanced tools. There are many cases in which organizations have introduced practices ahead of their time.

Even at R. G. Barry, the balance-sheet approach which was developed is leaps ahead of the company's overall human resource planning. At Xerox, the cost-benefit analysis and budgeting process which was developed is apparently not being used on a continuing, valid basis. Too often, new, state-of-the-art techniques are introduced with initial interest, and promoted. Then, as the practical applications of the results lag, the technique loses its sparkle and falls into disuse and possibly disrepute (loses its support) among operating personnel. Then it is time to move on to another "new" tool or to return to basics. It is the latter that makes sense from the approach outlined here.

The steps to be followed for evaluating the practical effectiveness of human resource planning applications are as follows:

1. Determine the objectives of the human resource planning process in terms of the objectives and plans of the organization. This may require discussions with key executives, analysis of corporate long-range plans, and examination of characteristics of the organization, the available talent, the tasks performed, the technology or technologies involved, and the environmental conditions of the organization.

2. Examine the various policies, systems, programs, and other elements of the human resource planning process—including all aspects of forecasting, programming, and information systems. Determine the overall pattern of human resource planning in relation to the four-stage framework presented in Exhibits I, II, and III. Identify the practices that appear to be consistent, within one of the stages described. Identify also those practices that appear to be more basic or more advanced by comparison with the predominant pattern.

3. Compare the current pattern of human resource planning practices with the objectives of the process and the needs of the organization (step one). Determine in which stage (or combination of stages, if appropriate) the organization should be conducting its human resource planning. As the organization grows and matures in the years immediately ahead, toward which stage of human resource planning should the organization be moving? These judgments are critical to the evaluation process. The framework presented here is designed to help managers make these judgments.

4. Apply specific evaluation tools and techniques, as outlined in Exhibit IV, for the review of the effectiveness of the practices involved in the stage determined to be suited to the organization's needs and objectives. This specific evaluation uses measures and

assessments that fit the stage of human resource planning practice. As discussed, subjective review and intuitive evaluation are appropriate techniques in organizations operating with Stage I human resource planning.

Public reporting of human resource data appears suited only to organizations with the most advanced human resource planning practices. In the mid-range, specific tools appear applicable where necessary supporting information is available and practices are amenable to particular types of evaluation.

This framework for viewing the human resource planning process, including the evaluation of human resource applications, is tentatively proposed and is subject to further refinement and testing. In the organizations where it has been applied, however, it has been a useful tool for examining and improving human resource planning.

At a time when managers are looking for simple answers to complex problems, when personnel professionals are increasingly specialized and (unfortunately) program and technique-oriented, and when advanced resource accounting concepts are of high topical interest, a broad systematic diagnostic approach for evaluation is needed. It's hoped this framework contributes to the satisfaction of this need.

REFERENCES

Alexander, Michael O., "Investment in People," *The Canadian Chartered Accountant*, July 1971.

Bassett, Glenn A., "Employee Turnover Measurement and Human Resource Accounting," *Human Resource Management*, Fall 1972, pp. 21-30.

Brummet, R. Lee, William C. Pyle, and Eric G. Flamholtz., "Human Resource Accounting in Industry," *Personnel Administration*, July-August 1969, pp. 34-46.

Burack, Elmer H. and James W. Walker (Eds.), *Manpower Planning and Programming*, Boston: Allyn & Bacon, 1972.

Cheek, Logan, "Cost-Effectiveness Comes to the Personnel Function," *Harvard Business Review*, May-June 1973.

Flamholtz, Eric G., "A Model for Human Resource Valuation: A Stochastic Process with Service Rewards," *The Accounting Review*, April 1971.

Flamholtz, Eric G., "Should Your Organization Attempt to Value Its Human Resources?" *California Management Review*, Winter 1971, pp. 40-45.

Flamholtz, Eric G., "Toward a Theory of Human Resource Value in Formal Organizations," *The Accounting Review*, October 1972, pp. 666-678.

Gordon, Michael E., "Three Ways to Effectively Evaluate Personnel Programs," *Personnel Journal*, July 1972.

Greiner, Larry, "Evolution and Revolution as Organizations Grow," *Harvard Business Review*, July-August 1972, pp. 37-46.

Lee, J. Finley, F. H. Barron, and Jerry S. Rosenbloom, "Evaluating and Protecting Human Resources," *Financial Executive*, March 1972.

Likert, Rensis, "The Human Organization: Its Management and Value," New York, McGraw-Hill Book Co., 1967.

Likert, Rensis and David G. Bowers, "Improving the Accuracy of P/L Reports by Estimating the Change in Dollar Value of the Human Organization," *Michigan Business Review*, March 1973, pp. 15-24.

Pyle, William C., "Monitoring Human Resources—'On Line'," *Michigan Business Review*, July 1970, pp. 19-32.

Rohan, Thomas, "Who's Worth What Around Here?" *Industry Week*, November 6, 1972, pp. 19-26.

Stone, Florence, "Investment in Human Resources at AT&T," *Management Review*, October 1972, pp. 23-27.

Thomas, B., J. Moxham, and J. Jones, "A Cost-Benefit Analysis of Industrial Training," *British Journal of Industrial Relations*, July 1969, pp.231-264.

Walker, James W., "Manpower Planning: How Is It Really Applied?" *European Business*, January 1973 a, pp, 72-78.

Walker, James W., "Individual Career Planning," *Business Horizons*, February, 1973, pp. 65-72.

Waters, James G., "A Practical Application of Human Resource Accounting Techniques," *Personnel Administration*, May-June 1972, 41-47.

Cost Effectiveness Comes to the Personnel Function
Logan M. Cheek

Business and government leaders are increasingly concerned over what has come to be called the "productivity crisis." A host of economic ills are ascribed to it—squeezed profit margins, moderating revenue growth, inflation, economic sluggishness, and the evaporation of the U.S. balance-of-trade surplus. Moreover, some disturbing figures underscore this concern:

- After averaging gains of 3% a year between 1950 and 1965, the U.S. productivity growth rate dropped to a 2.1% annual average between 1965 and 1970. Had the latter rate prevailed during the entire postwar period, the improvement in U.S. living standards would have been reduced by 30%.
- While the 1971 productivity rate jumped sharply by about 4%, this recovery-year improvement compares unfavorably with the 4.5% gain of 1955 and the 4.7% gain of 1962.
- For the long term, a well-publicized Bureau of Labor Statistics estimate forecasts a net potential decline of 0.2% in the rate. Translated into dollars, this could represent a $120 billion reduction of economic output in the 1970's.

Aware of the need for a substantial increase in productivity growth rates, business and labor leaders have been turning with increasing frequency to such techniques as job enrichment and redesign, group incentive pay plans, manpower planning for adjustment and upward mobility, and joint, labor-management productivity teams at the plant level.

Clearly, the primary responsibility for developing such manpower-related programs falls within the charter of the personnel department. Yet, while many techniques are being implemented, the overall effort to improve productivity in most companies appears to be only marginally successful. More often than not, this lack of success can be attributed to the personnel department itself, for these reasons:

Logan M. Cheek is Manager, Plans, Control, and Analysis, for Xerox's Information Systems Group in Rochester, New York.

- In a given year, a number of proposals emanate from such varied personnel functions as employment, compensation, training, planning, and systems. At the same time, any number of outside consultants' recommendations may have to be evaluated. Unless these proposals are rigorously scrutinized, many programs having only a marginal impact on productivity may be selected. As a result, the staff becomes stretched, profits suffer, and the long-term effect is a personnel function focused on activity rather than results.

- Because of the impact of behavioral science, personnel departments have moved increasingly in recent years into such complex and sophisticated areas as job enrichment, selection research, assessment centers, and executive career planning and development. Consequently, the problem of managing the personnel function has been compounded. Indeed, one might say that the sophistication of personnel programs has increased arithmetically, while the complexity of choosing the best ones and managing them has increased geometrically.

- While all personnel costs are direct and visible, most benefits derived from their effective operation are indirect and often intangible. For example, the linkage between improved profits and the costs of undertaking a comprehensive clerical job enrichment effort is elusive at best. Because of this difficulty, personnel is one of the last areas to be augmented in an economic upswing and one of the first to be trimmed in hard times. (Such management actions are particularly shortsighted. The manpower element constitutes between 40% and 70% of the total costs in most businesses. Yet personnel staff costs usually range between 1% and 2% of the payroll. The leverage implied suggests that productivity increases resulting from more effective and relevant personnel action programs can significantly impact on revenue and profits.)

Because of these and other problems, there is a clear need for personnel departments to develop the kinds of program-management techniques that will allow them to meet the productivity crisis in a direct and systematic manner. From a bewildering array of alternatives, they must be able to select the programs that will improve productivity and profits; then they must be able to continuously allocate staff resources only to those programs.

The purpose of this article is to describe a framework which top operating and personnel executives can use to channel the resources of the personnel function to the most worthwhile undertakings. This framework, first implemented at Xerox in 1971 as part of a long-range manpower planning strategy, is currently being used to develop operating budget proposals for selected personnel units throughout the company. Here are the key procedural steps that I shall discuss:

1. Define and describe each personnel program—whether proposed or ongoing—in a discrete package.
2. Separate for special treatment those programs that are legally required.
3. Evaluate all programs on the basis of these factors: (a) "state of the art," (b) ease of implementation, (c) net economic benefits, (d) economic risks of not acting.
4. Rank all programs, and allocate and deploy staff resources accordingly.

DEVELOPING A FRAMEWORK

Our efforts to systematically evaluate and rank personnel programs began as a follow-up to a recent long-range planning cycle. The president of our business products group asked us to review our manpower requirements and to indicate what programs were underway or were needed to ensure achievement of the plan. To accomplish this objective, we had to:

- Review our group's present and projected revenue and profit economics.
- Identify and understand the ways that major groups of employees (managers, scientists, salesmen, servicemen, clericals, and hourlies) affected our economic situation.
- Specify action programs that could increase productivity or help avoid major manpower risks and unnecessary costs.

While a discussion of how we conducted the diagnosis is beyond the scope of this article, I should note that over 120 possible program opportunities were identified. Many were already underway, some were on the drawing boards, and a few were entirely new opportunities. Given the constraints of our budget, however, it was clear that all programs could not be undertaken. Some sort of resource-allocation technique was necessary, one that would permit us to systematically sort out all the proposals as well as manage and control the implementation of the more desirable ones.

There is nothing fundamentally new about the four-part approach we developed.[1] For years, bankers have used systematic screening standards to evaluate credit worthiness. More recently, managers in virtually every business function other than personnel have used decision frameworks or models to assist them in selecting alternate investment or project opportunities. Usually, these techniques are quantitative; sometimes they are subjective. But in either case, they share a systems approach.

The idea, then, was to apply the systems approach and program management concepts to our personnel operations. Let us now turn to an examination of the key steps in Xerox's program management framework.

1. Define and Describe

The first step is for each staff specialist responsible for a particular program to describe his efforts—whether ongoing or proposed—in discrete packages. He specifies the program's objectives, target population, implementation schedule, and any other considerations that might impact on the program's success. (*Exhibit I* shows a condensed form of the basic document used in our evaluation process for all programs. It contains data on a job enrichment effort, a program that I will refer to throughout this article to illustrate our approach.)

The personnel program manager, who is responsible for coordinating the entire departmental effort, assists the staff specialist. The two work as a team, so that each individual's capabilities complement the other's. For example:

- On the one hand, the staff specialist (in the case of *Exhibit I*, a job enrichment specialist) is the most knowledgeable about the program's objectives and technical aspects, the behavioral subtleties of the target population, and the scheduling problems that might inhibit timely implementation.
- On the other hand, the personnel program manager can provide details on manpower levels, salaries, productivity, absenteeism and turnover rates, and spans of control, as well as the costs and profit economics implied by each.

2. Identify Legal Requirements

Many of the resources of a personnel staff must be allocated to programs required by law. Most manpower legislation and regulations have been enacted in the past decade in such areas as pension plans, minority hiring, labor relations, and wage controls. Moreover, such legal requirements will probably increase in future years, particularly among larger organizations, as the traditional economic role of business is enlarged to include a social one.

Obviously, the job enrichment program detailed in *Exhibit I* is not

Exhibit I. Program Evaluation Form

1. Define and describe the program.

2. Identify and segregate legally required efforts.

3. Evaluate feasibility
(a) State-of-the-art implications.
(b) Ease of implications.
(c) Net economic benefits . . .

PROGRAM NAME: Service Force Job Enrichment Program		Program No. 16

DESCRIPTION   (objectives, target population, implementation schedule):

To extend the job enrichment program for the service force — as piloted in   Spring Falls, Avon Hills, and Maplewood branches — to all branches between 1972 and 1976.

Is program legally required?   ☐ Yes   ☒ No

STATE OF THE ART	☒High	☐Medium	☐Low
EASE OF IMPLEMENTATION	☐High	☐Medium	☒Low
ECONOMIC BENEFITS	☒High	☐Medium	☐Low

	Potential revenue impact	Probability of occurrence	Probable gross benefit (cost)
Identifiable benefits:			
Reduction in service force turnover of 1 point.	$ 450,000	.2	$ 90,000
Extension of 1.2 point reduction in absenteeism, as demonstrated in pilot project.	$ 2,132,500	.8	$ 1,706,000
Extension of 5% increase in service force productivity, as demonstrated in initial efforts.	$85,500,000	.1	$ 8,550,000
Total benefits	$88,082,500	.12	$10,346,000

Tangible costs to Xerox of acting:
Group personnel staff time to develop program, and line management time to implement program in all branches.

($ 472,950)	.9	$ 425,655

Total costs	($ 472,950)	.9	$ 425,655
Probable net benefits (cost)			$ 9,920,345

... and intangibles.

Intangible benefits

Increased morale in service force, with improved customer service and satisfaction.

"Contagious effect" of job enrichment to other groups, e.g., sales and clericals.

Improved service manager development with concurrent sharpening of their motivational skills. As an extreme example, one manager at Avon Hills increased his team's productivity 70%.

ECONOMIC RISKS   [x] High   [ ] Medium   [ ] Low

(d) Economic risks.

Possible consequences of not acting:
Continued escalation of service costs as a percent of revenue.

ASSUMPTIONS AND OTHER CONSIDERATIONS:

Cost estimates assume 4.4 man years of group staff time, .26 man years of branch manager time, and 15.8 man years of service manager time to implement program in a population of 1,053 service managers.

Benefit estimates assume elimination of 3 days absenteeism per month for each of 1,053 service teams, favorable productivity, and that turnover experience in pilot branches can be cascaded to all branches.

a statutory necessity. But other programs—in areas such as labor relations, minority relations and reporting, and payroll—clearly are legal requirements. Moreover, such programs rarely have any net economic benefit to a company; their benefits are usually intangible in nature. Yet the potential legal exposure and the consequent impact on the company image dictate a need for special treatment. Accordingly, legally required efforts are handled separately from all other proposals and assigned the highest priority. Here are just a few illustrations from the spectrum of manpower regulation:

- Reporting programs to maintain records of hours, earnings, overtime, union dues collected and the financial health of existing or proposed pension plans.
- Affirmative action plans to hire and upgrade the skills of minority groups and women.
- Any validation efforts needed to insure that pre-employment selection tests or standards comply with the guidelines set by the federal government.
- Programs to insure a safe work environment and to eliminate recognized hazards likely to cause death or injury.[2]

Having identified and segregated such legally required efforts, we are ready to focus on the heart of the process—and its most challenging aspect—the feasibility evaluation.

3. Evaluate Feasibility

The feasibility evaluation of any program focuses on several distinct issues. These are:

Determining the state-of-the-art requirement. Are the necessary skills available?

Determining the ease of implementation. Will line management accept and execute the program?

Determining the net economic benefits. Will the program be cost-effective?

Determining the economic risks. Can the company afford not to act?

I suspect that, to one degree or another, these issues are considered intuitively by some top personnel executives. But let us now examine how each step of feasibility evaluation is handled systematically.

State of the Art: The resolution of this issue requires an in-depth assessment of a program's technical problems as well as the skills available within the personnel department or outside the company (e.g., consultants) needed to overcome these problems. If data processing support is necessary, programming complexity and the availability of equipment must also be determined.

In the case of the job enrichment program shown in *Exhibit I,* qualified technical talent was already available on our staff; thus we could evaluate the state of the art as "high." Three or four years ago, however, this evaluation probably would have been "medium," for we would have had to hire a qualified individual or retain an expert consultant. Ten years ago, the evaluation clearly would have been "low," since at that time job enrichment would have been a major state-of-the-art undertaking.

For comparative purposes, the technical feasibility of all programs must be consistently evaluated against the same standards. Part A of *Exhibit II* shows these standards, which I feel are generally applicable to most companies.

Ease of Implementation: This is the most critical stage of the feasibility evaluation. It involves such elements as line management attitudes, corporate policies, organization structure, operating environment, and management styles. These elements are difficult to change, particularly when programs are in new areas such as job enrichment, organization development, assessment centers, and selection research.

The key to successfully implementing such advanced concepts hinges on the willingness of line management to cooperate. Reorienting personality traits and management styles (which many of the new techniques require) is more challenging than gaining acceptance of a new production process, a new marketing program, or a new billing system. Most of the latter are more tangible and can be "sold" exclusively on their economic merits. But convincing managers of the need to change their behavior is not only difficult but also crucial to program implementation. Let us see how this issue was treated in the job enrichment program:

From an earlier pilot program, we had learned that selling the concept to management was sometimes an uphill fight, and that overall cooperation could be difficult to enlist. (A number of supervisors and key line managers balked at the idea of assigning greater responsibilities to their subordinates.) But we also knew that we had won converts and thus had increased the program's credibility throughout the organization. Because of the potential resistance, however, our evaluation of the ease-of-implementation factor was a qualified "low"—a mark that injected a sobering element should the program pass its other tests and be given the green light. In other words, the program would be warranted only if the risks identified in this stage were clearly offset by exceptionally high evaluations in other stages.

Exhibit II. Standards for Feasibility Evaluation

Evaluation	A. State of the art Standards	B. Ease of implementation Standards
High	Program appears simple. Skilled manpower available in company. EDP programming is simple. Hardware available in company.	Implementing program requires little or no effort to effect a change in line management attitudes and styles, and in organization policies, structure, and operating environment. Implementing program does not imply a radical departure from historic company practices.
Medium	Program appears complex. Skilled manpower not available in company but is available outside. EDP programming is difficult. Hardware not available in company but is on the market.	Implementing program requires moderate efforts to effect a change in line management attitudes and styles, and in organization policies, structure, and operating environment. Implementing program implies some departure from historic company practices.
Low	Program involves new or unfamiliar effort. Personnel not available on staff or outside company. EDP programming is very complex. Hardware not available.	Implementing program requires substantial efforts to effect a change in line management attitudes and styles, and in organization policies, structure, and operating. environment. Implementing program implies a radical departure from historic company practices.

Note: Standards for evaluation of the net economic benefits and the economic risks have not been included in this exhibit since they are not generally applicable to other companies.

Finally, as with the state-of-the-art evaluation, consistent standards must be applied when evaluating programs for ease of implementation. These standards are shown in Part B of *Exhibit II*; again, I feel they are generally applicable to most business enterprises.

Net Economic Benefits: At this stage of the evaluation, we use cost/ benefit analysis, with modifications that are appropriate to the unique needs of manpower management, to determine whether a program will be cost-effective.

For the program shown in *Exhibit I*, our job enrichment specialist, assisted by the personnel program manager, identified potential benefits and costs, estimated the probable occurrence of each benefit and cost, and calculated the probable dollar impact. In this case we were fortunate. The pilot project mentioned earlier gave us quantitative data regarding job enrichment's effect on turnover, absenteeism, and productivity.

For many other programs, however, it is particularly difficult to estimate potential benefits and to establish a direct linkage between them and the programs. To overcome this problem, we estimate benefits by one of these two approaches:

1. *Identifiable benefits.* These are used whenever possible. They must be tangible and clearly attributable to implementing the program. An example of an identifiable benefit is the direct savings achieved by eliminating redundant functions in a proposed reorganization.

In other cases, we contrast the cost (for value) of the existing approach with that of the proposed approach. For example, one of our employment managers felt he could achieve a significant savings by relying less on outside employment agencies. His identifiable benefit was developed using the present cost of fees paid to these agencies. The projected costs of additional staff and advertising were subtracted from this present cost to develop a net economic benefit for his proposal.

Finally, if a pilot test has been conducted on a small group of employees with favorable results, a plausible benefits estimate can be developed by projecting the savings identified in the pilot test to the entire organization.

2. *Target benefits.* These are used in the absence of identifiable benefits. In essence, they are derived from a preliminary estimate of results to which the personnel manager is willing to commit himself, if he is given the resources to do a pilot test of his proposal. An example of a target benefit is a 1% increase in revenue or a one point decline in turnover projected for a given program.

In some cases, the personnel manager develops such estimates for each of his programs with assistance from the program manager, the controller's staff, or the long-range planning staff. In other cases, our staff managers are able to make sound cases for target benefits by consulting their colleagues in other companies or by reviewing the professional literature.

If, for some reason, management should challenge the estimated target benefit as being overly ambitious, it is critical that management should not become lost in quibbling over decimal accuracy. One must remember that this procedure is as much an exercise in allocating resources toward projects that are most likely to yield the greatest relative benefits as it is a means of committing oneself to results.

The benefits detailed for the job enrichment program in *Exhibit I* are identifiable benefits. They are based on the pilot project, and assume that the results of that effort can be extended to other locations.

Intangible benefits and risks are also described at this stage of the feasibility evaluation. While some of these items may appear to be platitudes, specifying them is nevertheless useful. When a choice must be made between two programs of almost equal merit, the intangibles—if properly framed—may become key factors that swing the decision.

Economic Risks: In the final stage of the feasibility evaluation, we consider the economic impact of not implementing the proposal. For example, a failure to continually reevaluate the company's pre-employment selection standards could result in the hiring of more marginal employees. (The costs of subsequent declines in productivity could be estimated.) Or a failure to increase productivity could result in unacceptable costs. (This approach was used to assess the job enrichment program.)

Our standards for classifying economic risks, ranging from over $1,000,000 for "high" to under $100,000 for "low," are unique to our company. Other companies may have higher or lower standards, depending on their size or industry. Banks and insurance companies, for example, would probably have substantially higher risk standards than oil or chemical companies have. (The revenues of the former are highly sensitive to payroll costs.) Similarly, sevice organizations, such as airlines, are more vulnerable to strike losses than are hard goods enterprises. (The latter can hedge such risks with inventory.)

4. Allocate and Deploy Resources

After each program has been evaluated on its own merits, its overall feasibility must be determined. The decision table shown in *Exhibit III* serves as a convenient tool to accomplish this. It allows each program to be categorized into one of the following overall feasibility categories: (a) very desirable, (b) moderately desirable, (c) marginally desirable, or (d) not worthwhile.

Note that the table is structured so that a high rating on any factor will not conclusively decide in favor of the program, but a low rating on any factor could eliminate the program from consideration. For example, *Exhibit III* shows that while the job enrichment proposal was rated "high" on three of the four individual feasibility characteristics, the single "low" rating (for ease of implementation) resulted in an overall feasibility assessment of only moderately desirable.

When all programs have been classified in the foregoing manner, they are ranked on the Program Priorities Schedule shown in *Exhibit IV*. The legally required programs appear at the top of the schedule. All other programs are ranked, within the appropriate overall feasibility category, according to their economic benefits. (Note that the job

Exhibit III. Decision Table for Determining Program Feasibility

Step 1. Evaluate feasibility and economic benefits/risks. Using predefined standards, separately evaluate each program's state-of-the-art implications, ease of implementation, net economic benefits, and economic risks of not acting. The Service Force Job Enrichment Program was evaluated (see Exhibit I) as follows:

State of the art	— High
Ease of implementation	— Low
Net economic benefits	— High
Economic risks	— High

Step 2. Compare technical (state-of-the-art) with operational (ease-of-implementation) feasibility.

1. The "high" state-of-the-art evaluation...is matched against "low" ease of implementation.

State of the art	Ease of implementation		
	HIGH	MEDIUM	LOW
HIGH	Very desirable	Very desirable	Marginally desirable
MEDIUM	Very desirable	Moderately desirable	Marginally desirable
LOW	Marginally desirable	Marginally desirable	Not worthwhile

Step 3. Compare Step 2 evaluation with net economic benefits.

2. Results of this evaluation are compared to "high" net economic benefits

Step 2 evaluation	Net economic benefits		
	HIGH	MEDIUM	LOW
Very desirable	Very desirable	Moderately desirable	Marginally desirable
Moderately desirable	Very desirable	Moderately desirable	Marginally desirable
Marginally desirable	Marginally desirable	Marginally desirable	Not worthwhile

Step 4. Compare Step 3 evaluation with economic risks to determine overall feasibility.

3. Results of this evaluation are matched against "high" risks....

Step 3 evaluation	Economic risks		
	HIGH	MEDIUM	LOW
Very desirable	Very desirable	Moderately desirable	Moderately desirable

Exhibit III (Continued)

	Moderately desirable	Moderately desirable	Moderately desirable	Marginally desirable
4. ...to determine overall feasibility category of "moderately desirable."	Marginally desirable	Moderately desirable	Marginally desirable	Not worthwhile

enrichment program is ranked third after the legally required programs.) Those programs evaluated as "not worthwhile" appear at the bottom of the schedule—for elimination. And, if management limits the budget or mandates an austerity program, other programs can be cut, starting with those of lowest priority.

The Program Priorities Schedule has become our basic tool for allocating and deploying staff resources. But to use it effectively, management must undertake these actions:

Trim Marginal Programs.   This is often difficult for management to do since it may involve cutting some sacred cows (e.g., the executive jet or weekend retreats). But the fact remains that eliminating marginal programs is one key way of achieving the primary objective of business—profitable operations.

Allocate and Deploy Staff Resources Toward the Most Worthwhile Projects.   Timely program implementation requires that staff resources be deployed only toward the higher-ranked projects. For some programs, staff members might be transferred from areas that have been trimmed; for other programs, particularly in highly technical areas, new people might have to be hired. Furthermore, additional resources might be allocated to worthwhile projects in order to speed up their implementation date. In our job enrichment program, for example, we were able to identify some highly favorable benefits. But with only one man assigned to the program, achieving them would have taken four years. Because of the ranking of this project and its potential payoff, we were able to justify additional resources to ensure earlier results.

Evaluate All New Program Proposals and Reorder Priorities as Necessary.   To be successful, the evaluation procedure must be viewed as dynamic and ongoing. As new proposals are developed, they must be evaluated and ranked, then accepted or rejected by the same standards applied to all other efforts. Thus priorities may be changed, and staff resources may be redeployed, as circumstances warrant.

Reevaluate Existing Programs. Programs priorities must be changed not only to accommodate new programs but also to reflect alterations of existing programs. For example, the appointment of a new key executive in an operating department may alter the ease-of-implementation evaluation of a particular program. Similarly, the personnel staff may achieve a key breakthrough that raises the state-of-the-art evaluation. In short, any of a number of events could trigger a chain reaction of reordered priorities by altering the feasibility evaluation on one aspect of a given program.

Monitor Progress.   The execution of each program must be carefully monitored to identify bottlenecks as they develop, chart alternatives where necessary, and ensure timely implementation and achievement of planned benefits. This task should be the permanent and ongoing responsibility of a personnel program manager or a manpower planning manager.

CONCLUSION

The framework for evaluation and ranking personnel programs has enabled us to allocate resources to those programs that should significantly improve productivity and profit performance. (A brief review of the benefits column in *Exhibit IV* underscores the magnitude of this improvement potential.) One of the key advantages of this framework is the discipline it instills in the personnel staff. It encourages staff members to rigorously assess their programs' benefits and to evaluate the likelihood of achieving them. The procedure is by no means perfect, but I doubt that an optimal approach will ever be developed-particularly for staff projects. However, it does provide personnel management with a simple and systematic way to allocate resources in an area where good intentions, hunches, and poor information have cost many companies heavily in lost opportunities.

Quite conceivably, the same concepts may be applied to other functional areas in future years. But whether or not that happens, I believe the approach I have described can be implemented now in the personnel operations of many organizations, particularly the larger ones. This approach would permit organizations to move away from "gut-feel" techniques and the intrigue and politics too often characteristic of budgeting and resource-allocation decisions. In a more positive vein, it can guide management to the gains in profit and productivity that come from personnel programs targeted on results.

Exhibit IV. Program Priorities Schedule

ACTION PROGRAM	Priority	Timing (1972–1977)	Net annual dollar benefit	Cost/benefit ratio (1:n)
LEGALLY REQUIRED PROGRAMS				
Labor Relations Strategy	x		($619)	n/a
Protect Right to Select Employees	x		($86)	n/a
Continue Validation of Selection Tests	x		$35,000	78.17
Redesign Personnel Data System	x		$273	1.78
Develop Part-Time Female Employment Approaches	x		$227	4.16
VERY DESIRABLE PROGRAMS				
Restructuring Service Force	1		$14,608	9.6
Service College Coop Program	2		$4,490	2.74
MODERATELY DESIRABLE PROGRAMS				
Service Job Enrichment	3		$9,920	24.3
Assessment Center	4		$4,946	15.40
Education & Training Center	5		$4,780	3.57
Clerical Selection Program	6		$1,799	19.94

Annotations:

1. Legally required efforts come first.
2. ...then other programs are ranked by overall feasibility category.
3. ...and within feasibility category by net benefits
4. Priorities are indicated here.

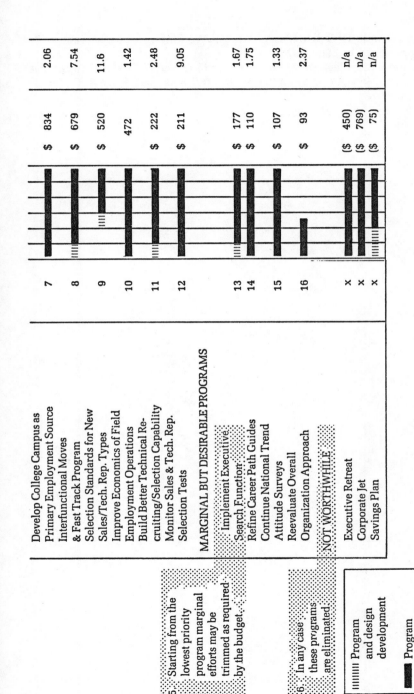

#	Program	Bar	$	Ratio
7	Develop College Campus as Primary Employment Source		$ 834	2.06
8	Interfunctional Moves & Fast Track Program		$ 679	7.54
9	Selection Standards for New Sales/Tech. Rep. Types		$ 520	11.6
10	Improve Economics of Field Employment Operations		472	1.42
11	Build Better Technical Recruiting/Selection Capability		$ 222	2.48
12	Monitor Sales & Tech. Rep. Selection Tests		$ 211	9.05

MARGINAL BUT DESIRABLE PROGRAMS

#	Program	Bar	$	Ratio
13	Implement Executive Search Function		$ 177	1.67
14	Refine Career Path Guides		$ 110	1.75
15	Continue National Trend Attitude Surveys		$ 107	1.33
16	Reevaluate Overall Organization Approach		$ 93	2.37

NOT WORTHWHILE

#	Program	Bar	$	Ratio
X	Executive Retreat		($ 450)	n/a
X	Corporate Jet		($ 769)	n/a
X	Savings Plan		($ 75)	n/a

5. Starting from the lowest priority program marginal efforts may be trimmed as required by the budget.

6. In any case these programs are eliminated.

||||||| Program and design development

■ Program Implementation

NOTES

1.See, for example, George R. Glaser, "Are You Working on the Right Problem?" *Datamation*, June 1967, p. 22.
2. For a more complete discussion of this subject, see Willard A. Lewis, "The Personnel Manager as Compliance Officer," *Personnel Journal*, December 1971, p. 907.

PART III

THE FUTURE OF HUMAN RESOURCE STRATEGIC PLANNING

A readings book which focuses on human resource strategic planning should obviously take into consideration the emergent trends that are redirecting thinking in this volatile area. Planning for the use of human resources has assumed eclectic dimensions over the past few decades. The observed trends in planning have evidenced as much variety as the types of private and public sector organizations that have attempted them.

It would appear that a trend of utmost significance in human resource planning is the growing recognition of it as a substantive effort in organizations from all sectors of the American economy. Such recognition has taken the form of a dollars-and-cents focus, inasmuch as personnel resources are assuming an ever-greater proportion of budgetary allocations.

In addition, studies have demonstrated that there are substantial costs associated with inadequate management, shortsighted personnel policies, and lack of planning and coordination that often result in excessive staffing. This realization is leading to more intensive scrutiny into ways and means of improving managerial styles, human resource utilization, and personnel career development.

These eclectic approaches to human resource planning generally assume a posture of "the past is prologue." It is virtually impossible for an organization to know where its human resources should go, can go, and ought to go unless the organization has a clear view of where it has been in the past. Using past data to attempt extrapolation into the future can be highly quantitative in focus or anecdotal in approach.

Whichever discrete approach is chosen by human resource planners in organizations—private or public, large or small—the fact exists that no longer can human resources be subordinated to an inconsequential element in the overall strategic planning equation. Explicit and implicit personnel costs in proportion to overall resource allocations have become significant in the attempts to achieve organizational goals effectively.

Organizational planners who ignore long-range, intermediate-range, and short-range human resource planning efforts do so at their own peril. It would appear that the more effective organizations capable of achieving their preestablished, predetermined goals are those that can measure in clear and irrefutable terms the degree to which their overall objectives have been attained. Evaluation of the effects of human resource planning is a substantive element in measuring these objectives.

Chapter Eight, the final chapter of this readings book, looks at the various trends seen to be emerging in human resource planning. It is evident that the only consistent thread that links these trends together is the growing awareness of the necessity to incorporate human resource planning into overall organizational strategic planning and environmental surveillance efforts.

CHAPTER 8
EMERGENT TRENDS IN HUMAN RESOURCE STRATEGIC PLANNING

Investing to Upgrade the Labor Force
Herbert E. Striner

This nation's dismal unemployment rate is inexcusable, politically and economically. While successive U.S. Administrations wring their hands over the problem, another major industrial country has rolled up its sleeves and dealt with it. Over the last decade, West Germany has outperformed us on employment, productivity, and inflation control, and we steadfastly refuse to learn the lesson. The West Germans, like most of the West European countries, view their work force as a form of "capital." They assume that this capital must be trained and retrained on a continuing basis to supply the changing spectrum of sophisticated skills needed by a high-technology nation. To do so requires a labor force "investment policy."

Beginning in 1964, West Germany has provided, *as a right* to every adult, whether employed or unemployed, up to two years of full-time training or retraining. All training costs plus an income subsidy, which can be as high as 90% of the last wage, are covered. The income subsidy varies inversely with the last wage. Thus, a low-wage employee loses little income in upgrading his or her skills and increasing productivity. A higher-paid worker will lose proportionately in income, thus guaranteeing there are no frivolous decisions to leave a job. The psychology works. Most people want to make more money rather than less. If they are given help to achieve this goal, they will do so. Those needing the most help, but with the most to gain, are the low-paid workers. Hence, they are subsidized the most. But the economy gains the most by their becoming higher-skilled workers. Moving allowances and short-term rental allowances to encourage moving where the good jobs are located are all included.

Herbert E. Striner is Dean of the College of Business Administration at The American University, Washington, D.C.

Because of the success of the West German approach, the French passed similar legislation in 1971, and the British followed in 1975. But even before the German legislation of 1963, the Danes and Swedes had already proven the efficacy of the "investment" approach.

Resisting an Effective Idea.   Meanwhile, the U.S. has continued to nibble around the edges of the unemployment problem, seeing it as a sort of disguised welfare problem involving people who should be urged to use their bootstraps with minimal help from unemployment payments. We view workers as an asset as long as they are employed. They become a liability when unemployed, and we are reluctant to spend too much money on them, hoping instead that the economy will improve or they will somehow find some sort of job.

We have had some training programs, of course, but our expenditures have been slight when compared with the relative efforts of West German, French, and since 1975, British programs. We have not, since the GI bill following World War II, provided both an adequate income supplement and a long enough period of training to do the job of maintaining a work force capable of supplying our advanced industrial and service sector needs. No U.S. Administration has really considered the European experience. Our key policymakers are most often "educated" by economic advisers about the inevitability of the Phillips curve and its trade-off between low unemployment rates and higher inflation. But these economic advisers seldom make the point that each country has a different Phillips curve, with ours being one of the worst.

The Wrong Emphasis.   We continue to spend money during the hot summers to cool off human tinder. We spend money for public service jobs that can be done by functional illiterates or by workers who can read and write but have too few skills for the better jobs that are vacant in both the public and the private sectors. We urge businessmen to design jobs for low-skilled workers. What a travesty! We perpetuate economic fraud in these efforts. In November, 1977, when the U.S. unemployment rate was about 7%, the Conference Board's index of help-wanted advertising reached an all-time peak. The jobs are there, but the trained people are not.

Until we adopt an investment approach to our labor force and spend funds that are really adequate for a continuing upgrading of this key resource, our unemployment rate will remain above acceptable levels. Our $2,000 billion economy probably needs an ongoing training program that covers about 2% of our work force each year.

Even when European unemployment rates are adjusted for U.S. data collection methods, the West German rate is around 4%, and the French is around 5%. Scandinavian rates are, of course, well below 3%.

Such a program should be modeled on the German system, which in turn follows the pattern set by our own GI program. It would provide payments and counseling to unskilled workers, but it would let them decide what sort of training they wanted and where they would get it. Private schools, public schools, and on-the-job training programs could then compete on the basis of efficiency.

It will cost a great deal more than we are accustomed to spending for education and training to deal adequately with the problem of an effective work force. But, as every successful businessman knows, you have to spend money to make money. Many of the industrial countries in Western Europe have learned that lesson with respect to their work forces, and their high economic performance has shown it. We have refused to learn from what they have done, especially the West Germans, and our low economic performance has shown it.

Increasing Organizational Effectiveness through Better Human Resource Planning and Development
Edgar H. Schein

INTRODUCTION

In this article I would like to address two basic questions. *First,* why is human resource planning and development becoming increasingly important as a determinant of organizational effectiveness? *Second,* what are the major *components* of a human resource planning and career development system, and how should these components be *linked* for maximum organizational effectiveness?

The field of personnel management has for some time addressed issues such as these and much of the technology of planning for and managing human resources have been worked out to a considerable degree.[1] Nevertheless there continues to be in organizations a failure, particularly on the part of line managers and functional managers in areas other than personnel, to recognize the true importance of planning for and managing human resources. This paper is not intended to be a review of what is known but rather a kind of position paper for line

---

Reprinted by permission from *Sloan Management Review*, Fall, 1977, pp.1-20.

Edgar H. Schein is Professor of Organizational Psychology and Management, Sloan School of Management, Massachusetts Institute of Technology.

managers to bring to their attention some important and all too often neglected issues. These issues are important for organizational *effectiveness*, quite apart from their relevance to the issue of humanizing work or improving the quality of working life.[2]

The observations and analyses made below are based on several kinds of information:

- Formal research on management development, career development, and human development through the adult life cycle conducted in the Sloan School and at other places for the past several decades;[3]
- Analysis of consulting relationships, field observations, and other involvements over the past several decades with all kinds of organizations dealing with the planning for and implementation of human resource development programs and organization development projects.[4]

WHY IS HUMAN RESOURCE PLANNING AND DEVELOPMENT (HRPD) INCREASINGLY IMPORTANT?

The Changing Managerial Job

The first answer to the question is simple, though paradoxical. Organizations are becoming more dependent upon people because they are increasingly involved in more complex technologies and are attempting to function in more complex economic, political, and sociocultural environments. The more different technical skills there are involved in the design, manufacture, marketing, and sales of a product, the more vulnerable the organization will be to critical shortages of the right kinds of human resources. The more complex the process, the higher the interdependence among the various specialists. The higher the interdependence, the greater the need for effective integration of all the specialities because the entire process is only as strong as its weakest link.

In simpler technologies, managers could often compensate for the technical or communication failures of their subordinates. General managers today are much more dependent upon their technically trained subordinates because they usually do not understand the details of the engineering, marketing, financial, and other decisions which their subordinates are making. Even the general manager who grew up in finance may find that since his day the field of finance has outrun him and his subordinates are using models and methods which he cannot entirely understand.

What all this means for the general manager is that he cannot any longer safely make decisions by himself; he cannot get enough information digested within his own head to be the integrator and decision maker. Instead, he finds himself increasingly having to manage the process of decision making, bringing the right people together around the right questions or problems, stimulating open discussion, insuring that all relevant information surfaces and is critically assessed, managing the emotional ups and downs of his prima donnas, and insuring that out of all this human and interpersonal process, a good decision will result.

As I have watched processes like these in management groups, I am struck by the fact that *the decision emerges out of the interplay*. It is hard to pin down who had the idea and who made the decision. The general manager in this setting is *accountable* for the decision, but rarely would I describe the process as one where he or she actually makes the decision, except in the sense of recognizing when the right answer has been achieved, ratifying that answer, announcing it, and following up on its implementation.

If the managerial *job* is increasingly moving in the direction I have indicated, managers of the future will have to be much more skilled in how to:

1. Select and train their subordinates,
2. Design and run meetings and groups of all sorts,
3. Deal with all kinds of conflict between strong individuals and groups,
4. Influence and negotiate from a low power base, and
5. Integrate the efforts of very diverse technical specialists.

If the above image of what is happening to organizations has any generality, it will force the field of human resource management increasingly to center stage. The more complex organizations become, the more they will be vulnerable to human error. They will not necessarily employ more people, but they will employ more sophisticated highly trained people both in managerial and in individual contributor, staff roles. The price of low motivation, turnover, poor productivity, sabotage, and intraorganizational conflict will be higher in such an organization. Therefore it will become a matter of *economic necessity* to improve human resource planning and development systems.

Changing Social Values
A second reason why human resource planning and development will become more central and important is that changing social values regarding the role of work will make it *more complicated to manage people*. There are several kinds of research findings and observations which illustrate this point.

First, my own longitudinal research of a panel of Sloan School graduates of the 1960s strongly suggests that we have put much too much emphasis on the traditional success syndrome of "climbing the corporate ladder."[5] Some alumni indeed want to rise to high-level general manager positions, but many others want to exercise their particular technical or functional competence and only rise to levels of functional management or senior staff roles with minimal managerial responsibility. Some want security, others are seeking nonorganizational careers as teachers or consultants, while a few are becoming entrepreneurs. I have called these patterns of motivation, talent, and values "career anchors" and believe that they serve to stabilize and constrain the career in predictable ways. The implication is obvious—organizations must develop multiple ladders and multiple reward systems to deal with different types of people.[6]

Second, studies of young people entering organizations in the last several decades suggest that work and career are not as central a life preoccupation as was once the case. Perhaps because of a prolonged period of economic affluence, people see more options for themselves and are increasingly exercising those options. In particular, one sees more concern with a balanced life in which work, family, and self-development play a more equal role.[7]

Third, closely linked to the above trend is the increase in the number of women in organizations, which will have its major impact through the increase of dual career families. As opportunities for women open up, we will see more new life-styles in young couples which will affect the organization's options as to moving people geographically, joint employment, joint career management, family support, etc.[8]

Fourth, research evidence is beginning to accumulate that personal growth and development is a life-long process and that predictable issues and crises come up in every decade of our lives. Organizations will have to be much more aware of what these issues are, how work and family interact, and how to manage people at different ages. The current "hot button" is *mid-career crisis*, but the more research we do the more we find developmental crises at *all* ages and stages.[9]

An excellent summary of what is happening in the world of values, technology, and management is provided in a recent text by Elmer Burack:

> The leading edge of change in the future will include the new technologies of information, production, and management, interlaced with considerable social dislocation and shifts in manpower inputs. These developments are without precedent in our industrial history.
>
> Technological and social changes have created a need for more education, training, and skill at all managerial and support levels. The lowering of

barriers of employment based on sex and race introduces new kinds of manpower problems for management officials. Seniority is coming to mean relatively less in relation to the comprehension of problems, processes, and approaches. The newer manpower elements and work technologies have shifted institutional arrangements: the locus of decision making is altered, role relationships among workers and supervisers are changed (often becoming more collegial), and the need to respond to changing routines has become commonplace ....

These shifts have been supported by more demanding customer requirements, increasing government surveillance (from product quality to anti-pollution measures), and more widespread use of computers, shifting power bases to the holders of specialized knowledge skills.[10]

In order for HRPD systems to become more responsive and capable of handling such growing complexity 'they must contain all the necessary components, must be based on correct assumptions, and must be adequately integrated.

COMPONENTS OF A HUMAN RESOURCE PLANNING AND DEVELOPMENT SYSTEM

The major problem with existing HRPD systems is that they are fragmented, incomplete, and sometimes built on faulty assumptions about human or organizational growth.

Human growth takes place through successive encounters with one's environment. As the person encounters a new situation, he or she is forced to try new responses to deal with that situation. Learning takes place as a function of how those responses work out and the results they achieve. If they are successful in coping with the situation, the person enlarges his repertory of responses; if they are not successful the person must try alternate responses until the situation has been dealt with. If none of the active coping responses work, the person sometimes falls back on retreating from the new situation, or denying that there is a problem to be solved. These responses are defensive and growth limiting.

The implication is that for growth to occur, people basically need two things: *new challenges* that are within the range of their coping responses, and *knowledge of results*, information on how their responses to the challenge have worked out. If the tasks and challenges are too easy or too hard, the person will be demotivated and cease to grow. If the information is not available on how well the person's responses are working, the person cannot grow in a systematic, valid direction but is forced into guessing or trying to infer information from ambiguous signals.

Organizational growth similarly takes place through successful coping with the internal and external environment.[11] But since the organization is a complex system of human, material, financial, and informational resources, one must consider how each of those areas can be properly managed toward organizational effectiveness. In this article I will only deal with the human resources.

In order for the organization to have the capacity to perform effectively over a period of time it must be able to plan for, recruit, manage, develop, measure, dispose of, and replace human resources as warranted by the tasks to be done. The most important of these functions is the *planning* function, since task requirements are likely to change as the complexity and turbulence of the organization's environment increase. In other words, a key assumption underlying organizational growth is that the nature of jobs will change over time, which means that such changes must be continuously monitored in order to insure that the right kinds of human resources can be recruited or developed to do those jobs. Many of the activities such as recruitment, selection, performance appraisal, and so on presume that some planning process has occurred which makes it possible to assess whether or not those activities are meeting *organizational needs,* quite apart from whether they are facilitating the individual's growth.

In an ideal HRPD system one would seek to match the organization's needs for human resources with the individual's needs for personal career growth and development. One can then depict the basic system as involving both individual and organizational planning, and a series of matching activities which are designed to facilitate mutual need satisfaction. If we further assume that both individual and organizational needs change over time, we can depict this process as a developmental one as in Figure 1.

In the right-hand column we show the basic stages of the individual career through the life cycle. While not everyone will go through these stages in the manner depicted, there is growing evidence that for organizational careers in particular, these stages reasonably depict the movement of people through their adult lives.[12]

Given those developmental assumptions, the left-hand side of the diagram shows the organizational planning activities which must occur if human resources are to be managed in an optimal way, and if changing job requirements are to be properly assessed and continuously monitored. The middle column shows the various matching activities which have to occur at various career stages.

The components of an effective HRPD system now can be derived from the diagram. *First,* there have to be in the organization the overall planning components shown on the left-hand side of Figure 1. *Second,* there have to be components which insure an adequate process of staffing the organization. *Third*, there have to be components which plan for and monitor growth and development. *Fourth*, there have to be components which facilitate the actual process of the growth and development of the people who are brought into the organization; this growth and development must be organized to meet *both* the needs of the organization and the needs of the individuals within it. *Fifth*, there have to be components which deal with decreasing effectiveness, leveling off, obsolescence of skills, turnover, retirement, and other phenomena which reflect the need for either a new growth direction or a process of disengagement of the person from his or her job. *Finally*, there have to be components which insure that as some people move out of jobs, others are available to fill those jobs, and as new jobs arise that people are available with the requisite skills to fill them.

In the remainder of this article I would like to comment on each of these six sets of components and indicate where and how they should be linked to each other.

Overall Planning Components

The function of these components is to insure that the organization has an adequate basis for selecting its human resources and developing them toward the fulfillment of organizational goals.

Strategic Business Planning. These activities are designed to determine the organization's goals, priorities, future directions, products, markets growth rate, geographical location, and organization structure or design. This process should lead logically into the next two planning activities but is often disconnected from them because it is located in a different part of the organization or is staffed by people with different orientations and backgrounds.

Job/Role Planning. These activities are designed to determine what actually needs to be done at every level of the organization (up through top management) to fulfill the organization's goals and tasks. This activity can be thought of as a dynamic kind of job analysis where a continual review is made of the skills, knowledge, values, etc. which are presently needed in the organization *and will be needed in the future.* The focus is on the predictable consequences of the strategic planning for managerial roles, specialist roles, and skill mixes which may be needed to get the mission accomplished. If the organization already has a satisfactory system of job descriptions, this activity would concern itself with how those jobs will evolve and change, and what new jobs or roles will evolve in the future.[13]

This component is often missing completely in organizations or is carried out only for lower level jobs. From a planning point of view it is

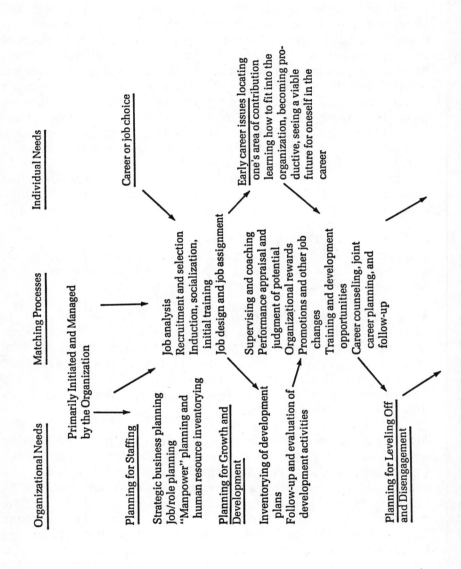

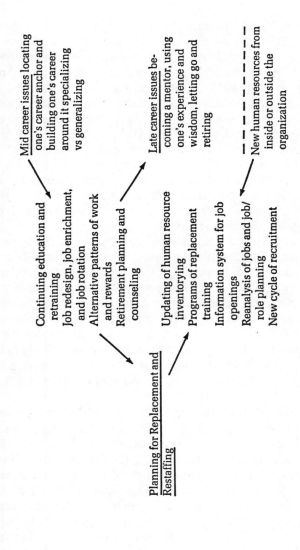

Figure 1. A Developmental Model of Human Resource Planning and Development

probably most important for the highest level jobs—how the nature of general and functional management will change as the organization faces new technologies, new social values, and new environmental conditions.

"Manpower Planning" and Human Resource Inventorying. These activities draw on the job/role descriptions generated in job/role planning and assess the capabilities of the present human resources against those plans or requirements. These activities may be focused on the numbers of people in given categories and are often designed to insure that under given assumptions of growth there will be an adequate supply of people in those categories. Or the process may focus more on how to insure that certain scarce skills which will be needed will in fact be available, leading to more sophisticated programs of recruitment or human resource development. For example, the inventorying process at high levels may reveal the need for a new type of general manager with broad integrative capacities which may further reveal the need to start a development program that will insure that such managers will be available five to ten years down the road.

These first three component activities are all geared to identifying the *organization's* needs in the human resource area. They are difficult to do and tools are only now beginning to be developed for job/role planning.[14] In most organizations I have dealt with, the three areas, if they exist at all, are not linked to each other organizationally. Strategic planning is likely to exist in the Office of the President. Job/role planning is likely to be an offshoot of some management development activities in Personnel. And human resource inventorying is likely to be a specialized subsection within Personnel. Typically, no one is accountable for bringing these activities together even on an ad hoc basis.

This situation reflects an erroneous assumption about growth and development which I want to mention at this time. The assumption is that if the organization develops its *present* human resources, it will be able to fill whatever job demands may arise in the future. Thus we do find in organizations elaborate human resource planning systems, but they plan for the present people in the organization, not for the organization per se. If there are no major changes in job requirements as the organization grows and develops, this system will work. But if jobs themselves change, it is no longer safe to assume that today's human resources, with development plans based on *today's* job requirements, will produce the people needed in some future situation. Therefore, I am asserting that more job/role planning must be done, independent of the present people in the organization.

The subsequent components to be discussed which focus on the matching of individual and organizational needs all assume that some sort of basic planning activities such as those described have been carried out. They may not be very formal, or they may be highly decentralized (e.g. every supervisor who has an open slot might make his own decision of what sort of person to hire based on his private assumptions about strategic business planning and job/role planning). Obviously, the more turbulent the environment, the greater the vulnerability of the organization if it does not centralize and coordinate its various planning activities, and generate its HRPD system from those plans.

Staffing Processes
The function of these processes is to insure that the organization acquires the human resources necessary to fulfill its goals.

Job Analysis.   If the organizational planning has been done adequately, the next component of the HRPD system is to actually specify what jobs need to be filled and what skills, etc. are needed to do those jobs. Some organizations go through this process very formally, others do it in an informal unprogrammed manner, but in some form it must occur in order to specify what kind of recruitment to do and how to select people from among the recruits.

Recruitment and Selection.   This activity involves the actual process of going out to find people to fulfill jobs and developing systems for deciding which of those people to hire. These components may be very formal including testing, assessment, and other aids to the selection process. If this component is seen as part of a total HRPD system, it will alert management to the fact that the recruitment selection system communicates to future employees something about the nature of the organization and its approach to people. All too often this component sends incorrect messages or turns off future employees or builds incorrect stereotypes which make subsequent supervision more difficult.[15]

Induction, Socialization, and Initial Training.   Once the employee has been hired, there ensues a period during which he or she learns the ropes, learns how to get along in the organization, how to work, how to fit in, how to master the particulars of the job, and so on. Once again, it is of a total process with long-range consequences for the attitudes of the employee.[16] The goal of these processes should be to facilitate the employees becoming productive and useful members of the organization both in the short run and in terms of long-range potential.

Job Design and Job Assignment.   One of the most crucial components of staffing is the actual design of the job which is given to the new employee and the manner in which the assignment is actually made. The issue is how to provide *optimal challenge,* a set of activities which will be neither too hard nor too easy for the new employee, and which will be neither too meaningless nor too risky from the point of view of the organization. If the job is too easy or too meaningless, the employee may become demotivated; if the job is too hard and/or involves too much responsibility and risk from the point of view of the organization, the employee will become too anxious, frustrated, or angry to perform at an optimal level. Some organizations have set up training programs for supervisors to help them to design optimally challenging work assignments.[17]

These four components are geared to insuring that the work of the organization will be performed. They tend to be processes that have to be performed by line managers and personnel staff specialists together. Line managers have the basic information about jobs and skill requirements; personnel specialists have the interviewing, recruiting, and assessment skills to aid in the selection process. In an optimal system these functions will be closely coordinated, particularly to insure that the recruiting process provides to the employee accurate information about the nature of the organization and the actual work that he or she will be doing in it. Recruiters also need good information on the long-range human resource plans so that these can be taken into account in the selection of new employees.

Development Planning

It is not enough to get good human resources in the door. Some planning activities have to concern themselves with how employees who may be spending thirty to forty years of their total life in a given organization will make a contribution for all of that time, will remain motivated and productive, and will maintain a reasonable level of job satisfaction.

Inventorying of Development Plans.   Whether or not the process is highly formalized, there is in most organizations some effort to plan for the growth and development of all employees. The planning component that is often missing is some kind of pulling together of this information into a centralized inventory that permits coordination and evaluation of the development activities. Individual supervisors may have clear ideas of what they will do with and for their subordinates, but this information may never be collected, making it impossible to determine whether the individual plans of supervisors are connected in any way. Whether it is done by department, division, or total company, some effort to collect such information and to think through its implications would be of great value to furthering the total development of employees at all levels.

Follow-up and Evaluation of Development Activities. I have observed two symptoms of insufficient planning in this area—one, development plans are made for individual employees, are written down but are never implemented, and two, if they are implemented they are never evaluated either in relation to the individual's own needs for growth or in relation to the organization's needs for new skills. Some system should exist to insure that plans are implemented and that activities are evaluated against both individual and organizational goals.

Career Development Processes

This label is deliberately broad to cover all of the major processes of managing human resources during their period of growth and peak productivity, a period which may be several decades in length. These processes must match the organization's needs for work with the individual's needs for a productive and satisfying work career. The system must provide for some kind of forward movement for the employee through some succession of jobs, whether these involve promotion, lateral movement to new functions, or simply new assignments within a given area.[18] The system must be based both on the organization's need to fill jobs as they open up and on employees' needs to have some sense of progress in their working lives.

Supervision and Coaching. By far the most important component in this area is the actual process of supervising, guiding, coaching, and monitoring. It is in this context that the work assignment and feedback processes which make learning possible occur, and it is the boss who plays the key role in molding the employee to the organization. There is considerable evidence that the first boss is especially crucial in giving new employees a good start in their careers,[19] and that training of supervisors in how to handle new employees is a valuable organizational investment.

Performance Appraisal and Judgment of Potential. This component is part of the general process of supervision but stands out as such an important part of that process that it must be treated separately. In most organizations there is some effort to standardize and formalize a process of appraisal above and beyond the normal performance feedback which is expected on a day-to-day basis. Such systems serve a number of functions—to justify salary increases, promotions, and other formal organizational actions with respect to the employee: to provide information for human resource inventories or at least written records of past accomplishments for the employee's personnel folder: and to provide a basis for annual or semiannual formal reviews between boss and subordinate to supplement day-to-day feedback and to facilitate information exchange for career planning and counseling. In some organizations so little day-to-day feedback occurs that the *formal* system bears the burden of providing the employees with knowledge of how they are doing and what they can look forward to. Since knowledge of results, of how one is doing, is a crucial component of any developmental process, it is important for organizations to monitor how well and how frequently feedback is actually given.

One of the major dilemmas in this area is whether to have a single system which provides both feedback for the growth and development of the employee and information for the organization's planning systems. The dilemma arises because the information which the planning system requires (e.g. "how much potential does this employee have to rise in the organization?", may be the kind of information which neither the boss nor the planner wants to share with the employee. The more potent and more accurate the information, the less likely it is to be fed back to the employee in anything other than very vague terms.

On the other hand, the detailed work-oriented, day-to-day feedback which the employee needs for growth and development may be too cumbersome to record as part of a selection-oriented appraisal system. If hundreds of employees are to be compared, there is strong pressure in the system toward more general kinds of judgments, traits, rankings, numerical estimates of ultimate potential, and the like. One way of resolving this dilemma which some companies have found successful is to develop two separate systems—one oriented toward performance improvement and the growth of the employee, and the other one oriented toward a more global assessment of the employee for future planning purposes involving judgments which may not be shared with the employee except in general terms.

A second dilemma arises around the identification of the employee's "development needs" and how that information is linked to other development activities. If the development needs are stated in relation to the planning system, the employee may never get the feedback of what his needs may have been perceived to be, and, worse, no one may implement any program to deal with those needs if the planning system is not well linked with line management.

Two further problems arise from this potential lack of linkage. One, if the individual does not get good feedback around developmental needs, he or she remains uninvolved in their own development and potentially becomes complacent. We pay lip service to the statement that only the individual can develop himself or herself, but then deprive the individual of the very information that would make sensible self-development possible. Two, the development needs as stated for the various employees in the organization may have nothing to do with the organization's needs for certain kinds of human resources in the future. All too often there is complete lack of linkage between the strategic or business planning function and the human resource development function resulting in potentially willy-nilly individual development based on today's needs and individual managers' stereotypes of what will be needed in the future.

Organizational Rewards—Pay, Benefits, Perquisites, Promotion and Recognition. Entire books have been written about all the problems and subtleties of how to link organizational rewards to the other components of a HRPD system to insure both short-run and long-run human effectiveness. For purposes of this short paper I wish to point out only one major issue—how to insure that organizational rewards are linked *both* to the needs of the organization for effective performance and development of potential. All too often the reward system is neither responsive to the individual employee nor to the organization, being driven more by criteria of elegance, consistency, and what other organizations are doing. If the linkage is to be established, line managers must actively work with compensation experts to develop a joint philosophy and set of goals based on an understanding of both what the organization is trying to reward and what employee needs actually are. As organizational careers become more varied and as social values surrounding work change, reward systems will probably have to become much more flexible both in time (people at different career stages may need different things) and by type of career (functional specialists may need different things than general managers).

Promotions and other Job Changes. There is ample evidence that what keeps human growth and effectiveness going is continuing optimal challenge.[20] Such challenge can be provided for some members of the organization through promotion to higher levels where more responsible jobs are available. For most members of the organization the promotion opportunities are limited, however, because the pyramid narrows at the top. An effective HRPD system will, therefore, concentrate on developing career paths, systems of job rotation. Changing assignments, temporary assignments, and other lateral job moves which insure continuing growth of all human resources

One of the key characteristics of an optimally challenging job is that it both draws on the person's abilities and skills and that it has opportunities for "closure." The employee must be in the job long enough to get involved and to see the results of his or her efforts. Systems of rotation which move the person too rapidly either prevent intitial involvement (as in the rotational training program), or prevent closure by transferring the person to a new job before the effects of his or her decisions can be assessed. I have heard many "fast track" executives complain that their self-confidence was low because they never really could see the results of their efforts. Too often we move poeple too fast in order to "fill slots" and thereby undermine their development.

Organizational planning systems which generate "slots" to be filled must be coordinated with development planning systems which concern themselves with the optimal growth of the human resources. Sometimes it is better for the organization in the long run not to fill an empty slot in order to keep the manager in another job where he or she is just beginning to develop. One way of insuring such linkage is to monitor these processes by means of a "development committee" which is composed of both line managers and personnel specialists. In such a group the needs of the organization and the needs of the people can be balanced against each other in the context of the long-range goals of the organization.

Training and Development Opportunities. Most organizations recognize that periods of formal training, sabbaticals, executive development programs outside of the company, and other educational activities are necessary in the total process of human growth and development. The important point about these activities is that they should be carefully linked both to the needs of the individual and to the needs of the organization. The individual should want to go to the program because he or she can see how the educational activity fits into the total career. The organization should send the person because the training fits into some concept of future career development. It should not be undertaken simply as a generalized "good thing," or because other companies are doing it. As much as possible the training and educational activities should be tied to job/role planning. For example, many companies began to use university executive development programs because of an explicit recognition that future managers would require a broader perspective on various problems and that such "broadening" could best be achieved in the university programs.

Career Counseling, Joint Career Planning, Follow-up, and Evaluation. Inasmuch as the growth and development which may be desired can only come from within the individual himself or herself, it is important that the organization provide some means for individual employees at all levels to become more proactive about their careers and some mechanisms for joint dialogue, counseling, and career planning.[21] This process should ideally be linked to performance appraisal, because it is in that context that the boss can review with the subordinate the future potential, development needs, strengths, weaknesses, career options, etc. The boss is often not trained in counseling but does possess some of the key information which the employee needs to initiate any kind of career planning. More formal counseling could then be supplied by the personnel development staff or outside the organization altogether.

The important point to recognize is that employees cannot manage their own growth development without information on how their own needs, talents, values, and plans mesh with the opportunity structure of the organization. Even though the organization may only have imperfect, uncertain information about the future, the individual is better off to know that than to make erroneous assumptions about the future based on no information at all. It is true that the organization cannot make commitments, nor should it unless required to by legislation or contract. But the sharing of information if properly done is not the same as making commitments or setting up false expectations.

If the organization can open up the communication channel between employees, their bosses, and whoever is managing the human resource system, the groundwork is laid for realistic individual development planning. Whatever is decided about training, next steps, special assignments, rotation, etc. should be jointly decided by the individual and the appropiate organizational resource (probably the supervisor and someone from personnel specializing in career development). Each step must fit into the employee's life plan and must be tied into *organizational needs*. The organization should be neither a humanistic charity nor an indoctrination center. Instead, it should be a vehicle for meeting both the needs of society and of individuals.

Whatever is decided should not merely be written down but executed. If there are implementation problems, the development plan should be renegotiated. Whatever developmental actions are taken, it is essential that they be followed up and evaluated both by the person and by the organization to determine what, if anything, was achieved. It is shocking to discover how many companies invest in major activities such as university executive development programs and never determine for themselves what was accomplished. In some instances, they make no plans to talk to the individual before or after the program so that it is not even possible to determine what the activity meant to the participant, or what might be an appropriate next assignment for him or her following the program.

I can summarize the above analysis best by emphasizing the two places where I feel there is the most fragmentation and violation of growth assumptions. First, too many of the activities occur without the involvement of the person who is "being developed" and therefore may well end up being self-defeating. This is particularly true of job assignments and performance appraisal where too little involvement and feedback occur. Second, too much of the human resource system functions as a personnel *selection* system unconnected to either the needs of the organization or the needs of the individual. All too often it is only a system for short-run replacement of people in standard type jobs. The key planning functions are not linked in solidly and hence do not influence the system to the degree they should.

Planning for the Managing Disengagment

The planning and management process which will be briefly reviewed here are counterparts of ones that have already been discussed but are focused on a different problem—the problem of the late career, loss of motivation, obsolescence, and ultimately retirement. Organizations must recognize that there are various options available to deal with this range of problems beyond the obvious ones of either terminating the employee or engaging in elaborate measures to "remotivate" people who may have lost work involvement.[22]

Continuing Education and Retraining. These activities have their greatest potential if the employee is motivated and if there is some clear connection between what is to be learned and what the employee's current or future job assignments require in the way of skills. More and more organizations are finding out that it is better to provide challenging work first and only then the training to perform that work once the employee sees the need for it. Obviously for this linkage to work well continuous dialogue is needed between employees and their managers. For those employees who have leveled off, have lost work involvement, but are still doing high quality work other solutions such as those described below are more applicable.

Job Redesign, Job Enrichment, and Job Rotation. This section is an extension of the arguments made earlier on job changes in general applied to the particular problems of leveled off employees. In some recent research, it has been suggested that job enrichment and other efforts to redesign work to increase motivation and performance may only work during the first few years on a job.[23] Beyond that the employee becomes "unresponsive" to the job characteristics themselves and pays more attention to surrounding factors such as the nature of supervision, relationships with co-workers, pay, and other extrinsic characteristics. In other words, before organizations attempt to "cure" leveled off employees by remotivating them through job redesign or rotation, they should examine whether those employees are still in a responsive mode or not. On the other hand, one can argue that there is nothing wrong with less motivated, less involved employees so long as the quality of what they are doing meets the organizational standards.[24]

Alternative Patterns of Work and Rewards.   Because of the changing needs and values of employees in recent decades, more and more organizations have begun to experiment with alternative work patterns such as flexible working hours, part-time work, sabbaticals or other longer periods of time off, several people filling one job, dual employment of spouses with more extensive childcare programs, etc. Along with these experiments have come others on flexible reward systems in which employees can choose between a raise, some time off, special retirement, medical, or insurance benefits, and other efforts to make multiple career ladders a viable reality. These programs apply to employees at all career stages but are especially relevant to people in mid and late career stages where their own perception of their career and life goals may be undergoing important changes.

None of those innovations should be attempted without first clearly establishing a HRPD system which takes care of the organization's needs as well as the needs of employees and links them to each other. There can be little growth and development for employees at any level in an *organization* which is sick and stagnant. It is in the best interests of both the individual and the organization to have a healthy organization which can provide opportunities for growth.

Retirement Planning and Counseling.   As part of any effective HRPD system, there must be a clear planning function which forecasts who will retire, and which feeds this information into both the replacement staffing system and the counseling functions so that the employees who will be retiring can be prepared for this often traumatic career stage. Employees need counseling not only with the mechanical and financial aspects of retirement, but also to prepare them psychologically for the time when they will no longer have a clear organizational base or job as part of their identity. For some people it may make sense to spread the period of retirement over a number of years by using part-time work or special assignments to help both the individual and the organization to get benefits from this period.

The counseling function here as in other parts of the career probably involves special skills and must be provided by specialists. However, the line manager continues to play a key role as a provider of job challenge, feedback, and information about what is ahead for any given employee. Seminars for line managers on how to handle the special problems of pre-retirement employees would probably be of great value as part of their managerial training.

Planning for and Managing Replacement and Restaffing
With this step the HRPD cycle closes back upon itself. This function must be concerned with such issues as:

1. Updating the human resource inventory as retirements or terminations occur;
2. Instituting special programs of orientation or training for new incumbents to specific jobs as those jobs open up;
3. Managing the information system on what jobs are available and determining how to match this information to the human resources available in order to determine whether to replace from within the organization or to go outside with a new recruiting program;
4. Continuously reanalyzing jobs to insure that the new incumbent is properly prepared for what the job *now* requires and *will* require in the future.

How these processes are managed links to the other parts of the system through the implicit messages that are sent to employees. For example, a company which decides to publicly post all of its unfilled jobs is clearly sending a message that it expects internal recruitment and supports self-development activities. A company which manages restaffing in a very secret manner may well get across a message that employees might as well be complacent and passive about their careers because they cannot influence them anyway.

SUMMARY AND CONCLUSIONS

I have tried to argue in this article that human reource planning and development is becoming an increasingly important function in organizations, that this function consists of multiple components, and that these components must be managed *both* by line managers and staff specialists. I have tried to show that the various planning activities are closely linked to the actual processes of supervision, job assignment, training, etc. and that those processes must be designed to match the needs of the organization with the needs of the employees throughout their evolving careers, whether or not those careers involve hierarchical promotions. I have also argued that the various components are linked to each other and must be seen as a total system if it is to be effective. The total system must be managed as a system to insure coordination between the planning functions and the implementation functions.

I hope it is clear from what has been said above that an effective human resource planning and development system is integral to the functioning of the organization and must, therefore, be a central concern of line management. Many of the activities require specialist help, but the accountabilities must rest squarely with line supervisors and top management. It is they who control the opportuntites and the rewards. It is the job assignment system and the feedback which employees get that is the ultimate raw material for growth and development. Whoever designs and manages the system, it will not help the organization to become more effective unless that system is *owned* by line management.

NOTES

1. See Pigors and Myers [24], and Burack [10].
2. See Hackman and Suttle [13], and Meltzer and Wickert[21].
3. See McGregor [20], Bennis [6], Pigors and Myers [24], Schein [29], Van Maanen [36], Bailyn and Schein [4], and Katz [18].
4. See Beckhard [5], Bennis [6], Schein [28], Galbraith [12], Lesieur [19], and Alfred [1].
5. See Schein [31].
6. See Schein [32].
7. See Bailyn and Schein [4], Myers [22], Van Maanen, Bailyn,and Schein [38], and Roeber [25].
8. See Van Maanen and Schein [39], Bailyn [3] and [2], and Kanter [17].
9. See Sheehy [33], Troll [35], Kalish [16], and Pearse and Pelzer [23].
10. See Burack [10], pp. 402-403.
11. See Schein [29].
12. See Dalton and Thompson [11], Super and Bohn [34], Hall [14], and Schein [32].
13. See Schein [32].
14. See Schein [32].
15. See Schein [26] and [32].
16. See Schein [27], and Van Maanen [36].
17. See Schein [26].
18. See Schein [30] and [32].
19. See Schein [26], Bray, Campbell, and Grant [9], Berlew and Hall [8], and Hall [14].
20. See Dalton and Thompson [11], and Katz [18].
21. See Heidke [15].
22. See Bailyn [2].
23. See Katz [18].
24. See Bailyn [2].

REFERENCES

Alfred, T. "Checkers or Choice in Manpower Management." *Harvard Business Review*, January-February 1967, pp. 157-169.

Bailyn, L. "Involvement and Accommodation in Technical Careers." In *Organizational Careers; Some New Perspectives*, edited by J. Van Maanen. New York: John Wiley & Sons, 1977.

Bailyn, L. "Career and Family Orientations of Husbands and Wives in Relation to Marital Happiness." *Human Relations* (1970): 97-113.

Bailyn, L., and Schein, E. H. "Life/Career Considerations as Indicators of Quality of Employment." In *Measuring Work Quality for Social Reporting*, edited by A. D. Biderman and T. F. Drury, New York: Sage Publications, 1976.

Beckhard, R. D. *Organization Development: Strategies and Models.* Reading, MA: Addison-Wesley. 1969.

Bennis, W. G. *Changing Organizations.* New York: McGraw-Hill, 1966.

Bennis, W. G. *Organization Development: Its Nature, Origins, and Prospects.* Reading, MA: Addison-Wesley, 1969.

Berlew, D., and Hall, D. T. "The Socialization of Managers." *Administrative Science Quarterly* 11 (1966): 207-223.

Bray, D. W.; Campbell, R. J.; and Grant, D. E. *Formative Years in Business.* New York: John Wiley & Sons, 1974.

Burack, E. *Organization Analysis.* Hinsdale, IL; Dryden, 1975.

Dalton, G. W., and Thompson, P. H. "Are R&D Organizations Obsolete?" *Harvard Business Review.* November-December 1976, pp. 105-116.

Galbraith, J. *Designing Complex Organizations.* Reading. MA: Addison-Wesley, 1973.

Hackman, J. R., and Suttle, J. L. *Improving Life at Work.* Los Angeles: Goodyear, 1977.

Hall, D. T. *Careers in Organizations.* Los Angles: Goodyear, 1976.

Heidke, R. *Career Pro-Activity of Middle Managers.* Master's Thesis. Massachusetts Institute of Technology, 1977.

Kalish, R. A. *Late Adulthood: Perspectives on Aging.* Monterey. CA: Brooks-Cole, 1975.

Kanter, R. M. *Work and Family in the United States.* New York: Russell Sage, 1977.

Katz, R. "Job Enrichment: Some Career Considerations." In *Organizational Careers: Some New Perspectives,* edited by J. Van Maanen. New York: John Wiley & Sons, 1977.

Lesieur, F. G. *The Scanlon Plan.* New York: John Wiley & Sons, 1958.

McGregor, D. *The Human Side of Enterprise.* New York: McGraw-Hill, 1960.

Meltzer, H., and Wickert, F. R. *Humanizing Organization Behavior.* Springfield. IL: Charles C. Thomas, 1976.

Myers, C. A. "Management and the Employee." In *Social Responsibility and the Business Predicament,* edited by J. W. McKie. Washington, D. C.: Brookings, 1974.

Pearse, R. F. and Pelzer, B. P. *Self-directed Change for the Mid-Career Manager.* New York: AMACOM, 1975.

Pigors P., and Myers, C. A. *Personnel Administration.* 8th ed. New York: McGraw-Hill, 1977.

Roeber, R. J. C. *The Organization in a Changing Environment.* Reading. MA: Addison-Wesley, 1973.

Schein, E. H. "How to Break in the College Graduate" *Harvard Business Review.* 1964, pp. 68-76.

Schein, E. H. Organizational Socialization and the Profession of Management. *Industrial Management Review,* Winter 1968, pp. 1-16.

Schein, E. H. *Process Consultation: Its Role in Organization Development.* Reading. MA: Addison-Wesley, 1969.

Schein, E. H. *Organizational Psychology.* Englewood Cliffs. NJ: Prentice-Hall, 1970.

Schein, E. H. The Individual, the Organization, and the Career: A Conceptual Scheme. *Journal of Applied Behavioral Science* 7 (1971): 401-426.

Schein, E. H. "How 'Career Anchors' Hold Executives to Their Career Paths." *Personnel* 52. no. 3 (1975): 11-24.

Schein, E. H. *The Individual, the Organization and the Career: Toward Greater Human Effectiveness.* Reading. MA: Addison-Wesley, forthcoming.

Sheehy, G. "Catch 30 and Other Predictable Crises of Growing Up Adult." *New York Magazine.* February 1974, pp. 30-44.

Super, D. E., and Bohn, M. J. *Occupational Psychology.* Belmont, CA: Wadsworth, 1970.

Troll, L. E. *Early and Middle Adulthood.* Monterey. CA: Brooks-Cole, 1975.

Van Maanen, J. "Breaking In: Socialization to Work." In *Handbook of Work, Organization, and Society,* edited by R. Dubin. Chicago: Rand McNally, 1976.

Van Maanen, J., ed. *Organizational Careers: Some New Perspectives.* New York: John Wiley & Sons, 1977.

Van Maanen, J.; Bailyn, L.; and Schein, E. H. "The Shape of Things to Come: A New Look at Organizational Careers." In *Perspectives on Behavior in Organizations,* edited by J. R. Hackman, E. E. Lawler, and L. W. Porter. New York: McGraw-Hill, 1977.

Van Maanen, J., and Schein, E. H. "Improving the Quality of Work Life: Career Development," In *Improving Life at Work,* edited by J. R. Hackman and J. L. Suttle. Los Angeles: Goodyear, 1977.

When Bosses Look Back to See Ahead

When former Harvard University Professor Harry Levinson, an acknowledged guru of behavioral science for business, first published his *Organizational Diagnosis* in 1972, it was as though a huge stone had dropped into a pond. The book—which stated that executives must take an extensive, introspective look at their company's history and goals in order to make sound management decisions—created ripples of talk throughout management and academic circles. Then, as suddenly, the whole discussion seemingly died off.

But one of those ripples reached Ebasco Services Inc., an old-line builder of power plants and the first company to try organizational diagnosis. Under the auspices of Andrew O. Manzini, director of manpower planning and development, Ebasco last year put 300 managers through intensive interviews, each lasting 90 minutes or more, to elicit their perceptions of where Ebasco has been, what kind of company it is now, and where it is heading.

The resulting report is a hernia-producing tome—515 pages of data analysis and 130 pages of summary and recommendations—that Ebasco's management is still trying to digest. But the report has already fanned some smoldering ideas for manpower planning within Ebasco, and it is helping the company sharpen its self-image.

SEEKING DEFINITIONS

Although financially sound, Ebasco has some profuse managerial and identity problems—in large part the result of its status as a perennial corporate foster child. Ebasco's original parent, Electric Bond & Share Co., was formed in 1905 as a subsidiary of General Electric Co. In 1925, Ebasco became independent, but was acquired by Boise Cascade Corp. in 1969. When Boise fell on hard times in the early 1970s, it divested itself of Ebasco, which was soon acquired by Halliburton Co. Halliburton was later forced by the Justice Dept. to divest itself of Ebasco, and in August, 1976, the power plant builder found its current home with Enserch Corp., a diversified energy company.

In the midst of all this moving around, Ebasco in 1969 started experimenting with matrix management (BW—Jan. 16, 1978), a system in which technical people—the mainstay of Ebasco's 4,500-person work force—were responsible for bottom-line results as well as for

---

engineering excellence. But that created new managerial problems. Lines of authority often became blurred. For example, a construction manager, used to choosing equipment only in terms of what works best from an engineering viewpoint, must now give equal priority to the project manager's budget concerns.

"Suddenly these people are expected not only to fulfill their discipline needs but to look at what they are doing in terms of the entire project on which they are working," explains John A. Scarola, Ebasco's president and chief executive officer. "We certainly needed a better definition of how different managers' functions interrelated."

To compound Ebasco's problems, after years of priding itself on being a top-of-the-line power plant builder, the company found its competitors increasingly underbidding it on lucrative projects, in good part because of its reluctance to give practical considerations to costs. "We have always thought of ourselves as the 'Cadillac of the power plant industry,' " notes an Ebasco executive. "But some of our customers want Chevies, not Cadillacs." The organizational diagnosis was necessary, he says, because "we needed to understand our perception of ourselves before we could decide the proper trade-offs between quality and profitability."

UNCERTAINTY

Ebasco's management is convinced that the internal interviews have put the company on the right track toward solving these deep-rooted problems. For Scarola, who moved up to the top job from a position as executive vice-president of operations just in time to receive the report, it meant a quick eye-opener into some of the sensitivities prevalent at Ebasco—sensitivities Scarola admits he ignored as a vice-president. "When you get to talk to this many people," he says, "you see that some problems have to be handled."

Among other things, Scarola notes that the study showed widespread concern and uncertainty about staffing plans and about individual futures. This led the company to accelerate the development of its embryonic plans for predicting future manpower needs and for determining where existing personnel fit into that scheme.

Ebasco has also started relating performance appraisals to specific jobs rather than to more general performance standards that might not be important for certain tasks. It also now does "potential appraisals," which outline an employee's projected upward path.

The survey also uncovered considerable confusion about matrix management and strategic planning, and Ebasco has started holding more frequent training and orientation sessions to make employees more comfortable with these techniques. "We've finally accepted that our people must be made to understand more fully how they are expected to interrelate," Scarola explains.

EMPLOYEE VIEWS

Such understanding requires a full knowledge of company goals, and it is Levinson's theory that goals can be set only when a company has a sense of its own history—something he claims few companies have. "If they did," he says, "they wouldn't make the decisions they do." To illustrate, he points to a retailer that has always had a reputation for extreme integrity but whose store managers started indulging in bait-and-switch sales practices. "It wouldn't have happened," he maintains, "if they had recognized the company's long tradition of honest service."

In the introduction to the Ebasco report, Manzini and his manpower planning staff echo Levinson's emphasis on getting employee views of the company. "People's perceptions are reality to them, and their actions will be guided accordingly," it reads. "If enough people 'feel' the same way about certain issues, problems, and circumstances . . . such 'feelings' are generally indicative of what's really happening."

Levinson's recommended questionnaire, which Manzini adopted almost verbatim, is designed to elicit such feelings. The survey asks managers how Ebasco "got to be the way it is today," what "sort of place is this to do your job," what are "the main rules around here that everyone has to follow," and what kinds of things is Ebasco "most interested in keeping up with." Interviewers also told managers to "make believe Ebasco is a person and describe that person." Scarola isolates one question that might easily have opened a Pandora's box: "Suppose Ebasco had to stop doing some of the things it now does— what should not be changed!"

THE 'CRITICAL MASS'

In actuality, both Scarola and other top executives say that while Ebasco got less than overall kudos from its managers, the responses were more often confused than negative. For example, Benjamin E. Tenzer, director of materials engineering and quality assurance, says he was "surprised how ignorant employees were about financial aspects of Ebasco, and how egocentric some people are about their own areas of the company." But he adds: "I was pleasantly surprised at the conviction that the company was better than any of its people. It was akin to someone saying, "The President stinks, Congress stinks, but America's a great country.' "

Tenzer's enthusiasm is particularly pleasing to Manzini, for Tenzer was one of 23 people he pegged at the outset as crucial to the project's success. To prepare the way for the organizational diagnosis, Manzini conducted a novel power analysis, searching for those people considered the key decision makers within Ebasco. Given the political dynamics inherent in most large companies, such a prelude may have taken more daring than the main study itself. "We simply went around asking employees who they thought had the power around here," says Manzini. "Then we asked those individuals, 'Do you think you have the power?'"

The process turned up 23 people who Manzini calls the "critical mass"—those executives with the power to make or break the diagnosis project. But Manzini went beyond getting their support for the main effort: He gave them a crash course in organizational diagnosis and enlisted their aid as interviewers.

A $74,000 TAB

Despite its scope and longevity, the project was relatively inexpensive. Manzini estimates the total cost—including the management time involved—at $74,000. But the drudgery of the project almost led to its being scuttled halfway through. The data gleaned from the interview tapes filled more than 40,000 index cards. "We were suffering from acute data overload," Manzini recalls. "It took us almost a year from start to finish, and only a small part of that time was spent on the interviewing itself."

Still, nearly all the managers involved concede that the diagnosis not only identified the company's problems but also changed their own management styles and concepts. "I pay more attention to trying to communicate information," notes John L. Leporati, vice-president of Ebasco's Envirosphere Co. Adds Joe R. Crespo, president of Ebasco's Business Consulting Co.: "It's keeping us focused on some of the main problems—the conflicts between emphasizing quality and keeping costs down, for example." And Tenzer notes: "I learned what a diversity of points of view people can have about subjective questions—a shock for me, since I've always tended to be literal-minded."

For Manzini, though, the project's biggest contribution is in breaking down communications barriers between engineer-managers and their employees. "It's now easier to get company management to address issues not normally pursued," he concludes, "because we've gotten people with engineering backgrounds to work comfortably with psychological processes."

HRIS: Introduction to Tomorrow's System for Managing Human Resources

Albert C. Hyde and Jay M. Shafritz

A NEW CONCEPT

Organizations understandably place considerable value on achieving the optimum use of their resources in order to accomplish their program objectives. To do otherwise would mean that resources would be wasted or that objectives might not be achieved. Given the fact that human resources constitute such an important part of any organization's resource base, the development of an information system that provides an ongoing assessment of the utilization of these resources is a natural reaction to an essential managerial need. The Department of State, perhaps more than most organizations, places a premium value on its most important resource—its employees. Having long perceived the need for a signficant systems advancement in its accounting, control, and planning for the use of human resources, the department has initiated an experiment with a new concept in management information systems for personnel resources. This work has been carried out via a special development project appropriately entitled Human Resources Information Systems, or, more simply, HRIS.

Any human resource information system is logically an inventory of the positions and skills extant in a given organization. However, HRIS is more than a simple aggregation mechanism for inventory control and accounting; it is the foundation for a set of management tools enabling managers to establish objectives for the use of their organization's human resources and to measure the extent to which those objectives have been achieved. As managers come to recognize both the essentiality and feasibility of sophisticated management information systems for monitoring human resources, more and more computerized personnel management information systems such as HRIS will be installed. Public personnel offices have long been using computers to facilitate their bookkeeping practices. The HRIS concept illustrates a

"HRIS: Introduction to Tomorrow's System for Managing Human Resources" by Albert C. Hyde and Jay M. Shafritz, Public Personnel Management, March-April, 1977. Reprinted by permission.

Albert C. Hyde is a foreign service officer with the U.S. Departmet of State and Jay M. Shafritz is associate professor of public affairs at the University of Houston, Clear Lake City.

further generation of computer usage in governmental personnel operations: beyond bookkeeping to management science.

HRIS OBJECTIVES

The specific objectives of HRIS were developed around an extensive review of perceived organizational needs. Two such needs were immediately apparent. First, data bases on both people and positions had to be rebuilt to provide the specific information required for human resource management needs. The major problem here was the gross labels used by the traditional personnel-related inventories. Many of these labels—job titles, for example—were either so ambiguous as to be virtually meaningless or were incorrect simply because they were outdated. Because of such factors, traditional personnel inventory data tend to be inherently incorrect. HRIS offers an alternative to the inherent weaknesses of the label concept. Its development is a recognition of the capacity of today's automated technology to input, maintain, retrieve, and analyze large amounts of specific data. Rather than crudely input data in some form of gross category, HRIS provides for data input in its most specific meaningful form. If a label is required for categorization purposes, HRIS can generate a name based on a preprogrammed decision rule applied to the grouped data.

The second objective, building in part upon the structure of the first, involves output processes entailing new reporting and inquiry methods for human resource management systems, such as resource allocation review, assignments matching, and intake and training projections, to name a few. These systems require comprehensive data on both positions and persons. HRIS can provide these data in reporting formats shaped to the specific objectives of each system.

Both data base and reporting format objectives must necessarily be modified to include universal evaluation criteria for the design of any computerized or manual management informative system: utility, cost-effectiveness, maintenance, validity probability, and installation costs and time. Essentially, these criteria form additional "objectives" upon which each module of HRIS must be evaluated. It has been recognized from the start that not all of the elements of a comprehensive HRIS can be developed and implemented concurrently. Therefore, HRIS is being developed as a modular system. Departmental priorities and budgetary considerations will determine which system components will first be implemented and with what speed.

THE DATA BASE

The HRIS data base has two major component parts-position data and personnel data.The latter, consisting of biographic information on individuals, is for the most part available from long-standing personnel files. Many of these data can be coded and stored in a computer file. For position data, one might logically go to the position classification system for the appropriate position descriptions; but these are so congenitally out of date that they are best ignored for HRIS purposes. Instead, a position data survey must be undertaken that would gather the following three categories of data:

1. *Organization identification:* the location and level of each position. For the State Department, this would necessarily include measures of the optimal length of position incumbency.
2. *Qualification levels and required experience:* describes the optimal requirements that the incumbent should possess to perform the requisite duties adequately. At a minimum, this should include education, experience, training, language proficiency, supervisory experience, and any special professional licenses.
3. *Functional job components:* a data array describing the basic tasks of each job with weights of time and relative importance.

One of the advantages of using functional job components is that traditionally restrictive labels for positions are discarded. In their place, a variety of component descriptions are used to more accurately illustrate the specific and varied duties actually performed by the incumbent. HRIS advances the technologically feasible concept that a position is more appropriately defined in terms of its component parts and that a computerized management information system can readily deal with such degrees of specification. The major problem of using job labels and titles that carry descriptions that are either too vague or so general as to accommodate virtually any possible type of work is that management has no rational way of making basic assignment, intake, training, or promotion decisions that reflect reality. HRIS represents an experiment in developing systems that can overcome this very common deficit.

REPORTING FORMATS

Once the profile of an organization's human assets—the HRIS core data base—is computerized, it becomes possible to use this as a reporting, analysis, or evaluation mechanism. A major example of such an application is resource allocation for budgetary purposes. An organization logically wants to know what activities its resources are devoted to and for what purpose. It is not enough to produce information stating that so many individuals are currently occupying positions that involve some general category of work. One individual may perform different functions for a variety of purposes, and these activities may change repeatedly. HRIS can provide specific reporting formats that break out the various activities being performed by purpose, time, and relative importance. When these data are aggregated by general functional or specific organization categories, it is possible to account very specifically for the current allocation of resources. Thus, instead of reporting that the Economic Bureau has X individuals performing economic work, HRIS could report X number of work years devoted to activity Y in the Economic Bureau. These activities can even be further broken down to very specific levels and categories.

For another example, consider the organization that may wish to measure just how equitable its advancement (promotion) policies have been, a particularly important consideration in the public sector. Equity in this instance is naturally examined in the aggregate rather than on a case-by-case basis. If equity truly exists, various employee categories (such as males/females, minorities/majorities, etc.) will have statistically similar rates of advancement. In order to evaluate the rate at which equity is being achieved, HRIS can provide a periodic reporting format that will provide basic measures such as the promotion rates of special status groups compared to those of the total population or of a control group. Particular groups may be presently advantaged or disadvantaged by current practices. HRIS, having no bias toward either overt or reverse discrimination, can provide the data that management needs to easily monitor trends in this area. In short, if an organization has a personnel management objective and that objective is operationalized, HRIS can be programmed to present the relevant data in whatever format is required. Management's task is to analyze the HRIS data, assess their implications, and make the appropriate policy decisions.

THE HRIS MODULES

Because HRIS is premised upon a computerized data base, it can perform a large variety of management and analysis tasks, many of which can impact upon each other. Each element or subsystem of the overall system is an independent module. However, the system is inherently interactive in that one module may contain information produced from other modules. Any given module integrates the available HRIS data to produce its decisional options. Theoretically, modularity enhances the viability of the total system for much longer periods of time; new modules can be added, or old modules can be deemphasized, merged into other modules, or even discarded. With a modular capability that is highly flexible, personnel inventories can be as detailed and dynamic as necessary. HRIS has a theoretical capacity for rapid change, to meet the changing needs of its host organization as required. As a management tool, it can be adjusted to both a changing organizational structure and an evolving computer technology.

Beyond redefining position and people data, HRIS becomes the foundation for a host of systems concepts that affect human resource management. For example, by adding an actuarial probability factor to specified HRIS personnel data for employees' age and time of service, an operating system can be created that will calculate attrition projections. By redividing and collapsing the functional job components data on HRIS position information—according to an arbitrary set of aggregation codes—a resource allocation analysis operation system can be created. All of the specific system objectives illustrated in Figure 1 represent potential operating systems that build off the basic HRIS data files— through manipulation either of separate person or position files or of the linked position/person files.

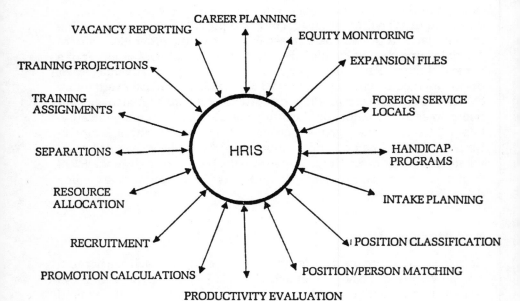

Figure 1. The HRIS Modules

The 16 modules delineated below illustrate the broad scope of HRIS. Because the modular concept allows for the timely addition and deletion of individual modules, any given list of modules is necessarily merely representative of the system's capabilities. Every organization implementing HRIS would have to choose or develop modules appropriate to the priority of its particular missions. The modules conceived for the State Department are presented below in alphabetical order:

Career Planning. This module will facilitate professional/career development planning for both the individual and the organization. It will chart future career paths for all categories of employees by specifying ranges of assignments and training opportunities for various career intervals. These career paths will be premised on the current and projected needs of the organization.

Equity Monitoring. This module will provide for automatic monitoring of special status groups within the organization to ensure that their career progression is comparable with that of the overall workforce and consistent with all legal mandates. It entails detailed periodic reporting and analysis of entrance, promotions, training and assignment opportunities, and separations for any special status categories of employees such as minorities, women, veterans, age categories, etc.

Expansion files. This module will enable organizational elements of the larger unit to develop and maintain supplemental file data within the basic HRIS system. Such files might contain data on the special capabilities or characteristics of employees—which builds on the core HRIS data—that would only be germane to that specific organizational element. For example, a security unit might require a more detailed profile of the characteristics of its employees.

Foreign Service Locals. This module entails developing a parallel data base and information system for various categories of peripheral employees. Specifically for the Department of State, an information system for its foreign service nationals employed abroad must be incorporated into the overall personnel management process.

Handicap Programs. This module examines and facilitates the employment and development of the physically handicapped. It identifies positions and work locations in terms of their suitability for the handicapped based on job content and physical requirements.

Intake Planning This module provides data for determining the organization's future workforce requirements and supply and for projecting intake needs for the future. It must calculate and monitor by specific work functions current imbalances, project changes in requirements, forecast attrition as well as net internal transfers, and produce intake recommendations for short- and long-range planning periods.

Position Classification. This module will provide an automated information system for position classification programs. It would entail the direct input and maintenance of position data by the position classification staff, automatic monitoring of the job content and level of positions, and computerized retrieval of data on classes or series of positions for evaluation.

Position/Person Matching. This module establishes a computerized process for the direct correlation of position requirements against personal qualifications and preferences for possible assignments. It creates a mechanism for scoring all employees as candidates for specific jobs and can identify either a top range of candidates for a specific position or a top range of potential positions for a single individual.

Productivity Evaluation. This module involves creating output measures of performance to be used in evaluating the productivity of specific programs, officers, or positions.

Promotion Calculations. This module allows for the determination and computation of opportunities for advancement. It provides necessary data on current workforce grade structures to calculate the number of promotion opportunities for specific job categories within the organization.

Recruitment. This module provides data for the analysis and evaluation of recruitment efforts. It will monitor the qualifications and special characteristics of new employees by various functional categories and analyze retention and development trends.

Resource Allocation. This module will establish a data base for the evaluation of the current distribution of resources—specifically human resources, by both organizational and functional breakdowns. It will make possible a budget analysis process that can actually identify what and how much work (human resource effort) is being performed and for what purposes.

Separations. This module involves collecting and analyzing data to provide cumulative statistics on separated employees by various categories. Such data will allow for the monitoring and verification of projected attrition calculations as well as planning for actuarial requirements.

Training Assignments. This module will provide for an automated position/person matching system to be employed in making training assignments. It entails integrating specific training possibilities with overall career development needs for both the individual and the organization.

Training Projections. This module will create a forecasting mechanism to enable the organization to recognize short-and long-term training needs. It involves basing training projections on current and future position requirements as correlated to the existing qualifications of the organizational workforce.

Vacancy Reporting. This module installs a process for identifying and monitoring present and potential vacancies within the orgnization. It specifies position vacancies by category and time to enable the organization to know when long-standing vacancies continue to exist.

SYSTEMS CONCEPTS

HRIS is an automated process that produces specific reports for managers for two purposes, accountability and planning. Its design was premised upon the basic assumption that effective planning is linked to accountability, an accurate assessment of current capabilities logically being an essential step in calculating future needs. Both processes meld to generate action proposals for reform or innovation. A prime feature of this linkage is that planning must be evaluated against some form of current assessment or feedback loop. Any system must have accountability measures if it is to be assured that its overall objectives are being implemented. The HRIS concept was developed around the two dimensions of operational accountability and operational planning specifically because the State Department's current information system was hard pressed to assist managers in either.

Figure 2 schematically illustrates the HRIS concept. The various module objectives and the core data on positions and persons are fed into HRIS for the dual purposes of planning and accountability. Data arrays or reports are thereupon produced in the format previously prescribed by the objectives. Feedback occurs when decisions based upon this output lead to the generation of new objectives.

It is important to distinguish between what HRIS will do by and of itself and what HRIS will provide in conjunction with other systems concepts. In a very simplified sense, HRIS is core data and their maintenance. It is the actual linked data arrays on positions and people and how that information is collected, changed, verified, updated, stored, retrieved, and deleted. These core data arrays become the data base foundations for a series of systems elements, each having distinct objectives and each representing specific human resource management programs. HRIS, as an integrated core data system, provides such information in the appropriate formats required for effective decision-making for all of the varied system elements. Because HRIS is an integrated information system, it can also delineate integrated decisional alternatives that involve more than one systems element.

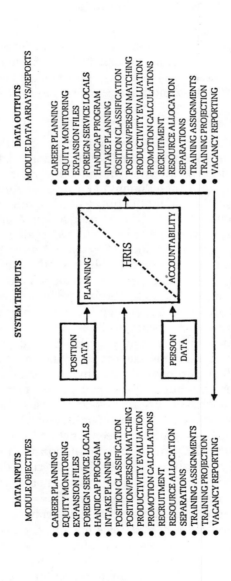

Figure 2. Human Resource Information Systems

A PERSONNEL MANAGEMENT TOOL

While HRIS can be a useful tool for a variety of policymakers and planners, its main function—at least during the initial phase of its installation—would be in support of the personnel management process HRIS would provide basic informational support for decisions on recruitment, placement, training, classification, and resource allocation, among others. In the past, personnel decisions were necessarily made using an incomplete data base. Subjective intuitive judgments simply had to be made. Decisions made using HRIS can be made using virtually all available data.

HRIS can provide management with a capability to avoid crises management because it can call attention to approaching human resource problems before they reach a crisis stage. The opportunity will exist to aggressively plan for (rather than anxiously react to) human resource management problems. By negating many of the ad hoc aspects of personnel decision making, HRIS would force consideration of the interrelationships of personnel functions. After all, the decision to take a manager off the line for training leads to a decision to replace him with a manager taken off another assignment, which leads to a decision to recruit for a temporary replacement, which leads to more and more decisions. The implications of any given personnel decision may sometimes seem infinite. HRIS, as an integrated personnel management information systems, could automatically chart the interactions of any given decisional option and report them as options to the decision-maker. That is the essential task and basic concept behind all management information systems.

The tone of personnel management in any organization is set by the dynamism and flux of the host organization. The worldwide operations of the State Department naturally create personnel complexities and problems with which few other governmental agencies must grapple: all the more reason for having a computerized information system capable of quickly delivering to policymakers basic data on the total manpower deployment and capabilities of the department. While global operations would alone justify the need for an HRIS program, the need is doubly apparent when the purview of modern personnel management programs is examined. In most large governmental jurisdictions, personnel operations are gradually but inexorably moving beyond personnel administration to personnel management. The difference is more than semantic. While the former is mainly concerned with the technical aspects of maintaining a full complement of employees, the latter concerns itself largely with the problems of the viability and vitality of its organization's human resources. Personnel management tends to go by default in most government agencies because the traditional administrative role of the personnel office creates an artificial and frequently self-imposed boundary on the scope of its activities and because the tools of a sophisticated personnel management program—computer and behavioral technology—have become available only comparatively recently. However, with the advent of affirmative action programs, the need for greater measures of governmental productivity, and the insistence of employees that they participate meaningfully in the decisional process that affect them, public sector executives have been increasingly demanding personnel management information systems that are accurate, speedy, and flexible enough to be used as decisional and control tools. HRIS, as a computer system, can be rapid and responsive, and its modular approach can offer almost unlimited flexibility. Consequently, HRIS will never be a "finished" system. To suggest that it can or should be completed is to imply that at some future date, personnel management innovation will cease.